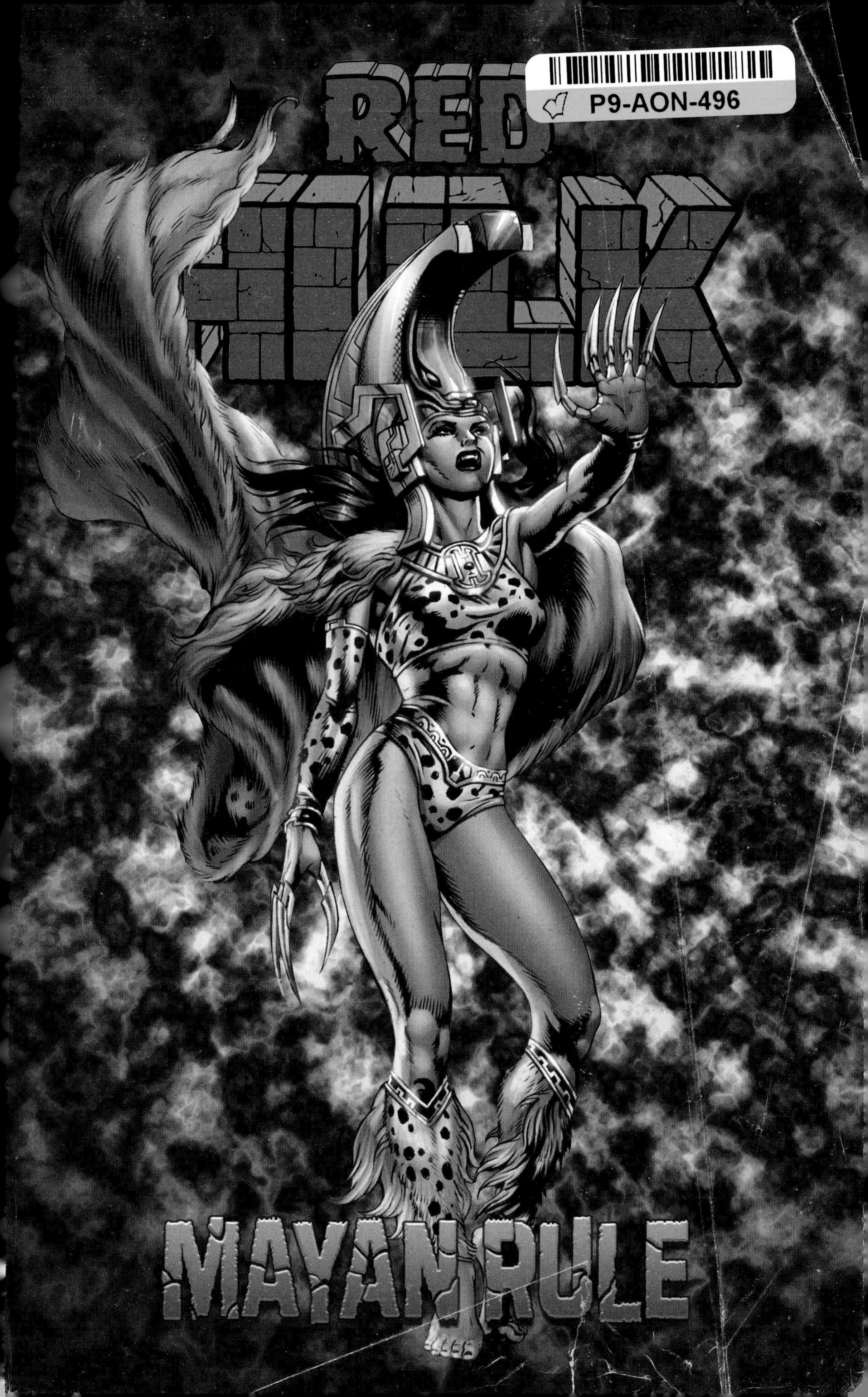
RED
HULK
MAYAN RULE

RED HULK
MAYAN RULE

WRITER: **JEFF PARKER**

ARTIST: **DALE EAGLESHAM**

COLOR ARTISTS: **JESUS ABURTOV** (ISSUES #53-54)

& **VAL STAPLES** (ISSUES #54-57)

LETTERER: **VC'S CLAYTON COWLES**

COVER ARTIST: **DALE EAGLESHAM**

WITH **JESUS ABURTOV** (ISSUES #53-54) & **VAL STAPLES** (ISSUES #55-57)

ASSISTANT EDITORS: **JAKE THOMAS** & **JON MOISAN**

EDITOR: **MARK PANICCIA**

COLLECTION EDITOR & DESIGN: **CORY LEVINE**

ASSISTANT EDITORS: **ALEX STARBUCK** & **NELSON RIBEIRO**

EDITORS, SPECIAL PROJECTS: **JENNIFER GRÜNWALD** & **MARK D. BEAZLEY**

SENIOR EDITOR, SPECIAL PROJECTS: **JEFF YOUNGQUIST**

SENIOR VICE PRESIDENT OF SALES: **DAVID GABRIEL**

SVP OF BRAND PLANNING & COMMUNICATIONS: **MICHAEL PASCIULLO**

EDITOR IN CHIEF: **AXEL ALONSO**

CHIEF CREATIVE OFFICER: **JOE QUESADA**

PUBLISHER: **DAN BUCKLEY**

EXECUTIVE PRODUCER: **ALAN FINE**

RED HULK: MAYAN RULE. Contains material originally published in magazine form as HULK #53-57. First printing 2012. ISBN# 978-0-7851-6097-7. Published by MARVEL WORLDWIDE, INC., a subsidiary of MARVEL ENTERTAINMENT, LLC. OFFICE OF PUBLICATION: 135 West 50th Street, New York, NY 10020. Copyright © 2012 Marvel Characters, Inc. All rights reserved. $16.99 per copy in the U.S. and $18.99 in Canada (GST #R127032852); Canadian Agreement #40668537. All characters featured in this issue and the distinctive names and likenesses thereof, and all related indicia are trademarks of Marvel Characters, Inc. No similarity between any of the names, characters, persons, and/or institutions in this magazine with those of any living or dead person or institution is intended, and any such similarity which may exist is purely coincidental. **Printed in the U.S.A.** ALAN FINE, EVP - Office of the President, Marvel Worldwide, Inc. and EVP & CMO Marvel Characters B.V.; DAN BUCKLEY, Publisher & President - Print, Animation & Digital Divisions; JOE QUESADA, Chief Creative Officer; TOM BREVOORT, SVP of Publishing; DAVID BOGART, SVP of Operations & Procurement, Publishing; RUWAN JAYATILLEKE, SVP & Associate Publisher, Publishing; C.B. CEBULSKI, SVP of Creator & Content Development; DAVID GABRIEL, SVP of Publishing Sales & Circulation; MICHAEL PASCIULLO, SVP of Brand Planning & Communications; JIM O'KEEFE, VP of Operations & Logistics; DAN CARR, Executive Director of Publishing Technology; SUSAN CRESPI, Editorial Operations Manager; ALEX MORALES, Publishing Operations Manager; STAN LEE, Chairman Emeritus. For information regarding advertising in Marvel Comics or on Marvel.com, please contact Niza Disla, Director of Marvel Partnerships, at ndisla@marvel.com. For Marvel subscription inquiries, please call 800-217-9158. **Manufactured between 9/13/2012 and 10/16/2012 by QUAD/GRAPHICS, DUBUQUE, IA, USA.**

10 9 8 7 6 5 4 3 2 1

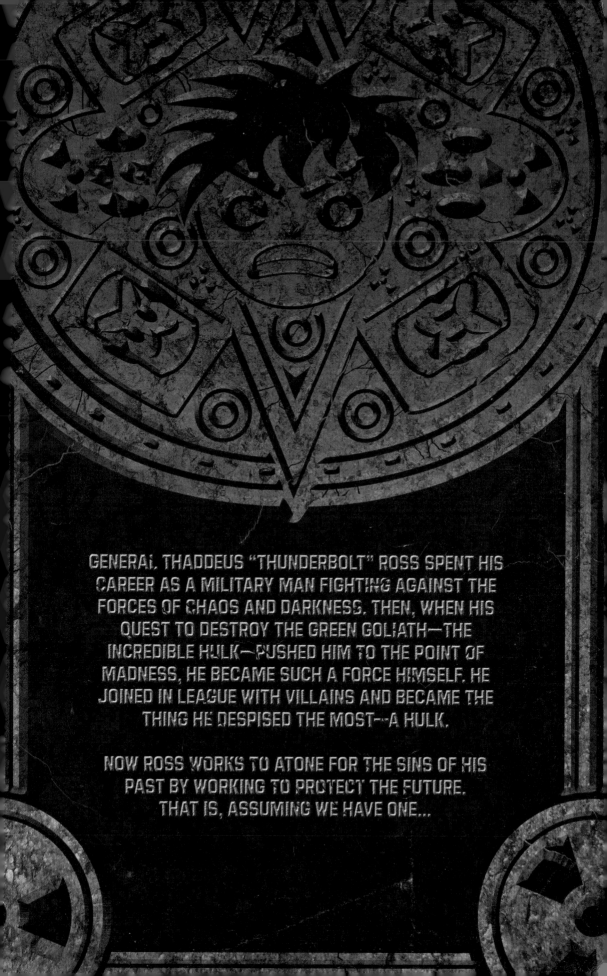

GENERAL THADDEUS "THUNDERBOLT" ROSS SPENT HIS CAREER AS A MILITARY MAN FIGHTING AGAINST THE FORCES OF CHAOS AND DARKNESS. THEN, WHEN HIS QUEST TO DESTROY THE GREEN GOLIATH—THE INCREDIBLE HULK—PUSHED HIM TO THE POINT OF MADNESS, HE BECAME SUCH A FORCE HIMSELF. HE JOINED IN LEAGUE WITH VILLAINS AND BECAME THE THING HE DESPISED THE MOST—A HULK.

NOW ROSS WORKS TO ATONE FOR THE SINS OF HIS PAST BY WORKING TO PROTECT THE FUTURE. THAT IS, ASSUMING WE HAVE ONE...

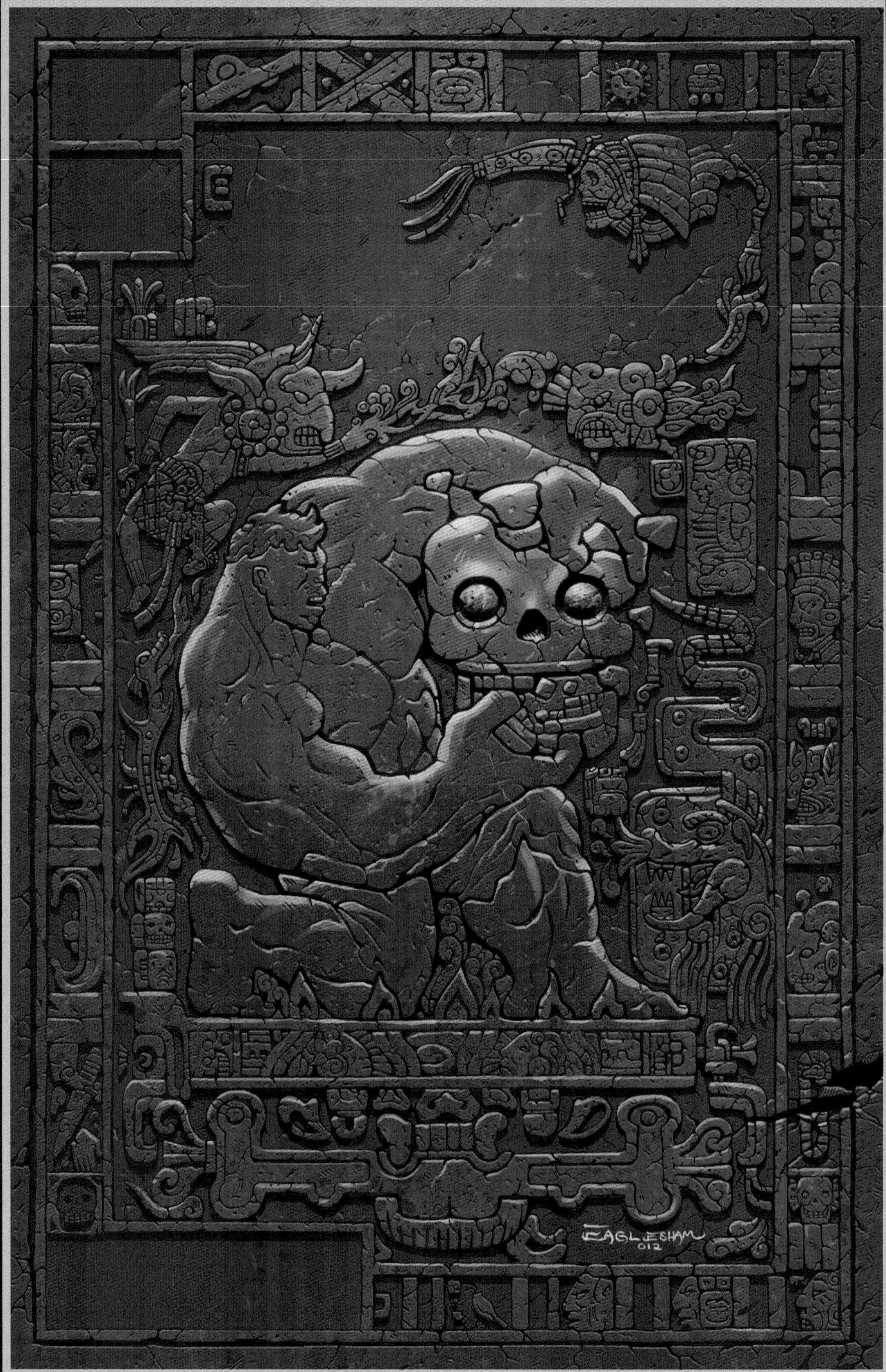
EAGLESHAM
012

HULK #53

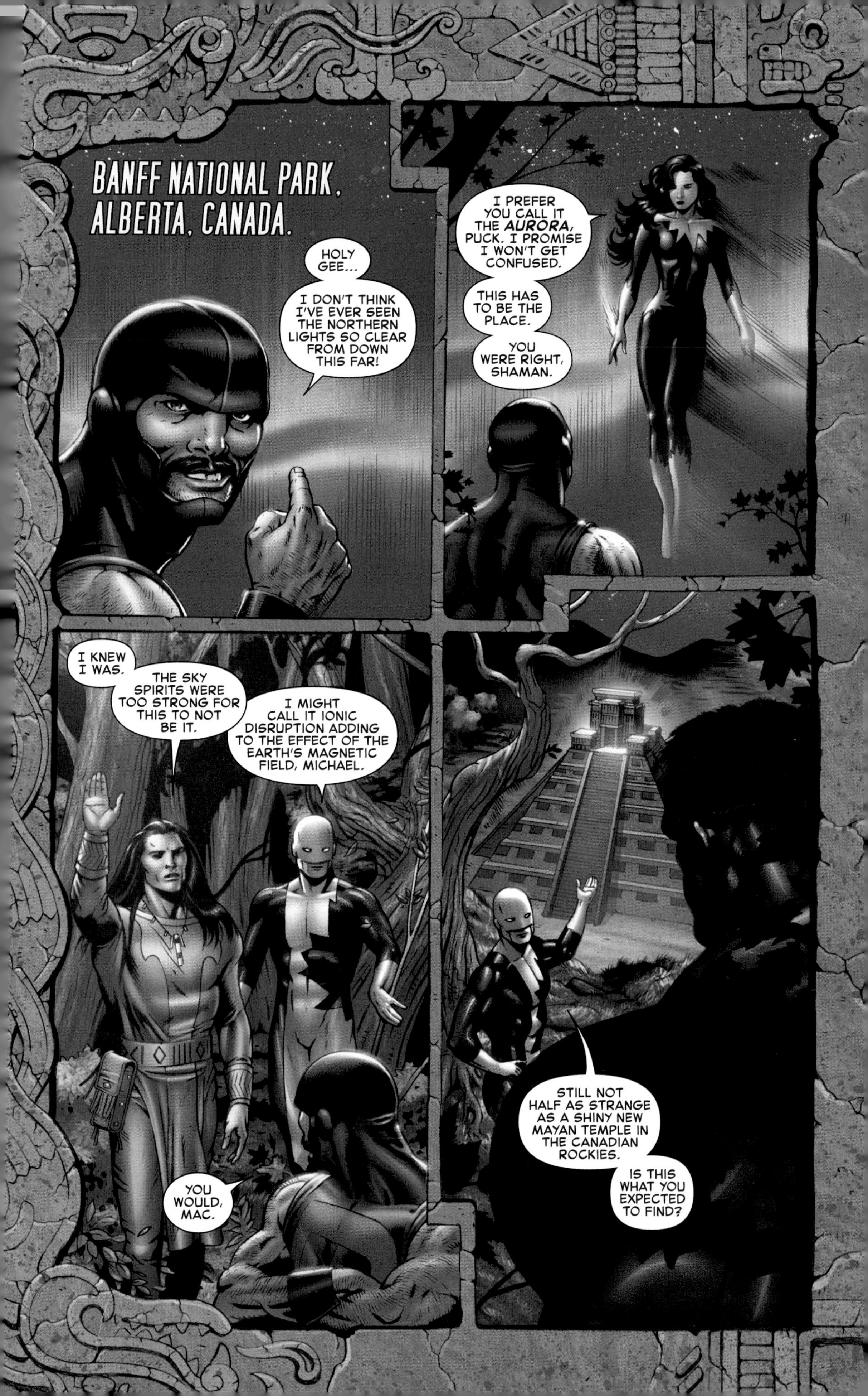
BANFF NATIONAL PARK, ALBERTA, CANADA.
HOLY GEE...
I DON'T THINK I'VE EVER SEEN THE NORTHERN LIGHTS SO CLEAR FROM DOWN THIS FAR!
I PREFER YOU CALL IT THE AURORA, PUCK. I PROMISE I WON'T GET CONFUSED.
THIS HAS TO BE THE PLACE.
YOU WERE RIGHT, SHAMAN.
I KNEW I WAS.
THE SKY SPIRITS WERE TOO STRONG FOR THIS TO NOT BE IT.
I MIGHT CALL IT IONIC DISRUPTION ADDING TO THE EFFECT OF THE EARTH'S MAGNETIC FIELD, MICHAEL.
YOU WOULD, MAC.
STILL NOT HALF AS STRANGE AS A SHINY NEW MAYAN TEMPLE IN THE CANADIAN ROCKIES.
IS THIS WHAT YOU EXPECTED TO FIND?

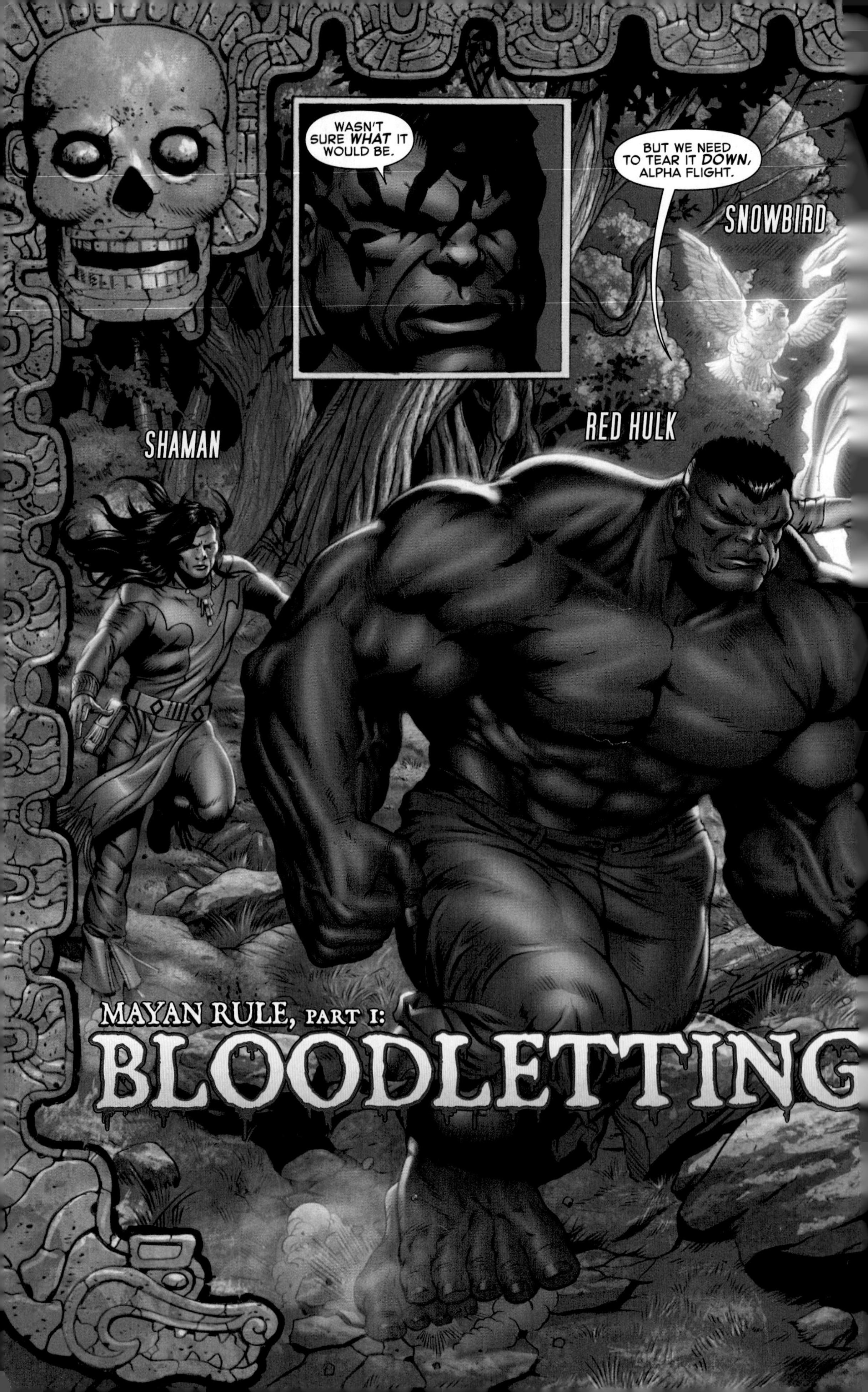

WASN'T SURE WHAT IT WOULD BE.
BUT WE NEED TO TEAR IT DOWN, ALPHA FLIGHT.
SNOWBIRD
SHAMAN
RED HULK
MAYAN RULE, PART I:
BLOODLETTING

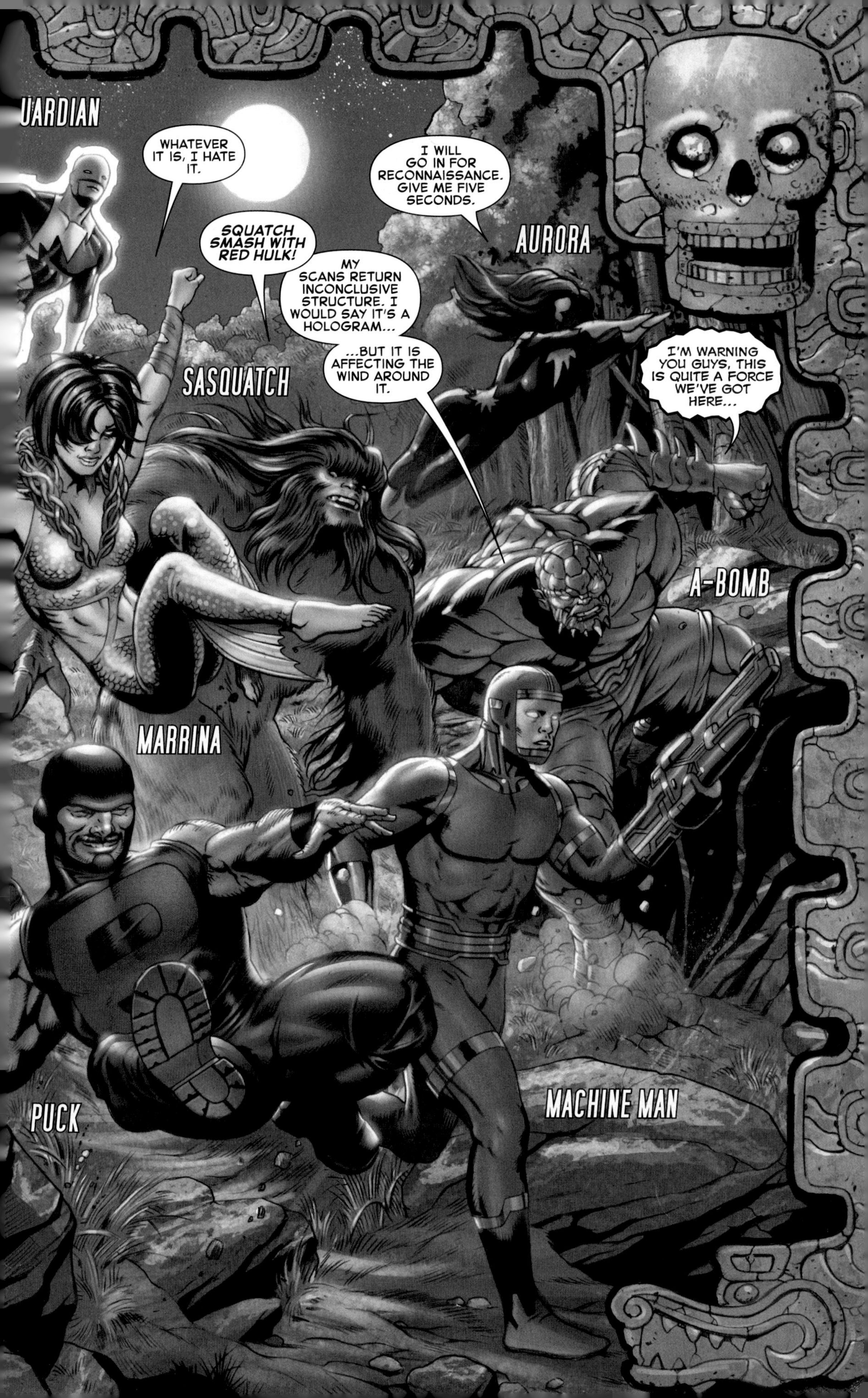
UARDIAN
WHATEVER IT IS, I HATE IT.
SQUATCH SMASH WITH RED HULK!
I WILL GO IN FOR RECONNAISSANCE. GIVE ME FIVE SECONDS.
AURORA
MY SCANS RETURN INCONCLUSIVE STRUCTURE. I WOULD SAY IT'S A HOLOGRAM...
...BUT IT IS AFFECTING THE WIND AROUND IT.
I'M WARNING YOU GUYS, THIS IS QUITE A FORCE WE'VE GOT HERE...
SASQUATCH
A-BOMB
MARRINA
PUCK
MACHINE MAN

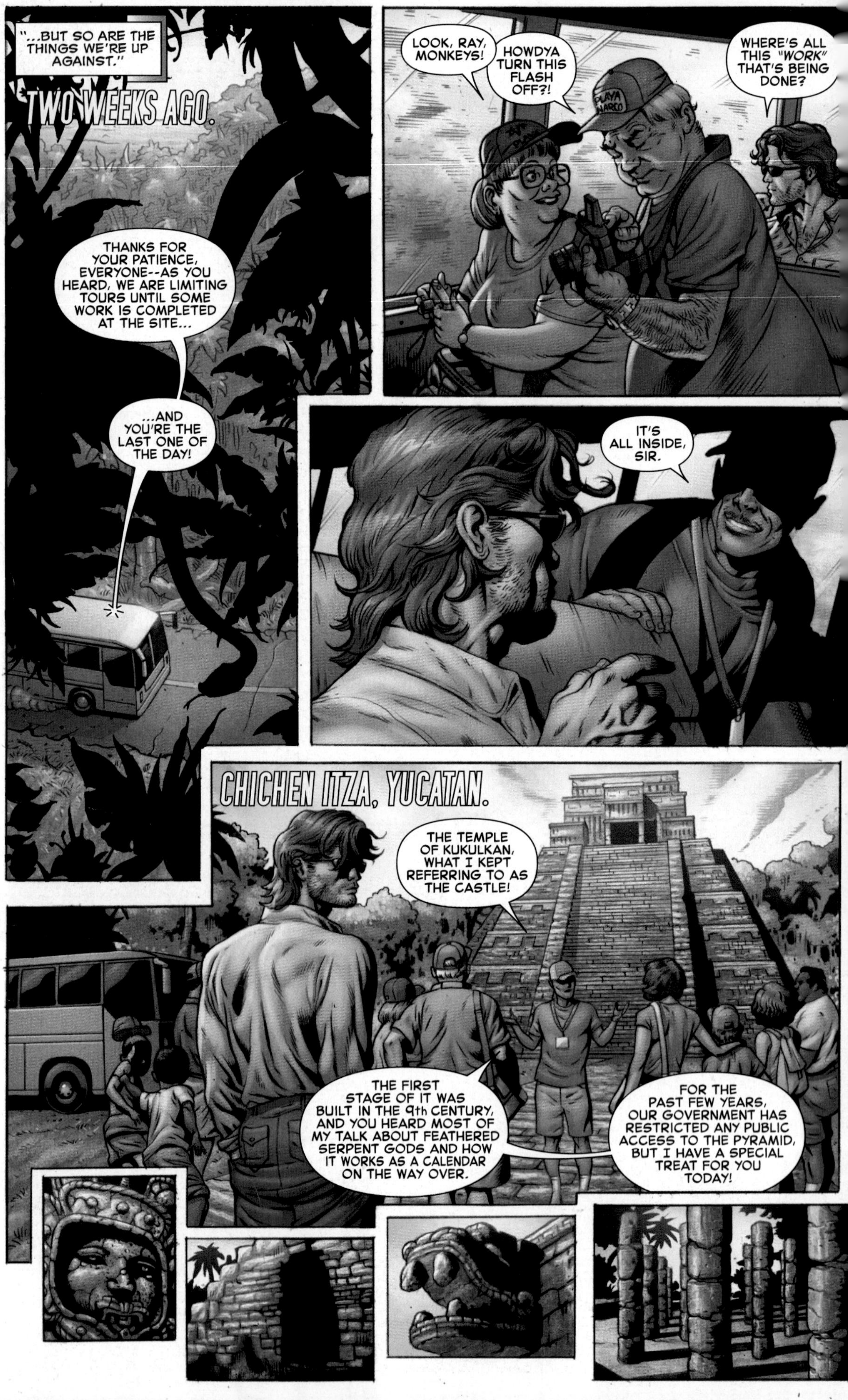
"...BUT SO ARE THE THINGS WE'RE UP AGAINST."
TWO WEEKS AGO.
THANKS FOR YOUR PATIENCE, EVERYONE--AS YOU HEARD, WE ARE LIMITING TOURS UNTIL SOME WORK IS COMPLETED AT THE SITE...
...AND YOU'RE THE LAST ONE OF THE DAY!
LOOK, RAY, MONKEYS!
HOWDYA TURN THIS FLASH OFF?!
PLAYA NARCO
WHERE'S ALL THIS "WORK" THAT'S BEING DONE?
IT'S ALL INSIDE, SIR.
CHICHEN ITZA, YUCATAN.
THE TEMPLE OF KUKULKAN, WHAT I KEPT REFERRING TO AS THE CASTLE!
THE FIRST STAGE OF IT WAS BUILT IN THE 9th CENTURY, AND YOU HEARD MOST OF MY TALK ABOUT FEATHERED SERPENT GODS AND HOW IT WORKS AS A CALENDAR ON THE WAY OVER.
FOR THE PAST FEW YEARS, OUR GOVERNMENT HAS RESTRICTED ANY PUBLIC ACCESS TO THE PYRAMID, BUT I HAVE A SPECIAL TREAT FOR YOU TODAY!

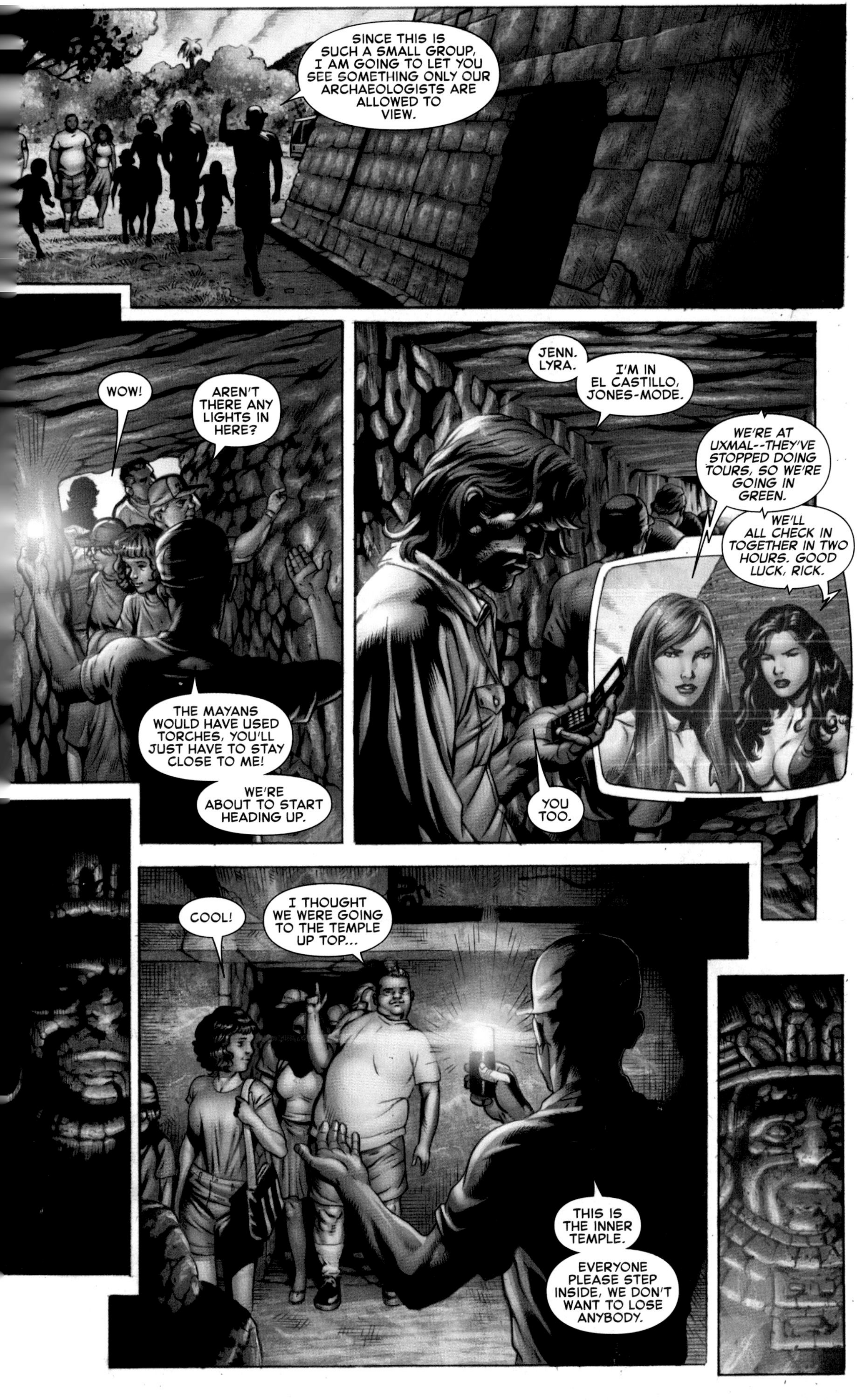
SINCE THIS IS SUCH A SMALL GROUP, I AM GOING TO LET YOU SEE SOMETHING ONLY OUR ARCHAEOLOGISTS ARE ALLOWED TO VIEW.
WOW!
AREN'T THERE ANY LIGHTS IN HERE?
THE MAYANS WOULD HAVE USED TORCHES, YOU'LL JUST HAVE TO STAY CLOSE TO ME!
WE'RE ABOUT TO START HEADING UP.
JENN. LYRA.
I'M IN EL CASTILLO, JONES-MODE.
WE'RE AT UXMAL--THEY'VE STOPPED DOING TOURS, SO WE'RE GOING IN GREEN.
WE'LL ALL CHECK IN TOGETHER IN TWO HOURS. GOOD LUCK, RICK.
YOU TOO.
COOL!
I THOUGHT WE WERE GOING TO THE TEMPLE UP TOP...
THIS IS THE INNER TEMPLE.
EVERYONE PLEASE STEP INSIDE, WE DON'T WANT TO LOSE ANYBODY.

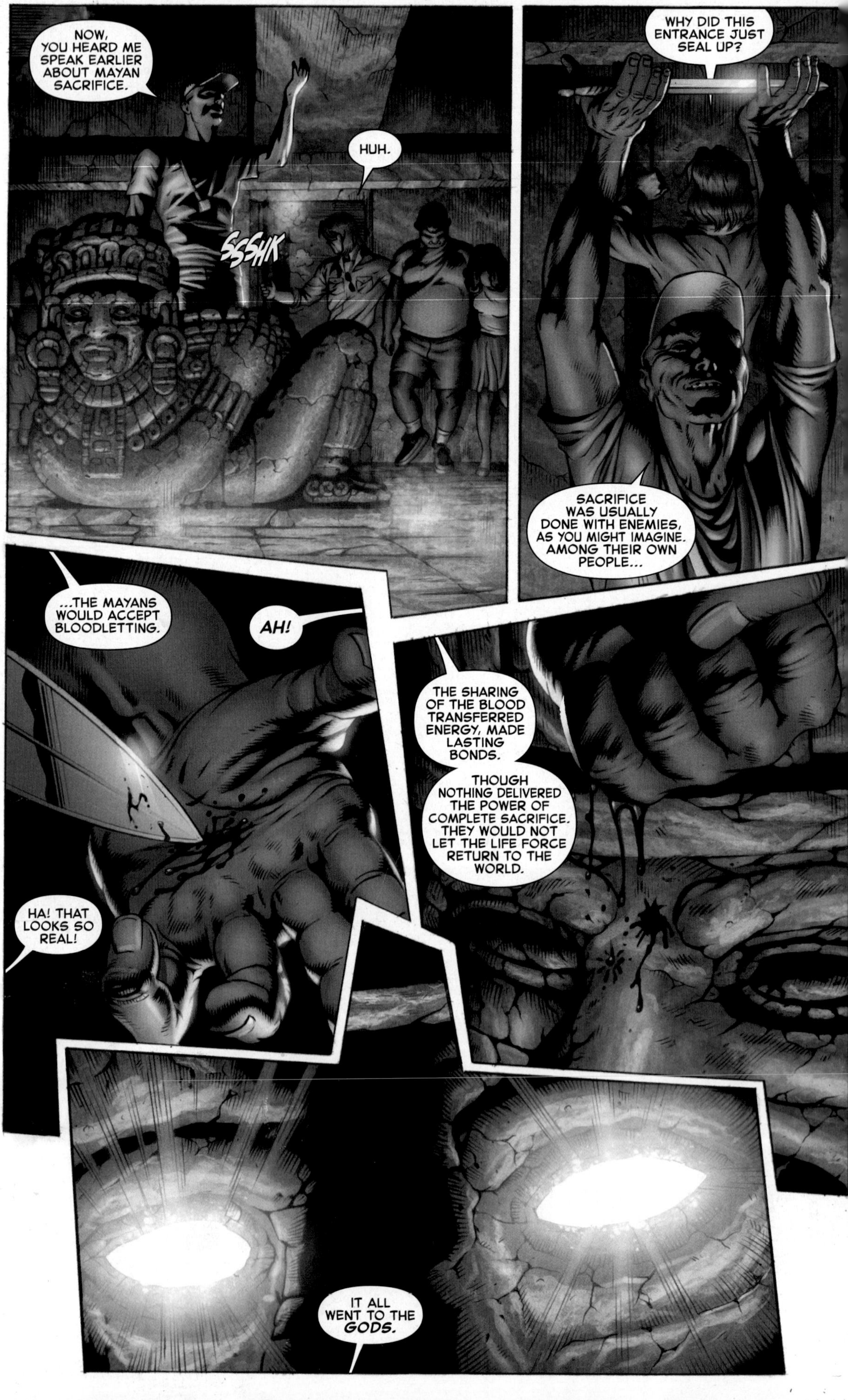

NOW, YOU HEARD ME SPEAK EARLIER ABOUT MAYAN SACRIFICE.
HUH.
SSSHK
WHY DID THIS ENTRANCE JUST SEAL UP?
SACRIFICE WAS USUALLY DONE WITH ENEMIES, AS YOU MIGHT IMAGINE. AMONG THEIR OWN PEOPLE...
...THE MAYANS WOULD ACCEPT BLOODLETTING.
AH!
HA! THAT LOOKS SO REAL!
THE SHARING OF THE BLOOD TRANSFERRED ENERGY, MADE LASTING BONDS.
THOUGH NOTHING DELIVERED THE POWER OF COMPLETE SACRIFICE. THEY WOULD NOT LET THE LIFE FORCE RETURN TO THE WORLD.
IT ALL WENT TO THE GODS.

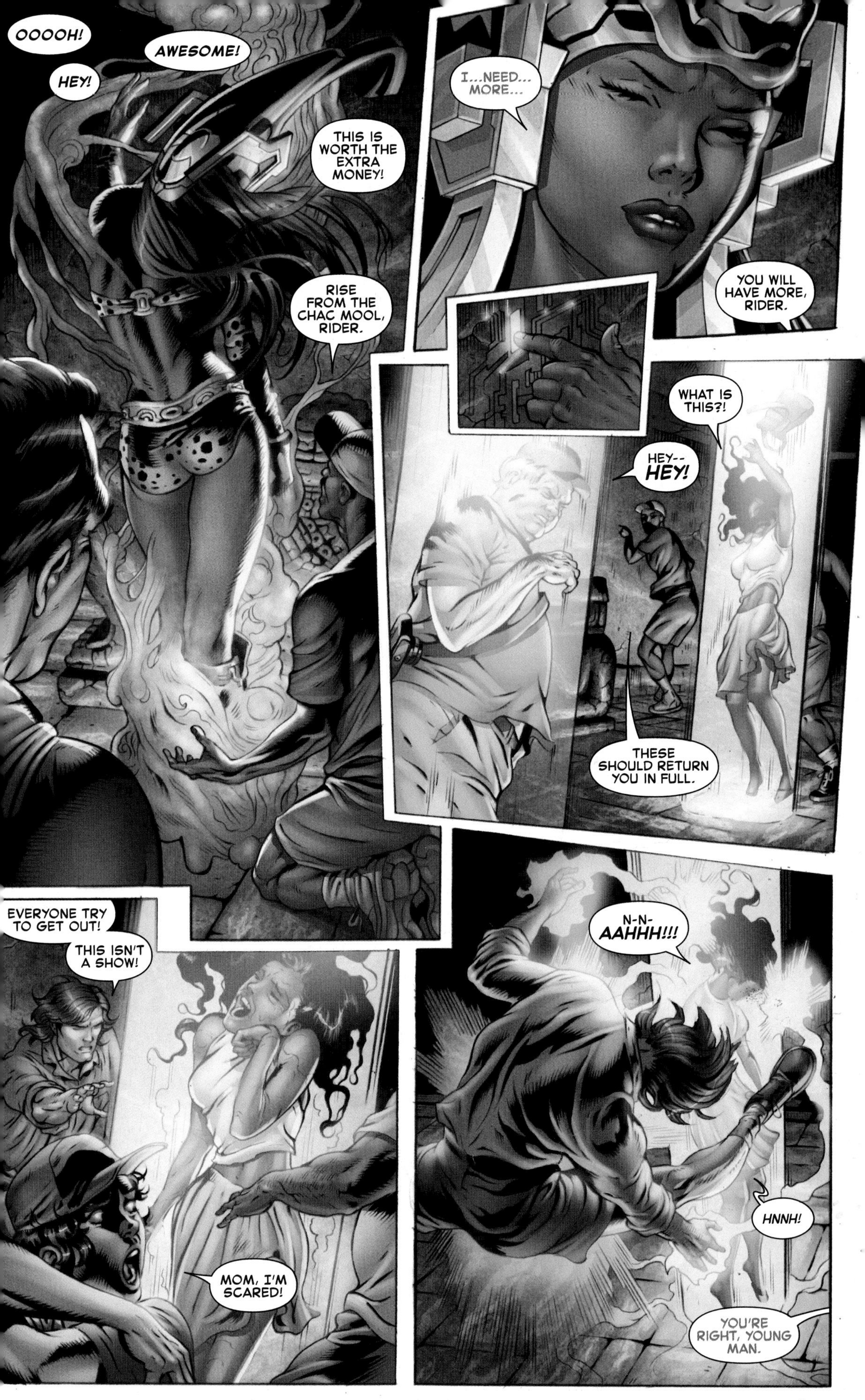
OOOOH!
HEY!
AWESOME!
THIS IS WORTH THE EXTRA MONEY!
RISE FROM THE CHAC MOOL, RIDER.
I...NEED... MORE...
YOU WILL HAVE MORE, RIDER.
WHAT IS THIS?!
HEY-- HEY!
THESE SHOULD RETURN YOU IN FULL.
EVERYONE TRY TO GET OUT!
THIS ISN'T A SHOW!
MOM, I'M SCARED!
N-N- AAHHH!!!
HNNH!
YOU'RE RIGHT, YOUNG MAN.

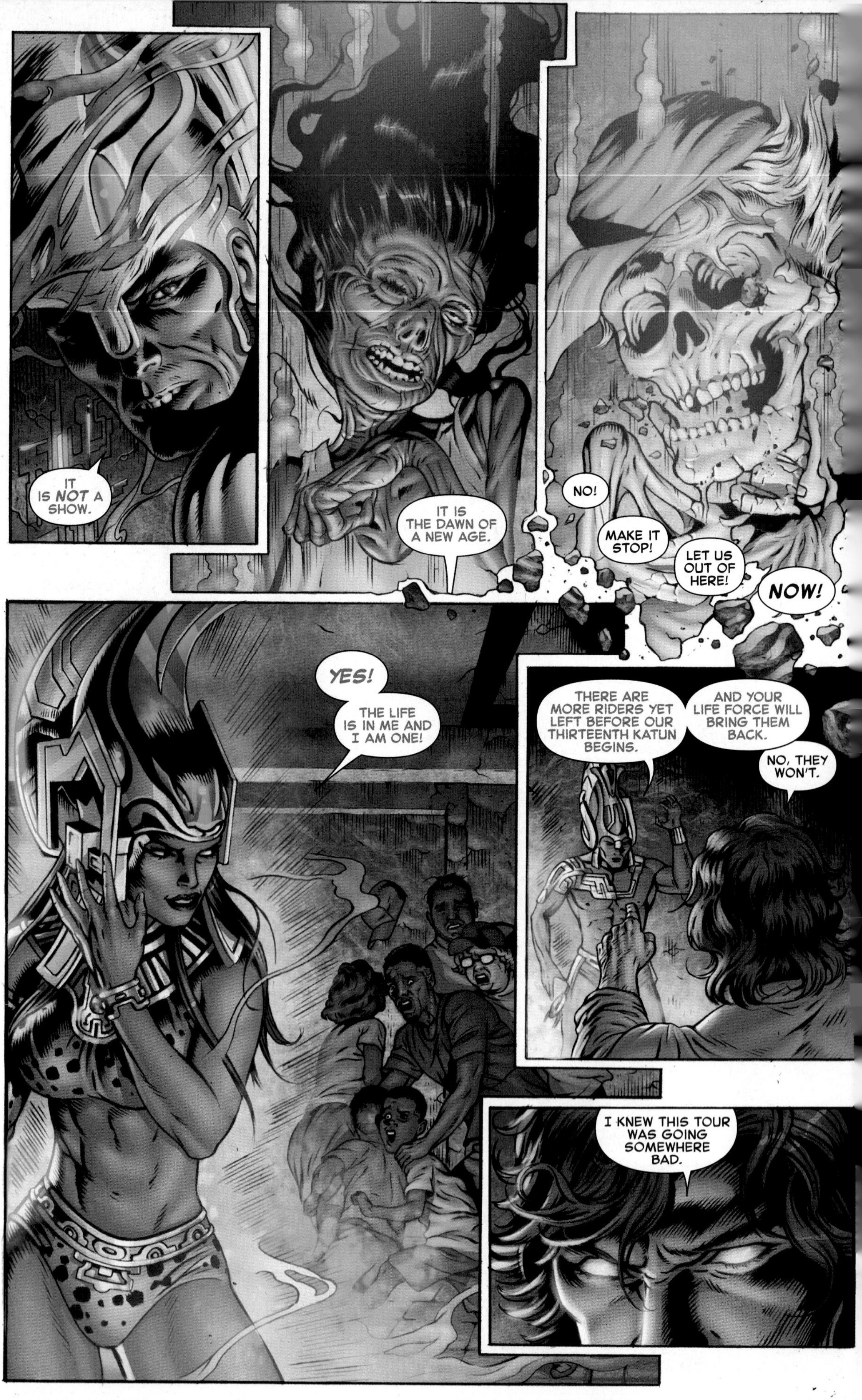
IT IS NOT A SHOW.
IT IS THE DAWN OF A NEW AGE.
NO!
MAKE IT STOP!
LET US OUT OF HERE!
NOW!
YES!
THE LIFE IS IN ME AND I AM ONE!
THERE ARE MORE RIDERS YET LEFT BEFORE OUR THIRTEENTH KATUN BEGINS.
AND YOUR LIFE FORCE WILL BRING THEM BACK.
NO, THEY WON'T.
I KNEW THIS TOUR WAS GOING SOMEWHERE BAD.

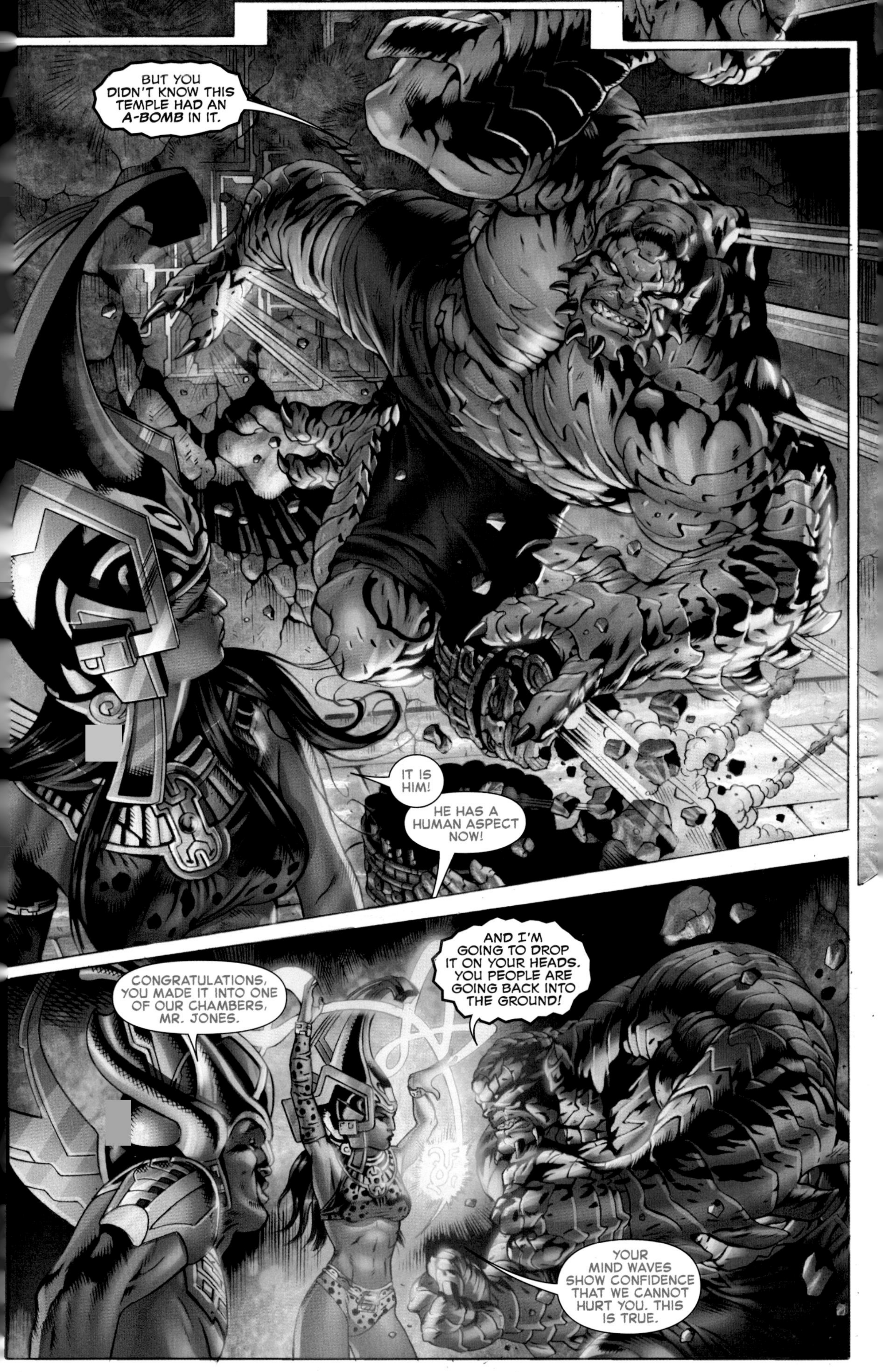
BUT YOU DIDN'T KNOW THIS TEMPLE HAD AN A-BOMB IN IT.
IT IS HIM!
HE HAS A HUMAN ASPECT NOW!
CONGRATULATIONS, YOU MADE IT INTO ONE OF OUR CHAMBERS, MR. JONES.
AND I'M GOING TO DROP IT ON YOUR HEADS. YOU PEOPLE ARE GOING BACK INTO THE GROUND!
YOUR MIND WAVES SHOW CONFIDENCE THAT WE CANNOT HURT YOU. THIS IS TRUE.

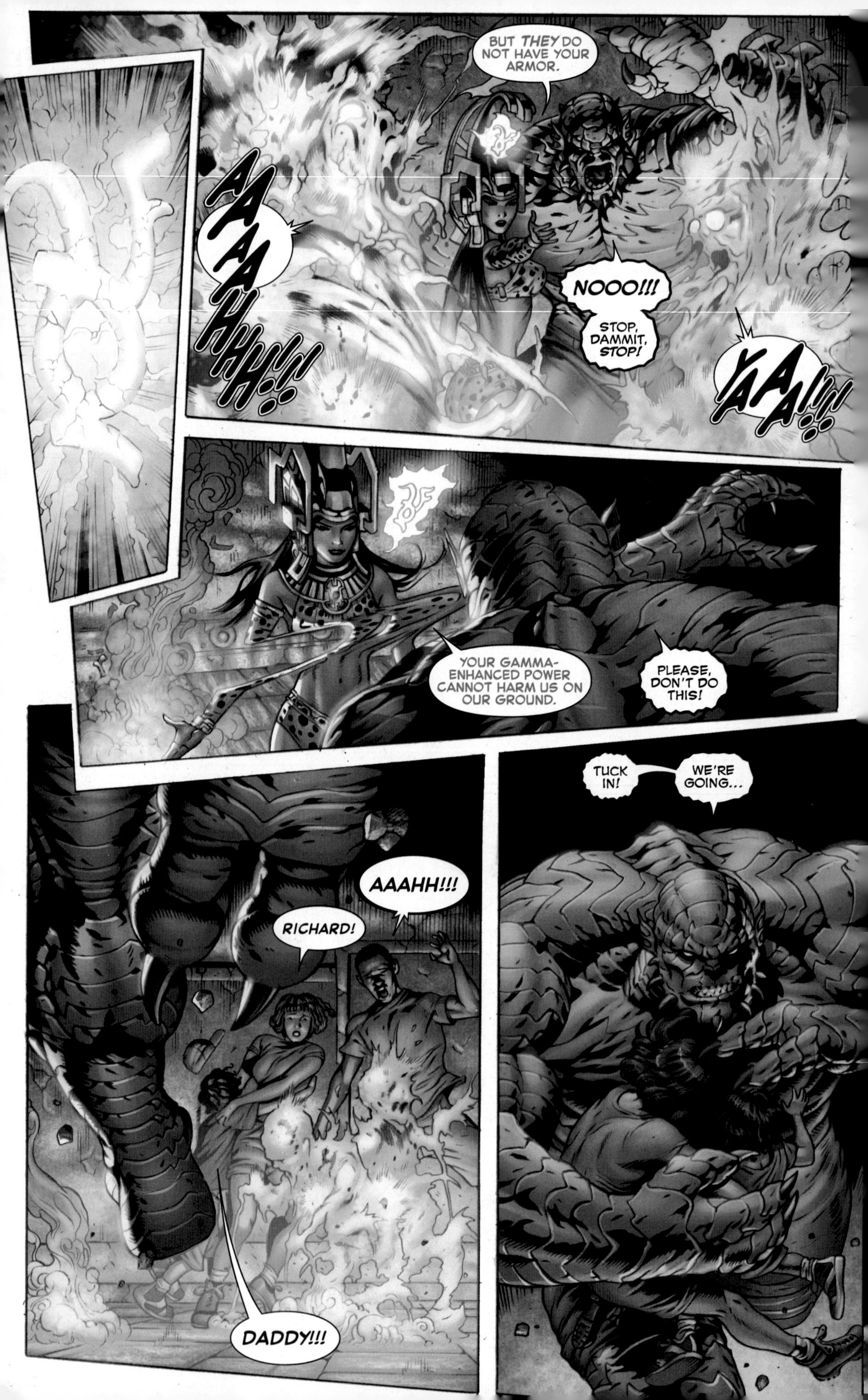
BUT THEY DO NOT HAVE YOUR ARMOR.
AAAAHHH!!!!
NOOO!!!
STOP, DAMMIT, STOP!
YAAA!!!!
YOUR GAMMA-ENHANCED POWER CANNOT HARM US ON OUR GROUND.
PLEASE, DON'T DO THIS!
AAAHH!!!
RICHARD!
DADDY!!!
TUCK IN!
WE'RE GOING...

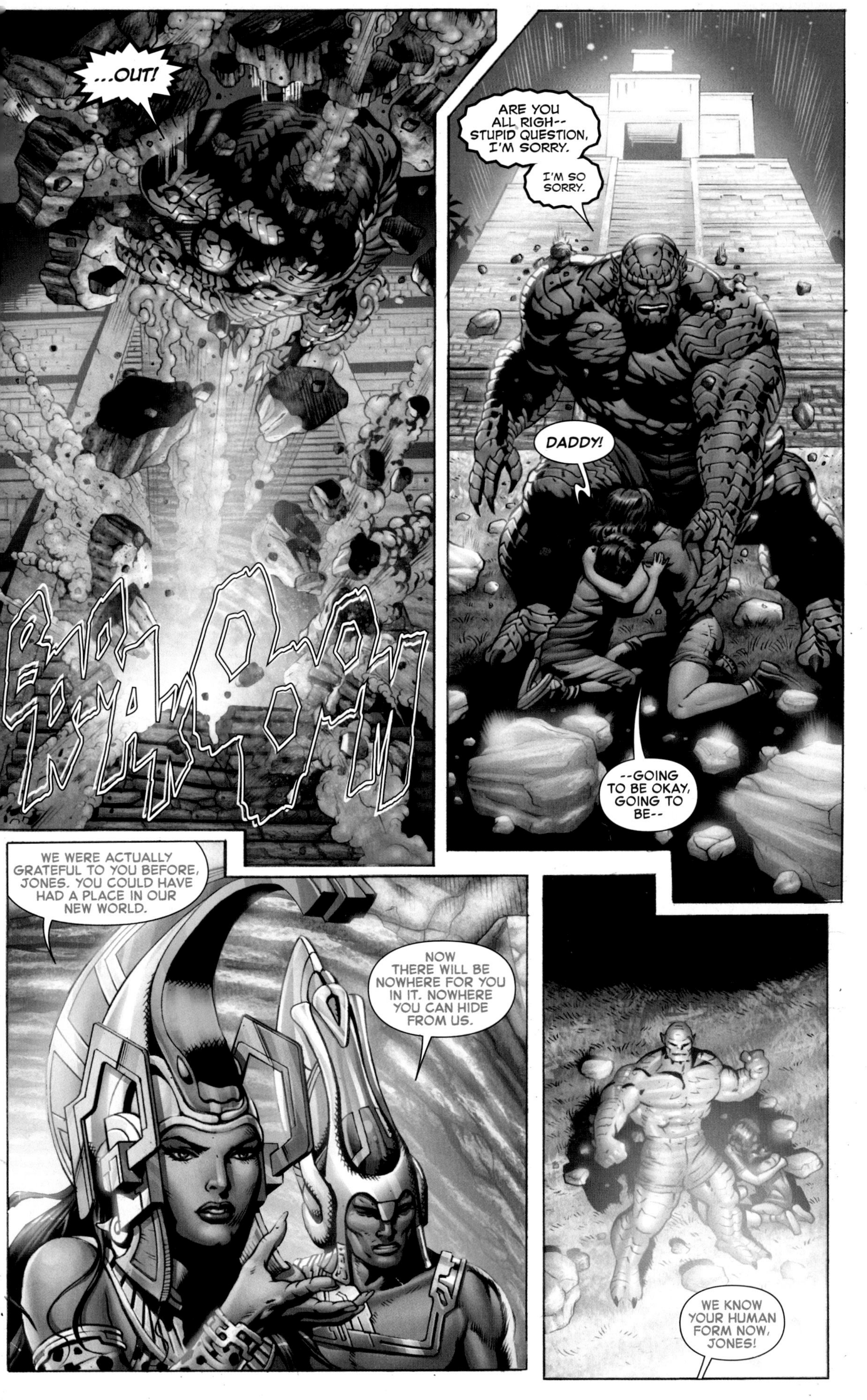
...OUT!
ARE YOU ALL RIGH-- STUPID QUESTION, I'M SORRY.
I'M SO SORRY.
DADDY!
--GOING TO BE OKAY, GOING TO BE--
WE WERE ACTUALLY GRATEFUL TO YOU BEFORE, JONES. YOU COULD HAVE HAD A PLACE IN OUR NEW WORLD.
NOW THERE WILL BE NOWHERE FOR YOU IN IT. NOWHERE YOU CAN HIDE FROM US.
WE KNOW YOUR HUMAN FORM NOW, JONES!

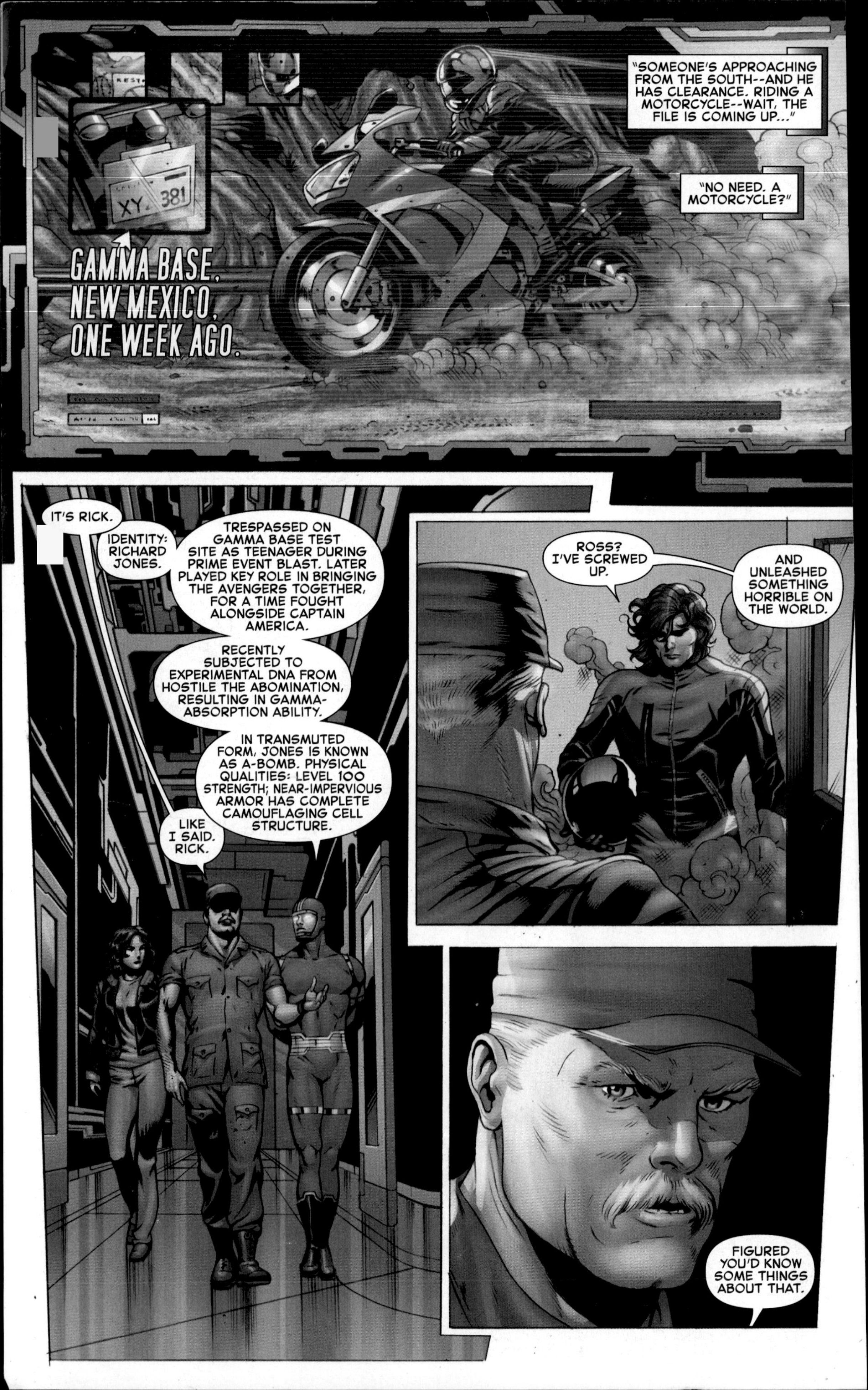
GAMMA BASE, NEW MEXICO, ONE WEEK AGO.
"SOMEONE'S APPROACHING FROM THE SOUTH--AND HE HAS CLEARANCE. RIDING A MOTORCYCLE--WAIT, THE FILE IS COMING UP..."
"NO NEED. A MOTORCYCLE?"
XY 381
IT'S RICK.
IDENTITY: RICHARD JONES.
TRESPASSED ON GAMMA BASE TEST SITE AS TEENAGER DURING PRIME EVENT BLAST. LATER PLAYED KEY ROLE IN BRINGING THE AVENGERS TOGETHER, FOR A TIME FOUGHT ALONGSIDE CAPTAIN AMERICA.
RECENTLY SUBJECTED TO EXPERIMENTAL DNA FROM HOSTILE THE ABOMINATION, RESULTING IN GAMMA-ABSORPTION ABILITY.
IN TRANSMUTED FORM, JONES IS KNOWN AS A-BOMB. PHYSICAL QUALITIES: LEVEL 100 STRENGTH; NEAR-IMPERVIOUS ARMOR HAS COMPLETE CAMOUFLAGING CELL STRUCTURE.
LIKE I SAID. RICK.
ROSS? I'VE SCREWED UP.
AND UNLEASHED SOMETHING HORRIBLE ON THE WORLD.
FIGURED YOU'D KNOW SOME THINGS ABOUT THAT.

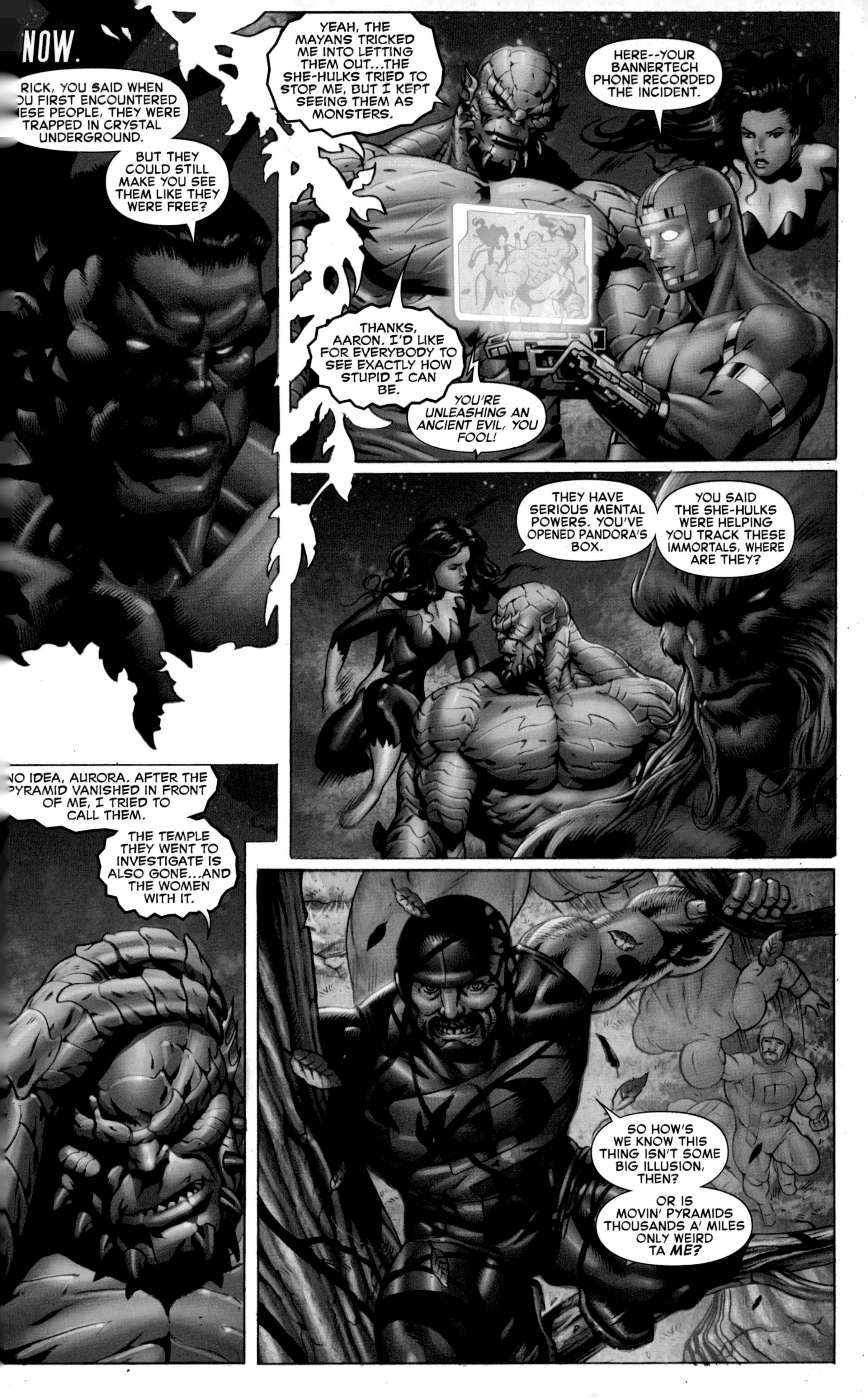
NOW.
RICK, YOU SAID WHEN OU FIRST ENCOUNTERED IESE PEOPLE, THEY WERE TRAPPED IN CRYSTAL UNDERGROUND.
BUT THEY COULD STILL MAKE YOU SEE THEM LIKE THEY WERE FREE?
YEAH, THE MAYANS TRICKED ME INTO LETTING THEM OUT...THE SHE-HULKS TRIED TO STOP ME, BUT I KEPT SEEING THEM AS MONSTERS.
HERE--YOUR BANNERTECH PHONE RECORDED THE INCIDENT.
THANKS, AARON. I'D LIKE FOR EVERYBODY TO SEE EXACTLY HOW STUPID I CAN BE.
YOU'RE UNLEASHING AN ANCIENT EVIL, YOU FOOL!
THEY HAVE SERIOUS MENTAL POWERS. YOU'VE OPENED PANDORA'S BOX.
YOU SAID THE SHE-HULKS WERE HELPING YOU TRACK THESE IMMORTALS, WHERE ARE THEY?
NO IDEA, AURORA. AFTER THE PYRAMID VANISHED IN FRONT OF ME, I TRIED TO CALL THEM.
THE TEMPLE THEY WENT TO INVESTIGATE IS ALSO GONE...AND THE WOMEN WITH IT.
SO HOW'S WE KNOW THIS THING ISN'T SOME BIG ILLUSION, THEN?
OR IS MOVIN' PYRAMIDS THOUSANDS A' MILES ONLY WEIRD TA *ME?*

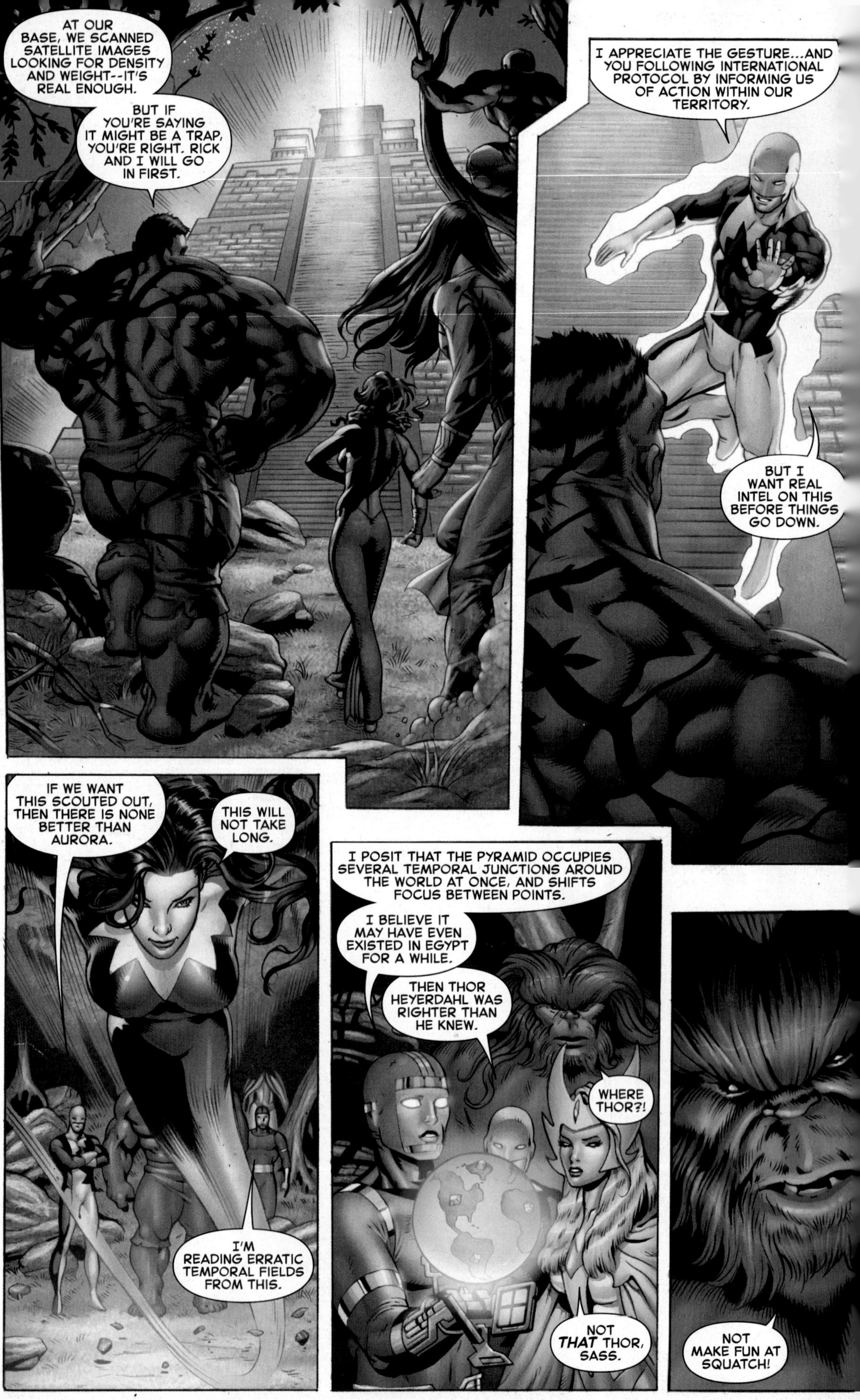
AT OUR BASE, WE SCANNED SATELLITE IMAGES LOOKING FOR DENSITY AND WEIGHT--IT'S REAL ENOUGH.
BUT IF YOU'RE SAYING IT MIGHT BE A TRAP, YOU'RE RIGHT. RICK AND I WILL GO IN FIRST.
I APPRECIATE THE GESTURE...AND YOU FOLLOWING INTERNATIONAL PROTOCOL BY INFORMING US OF ACTION WITHIN OUR TERRITORY.
BUT I WANT REAL INTEL ON THIS BEFORE THINGS GO DOWN.
IF WE WANT THIS SCOUTED OUT, THEN THERE IS NONE BETTER THAN AURORA.
THIS WILL NOT TAKE LONG.
I'M READING ERRATIC TEMPORAL FIELDS FROM THIS.
I POSIT THAT THE PYRAMID OCCUPIES SEVERAL TEMPORAL JUNCTIONS AROUND THE WORLD AT ONCE, AND SHIFTS FOCUS BETWEEN POINTS.
I BELIEVE IT MAY HAVE EVEN EXISTED IN EGYPT FOR A WHILE.
THEN THOR HEYERDAHL WAS RIGHTER THAN HE KNEW.
WHERE THOR?!
NOT **THAT** THOR, SASS.
NOT MAKE FUN AT SQUATCH!

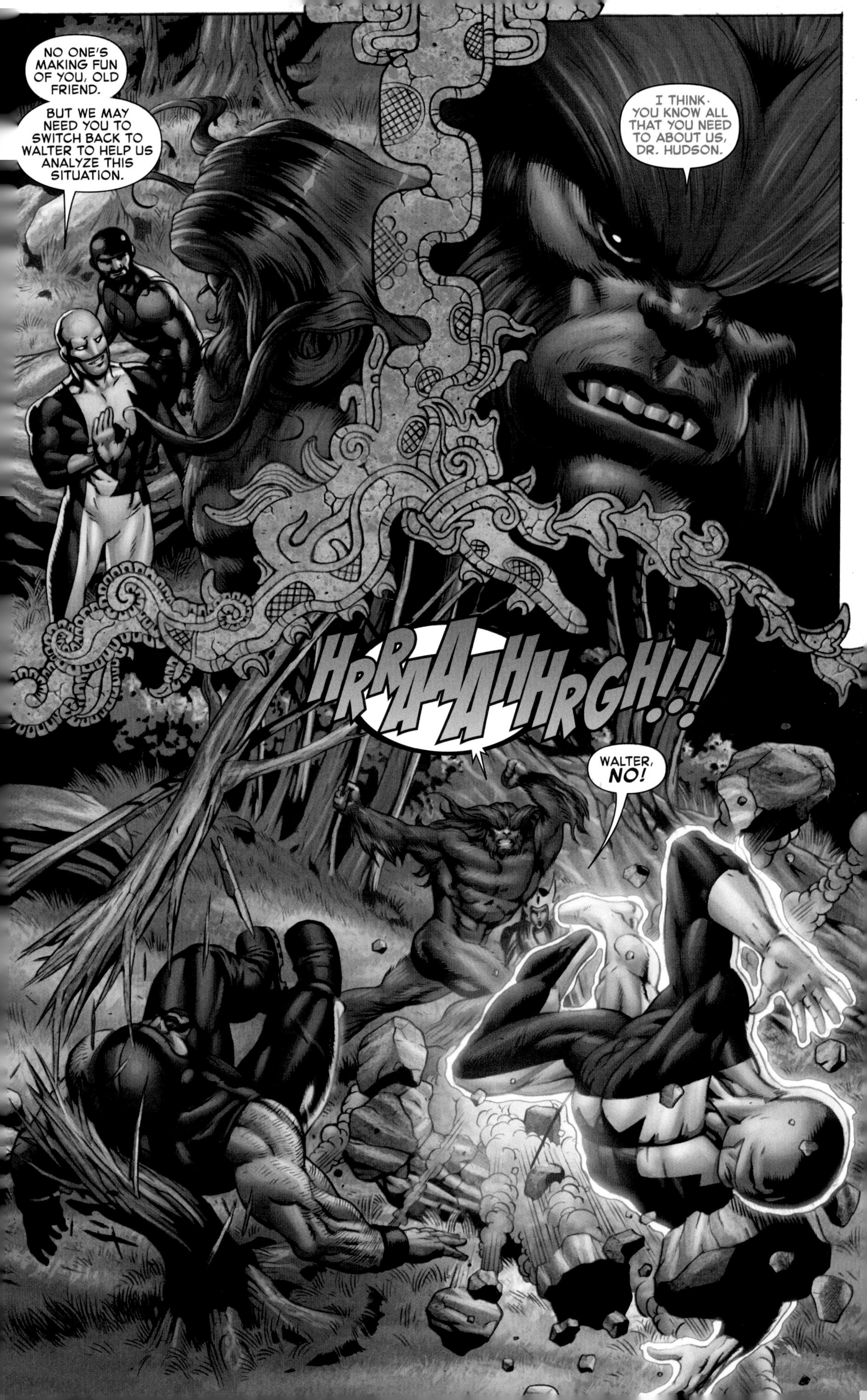
NO ONE'S MAKING FUN OF YOU, OLD FRIEND.
BUT WE MAY NEED YOU TO SWITCH BACK TO WALTER TO HELP US ANALYZE THIS SITUATION.
I THINK YOU KNOW ALL THAT YOU NEED TO ABOUT US, DR. HUDSON.
HRRAAAHHRGH!!!
WALTER, NO!

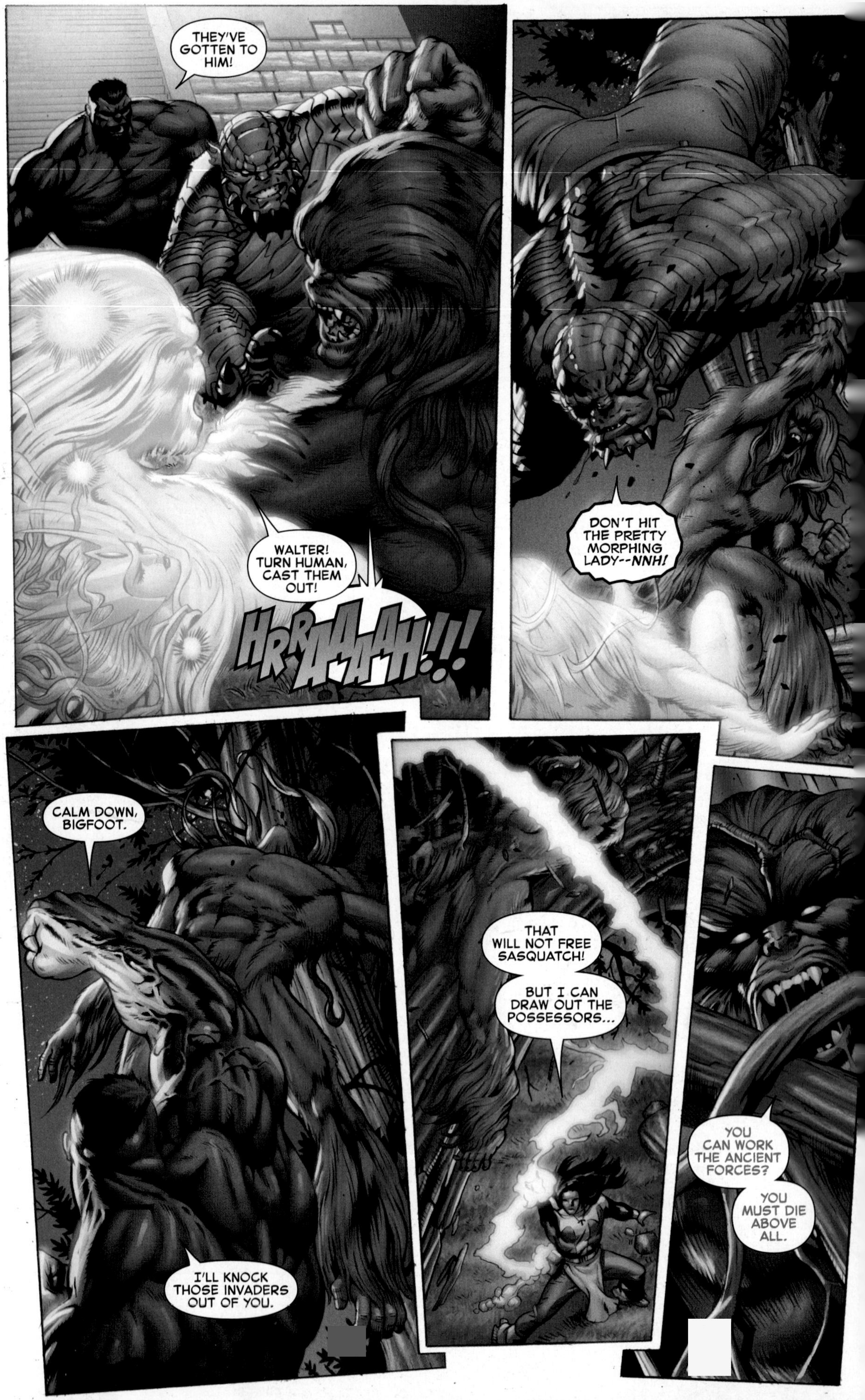
THEY'VE GOTTEN TO HIM!
WALTER! TURN HUMAN, CAST THEM OUT!
HRRAAAAH!!!
DON'T HIT THE PRETTY MORPHING LADY--NNH!
CALM DOWN, BIGFOOT.
I'LL KNOCK THOSE INVADERS OUT OF YOU.
THAT WILL NOT FREE SASQUATCH!
BUT I CAN DRAW OUT THE POSSESSORS...
YOU CAN WORK THE ANCIENT FORCES?
YOU MUST DIE ABOVE ALL.

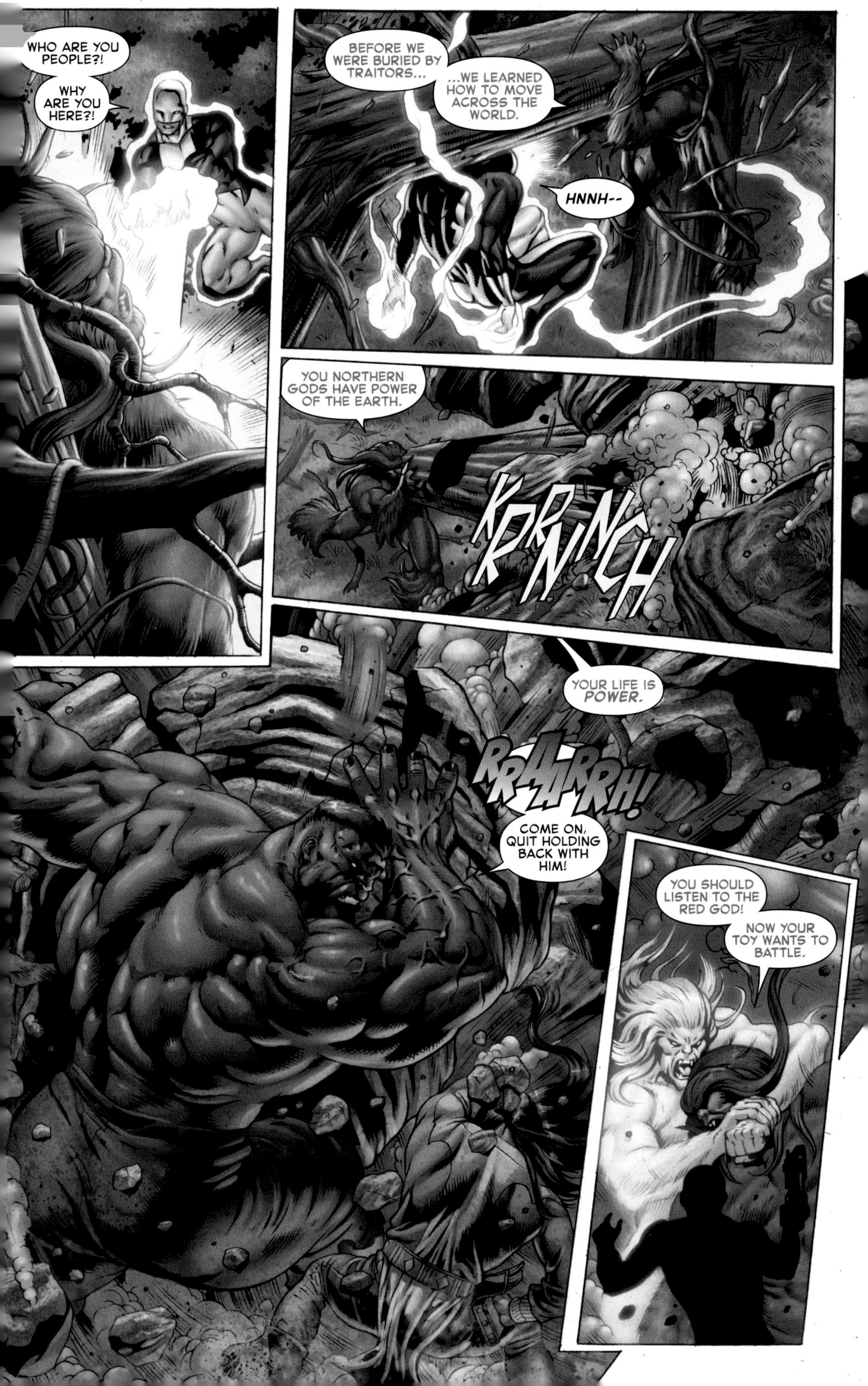
WHO ARE YOU PEOPLE?!
WHY ARE YOU HERE?!
BEFORE WE WERE BURIED BY TRAITORS...
...WE LEARNED HOW TO MOVE ACROSS THE WORLD.
HNNH--
YOU NORTHERN GODS HAVE POWER OF THE EARTH.
KKRRNNCH
YOUR LIFE IS POWER.
RRAARRH!
COME ON, QUIT HOLDING BACK WITH HIM!
YOU SHOULD LISTEN TO THE RED GOD!
NOW YOUR TOY WANTS TO BATTLE.

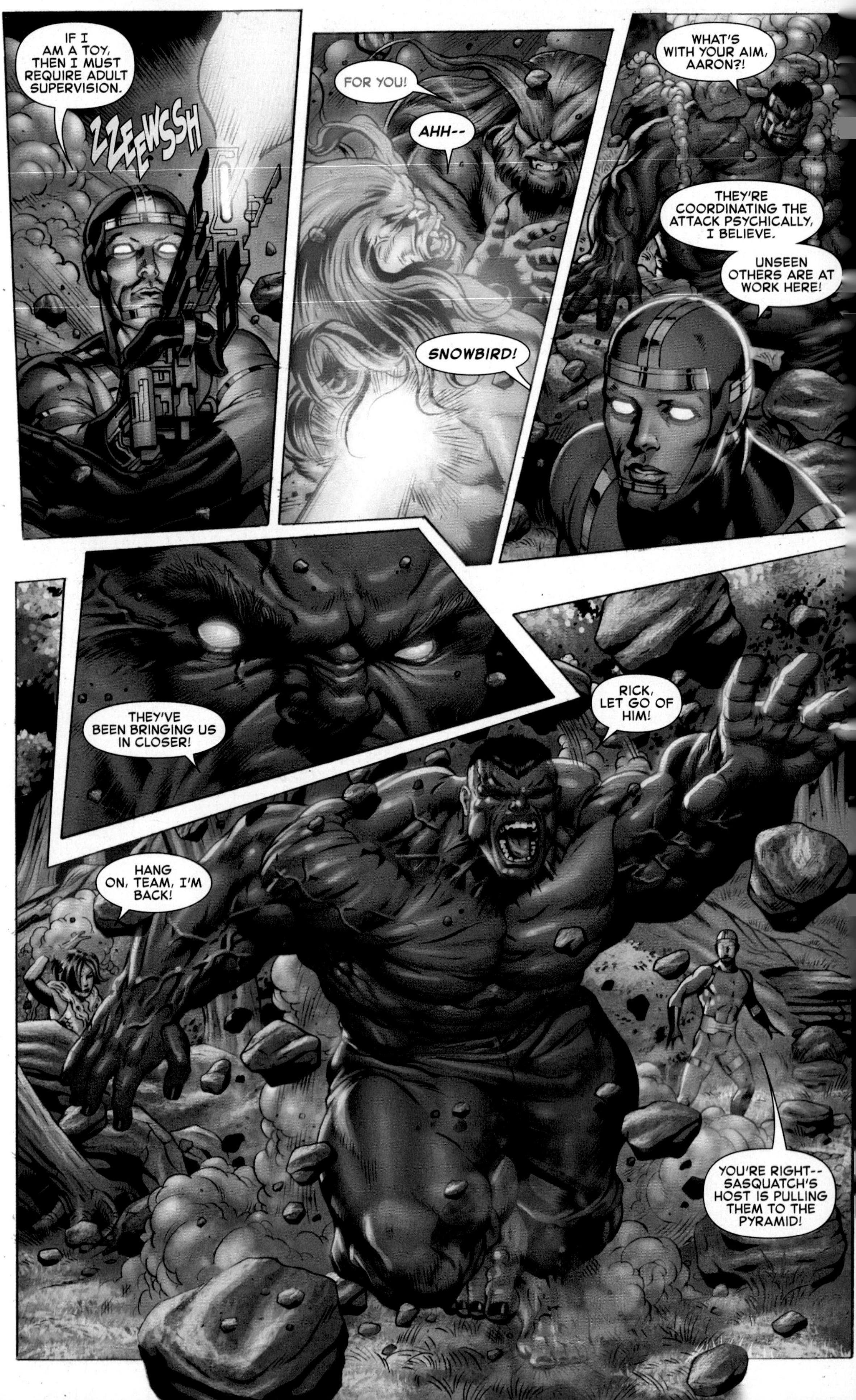
IF I AM A TOY, THEN I MUST REQUIRE ADULT SUPERVISION.
ZZEEWSSH
FOR YOU!
AHH--
SNOWBIRD!
WHAT'S WITH YOUR AIM, AARON?!
THEY'RE COORDINATING THE ATTACK PSYCHICALLY, I BELIEVE.
UNSEEN OTHERS ARE AT WORK HERE!
THEY'VE BEEN BRINGING US IN CLOSER!
RICK, LET GO OF HIM!
HANG ON, TEAM, I'M BACK!
YOU'RE RIGHT-- SASQUATCH'S HOST IS PULLING THEM TO THE PYRAMID!

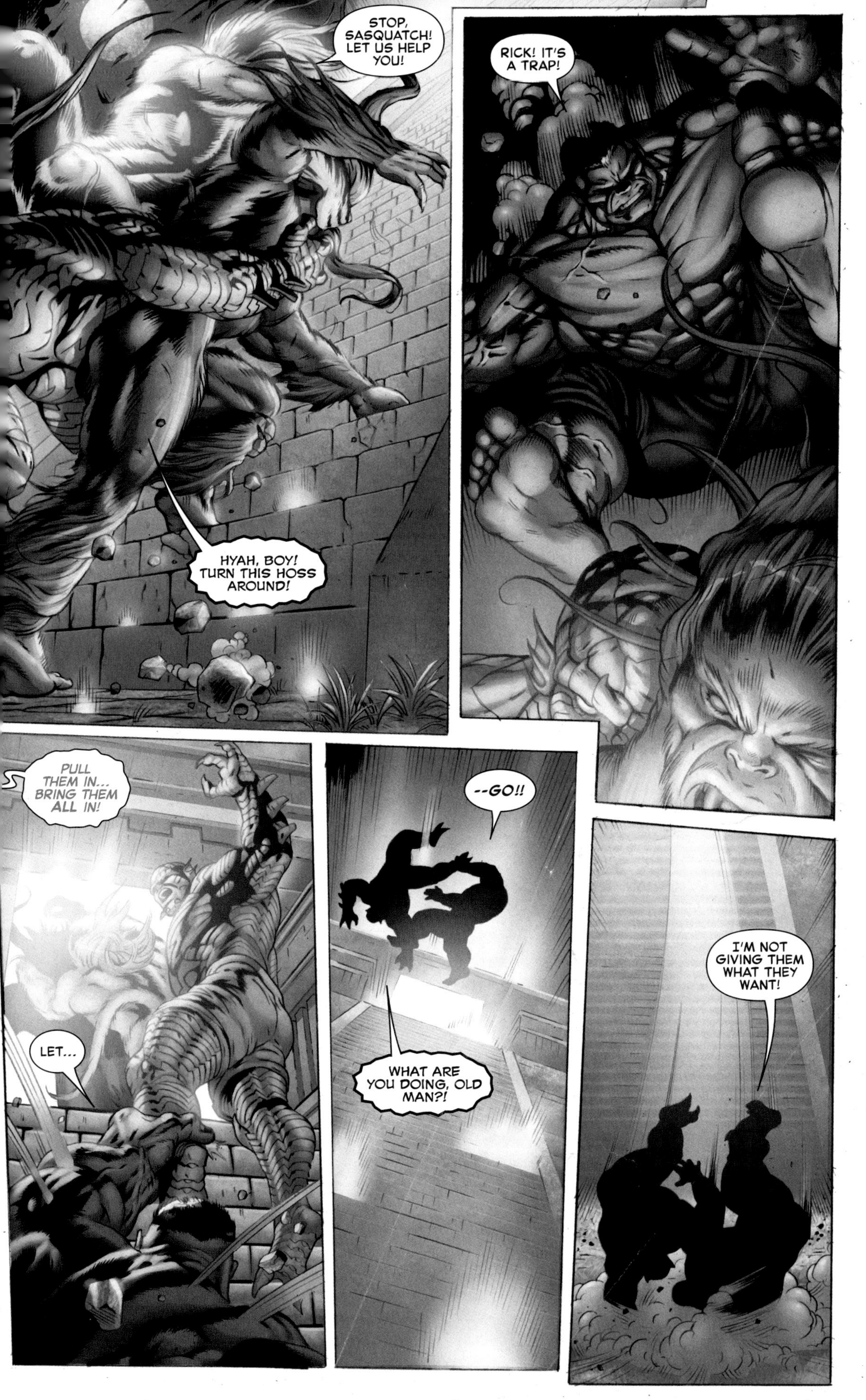
STOP, SASQUATCH! LET US HELP YOU!
HYAH, BOY! TURN THIS HOSS AROUND!
RICK! IT'S A TRAP!
PULL THEM IN... BRING THEM ALL IN!
LET...
--GO!!
WHAT ARE YOU DOING, OLD MAN?!
I'M NOT GIVING THEM WHAT THEY WANT!

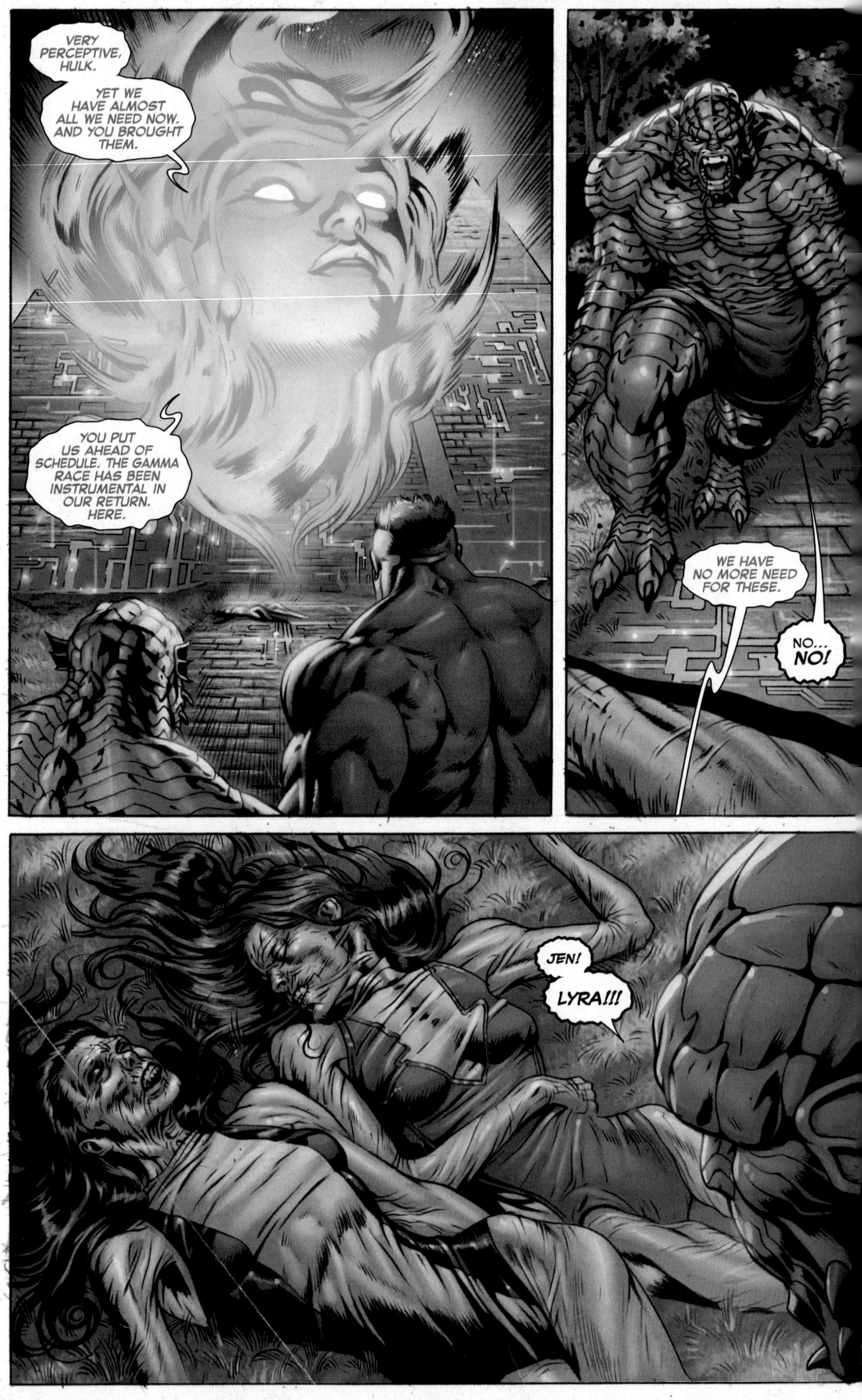
VERY PERCEPTIVE, HULK.
YET WE HAVE ALMOST ALL WE NEED NOW. AND YOU BROUGHT THEM.
YOU PUT US AHEAD OF SCHEDULE. THE GAMMA RACE HAS BEEN INSTRUMENTAL IN OUR RETURN. HERE.
WE HAVE NO MORE NEED FOR THESE.
NO... NO!
JEN!
LYRA!!!

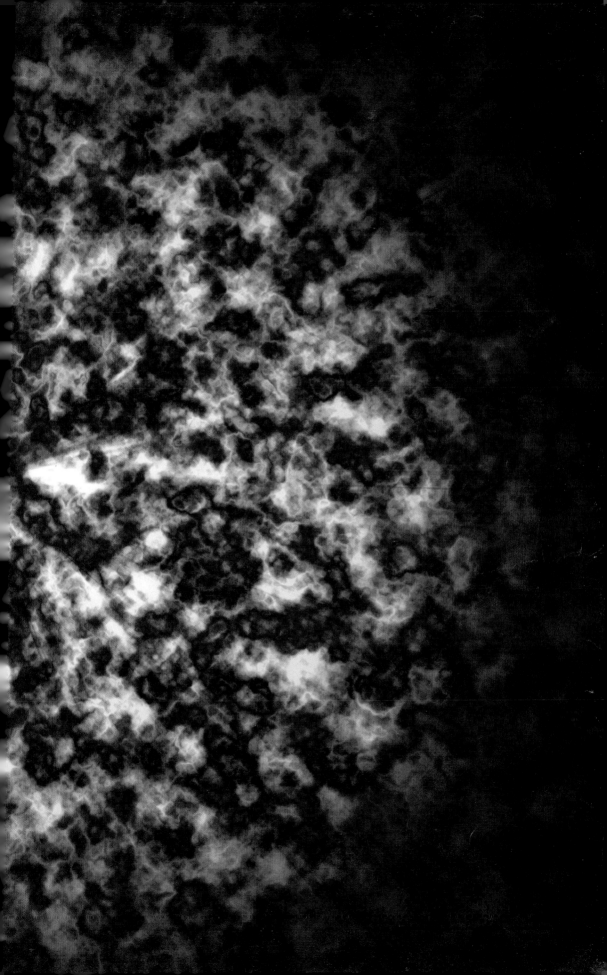

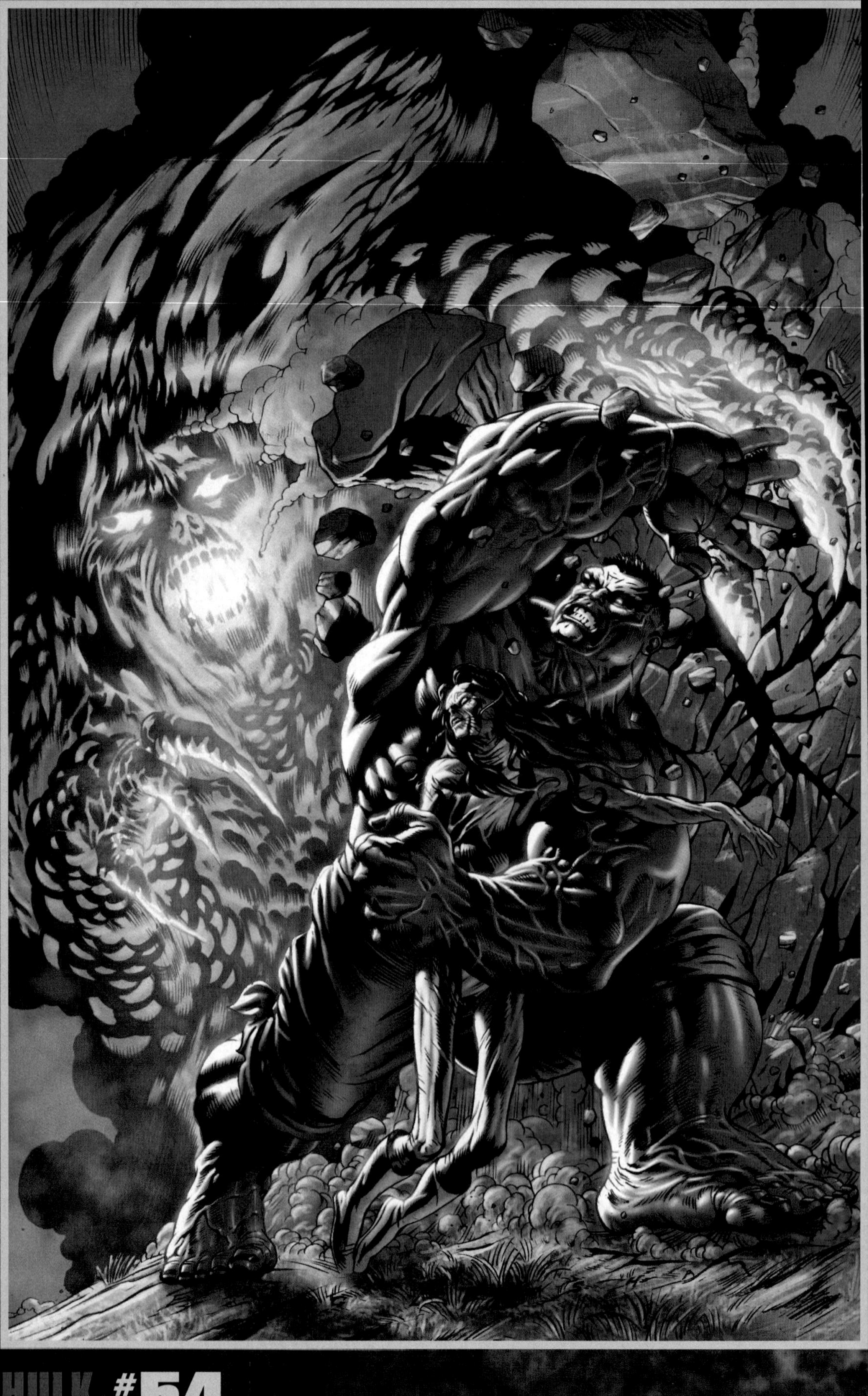

HULK #54

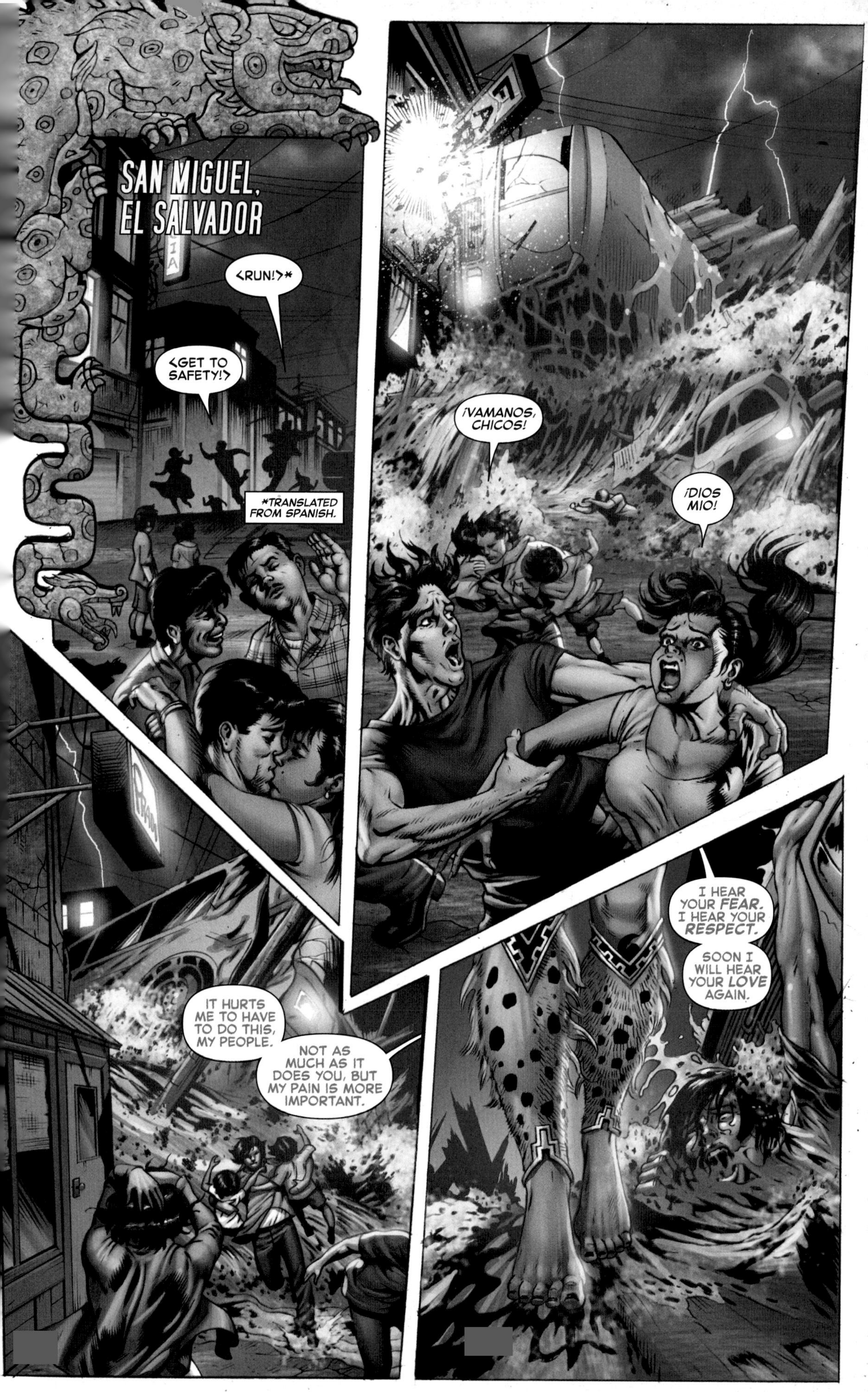
SAN MIGUEL, EL SALVADOR
<RUN!>*
<GET TO SAFETY!>
*TRANSLATED FROM SPANISH.
¡VAMANOS, CHICOS!
¡DIOS MIO!
IT HURTS ME TO HAVE TO DO THIS, MY PEOPLE.
NOT AS MUCH AS IT DOES YOU, BUT MY PAIN IS MORE IMPORTANT.
I HEAR YOUR FEAR. I HEAR YOUR RESPECT.
SOON I WILL HEAR YOUR LOVE AGAIN.

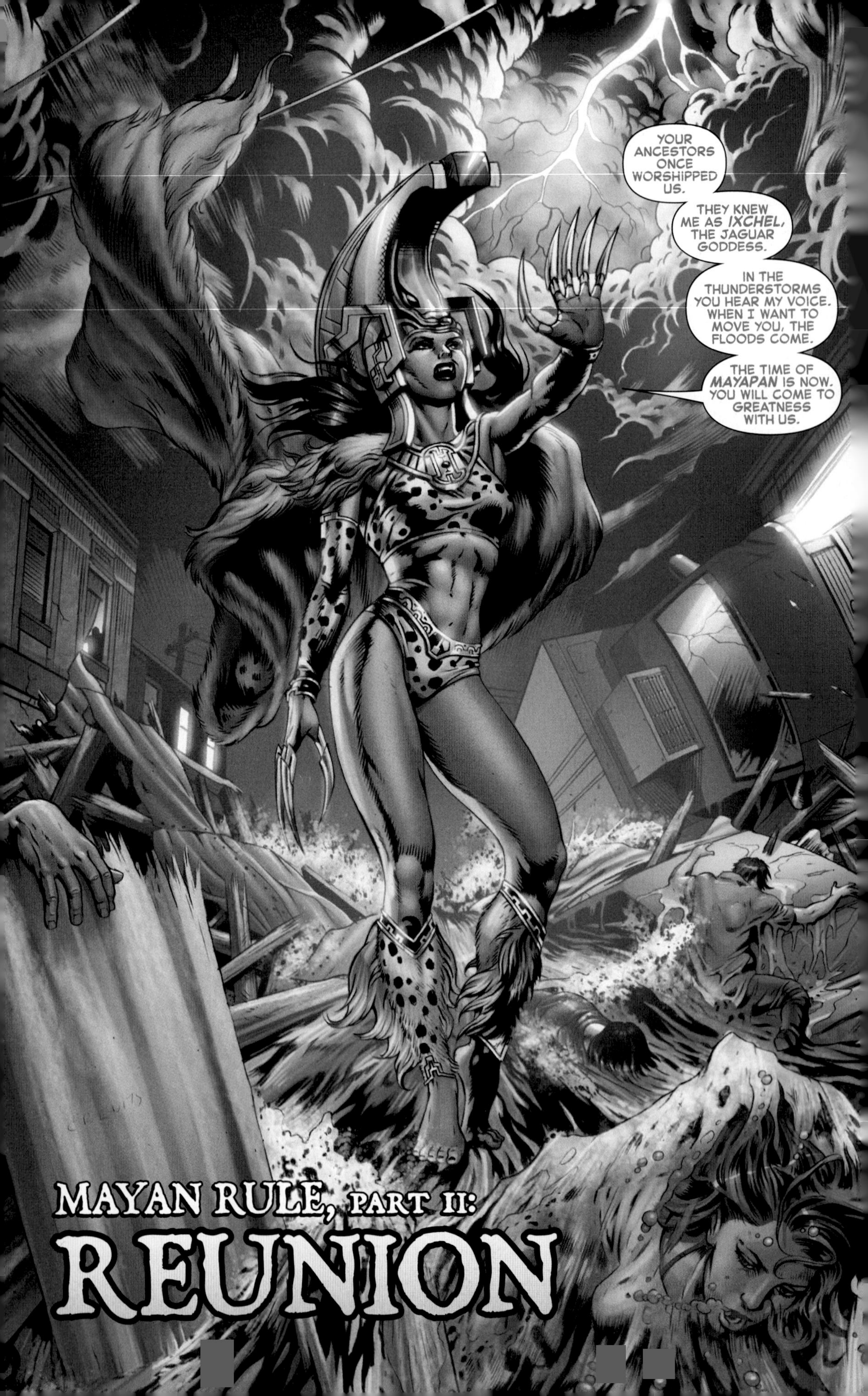
YOUR ANCESTORS ONCE WORSHIPPED US.
THEY KNEW ME AS IXCHEL, THE JAGUAR GODDESS.
IN THE THUNDERSTORMS YOU HEAR MY VOICE. WHEN I WANT TO MOVE YOU, THE FLOODS COME.
THE TIME OF MAYAPAN IS NOW. YOU WILL COME TO GREATNESS WITH US.
MAYAN RULE, PART II:
REUNION

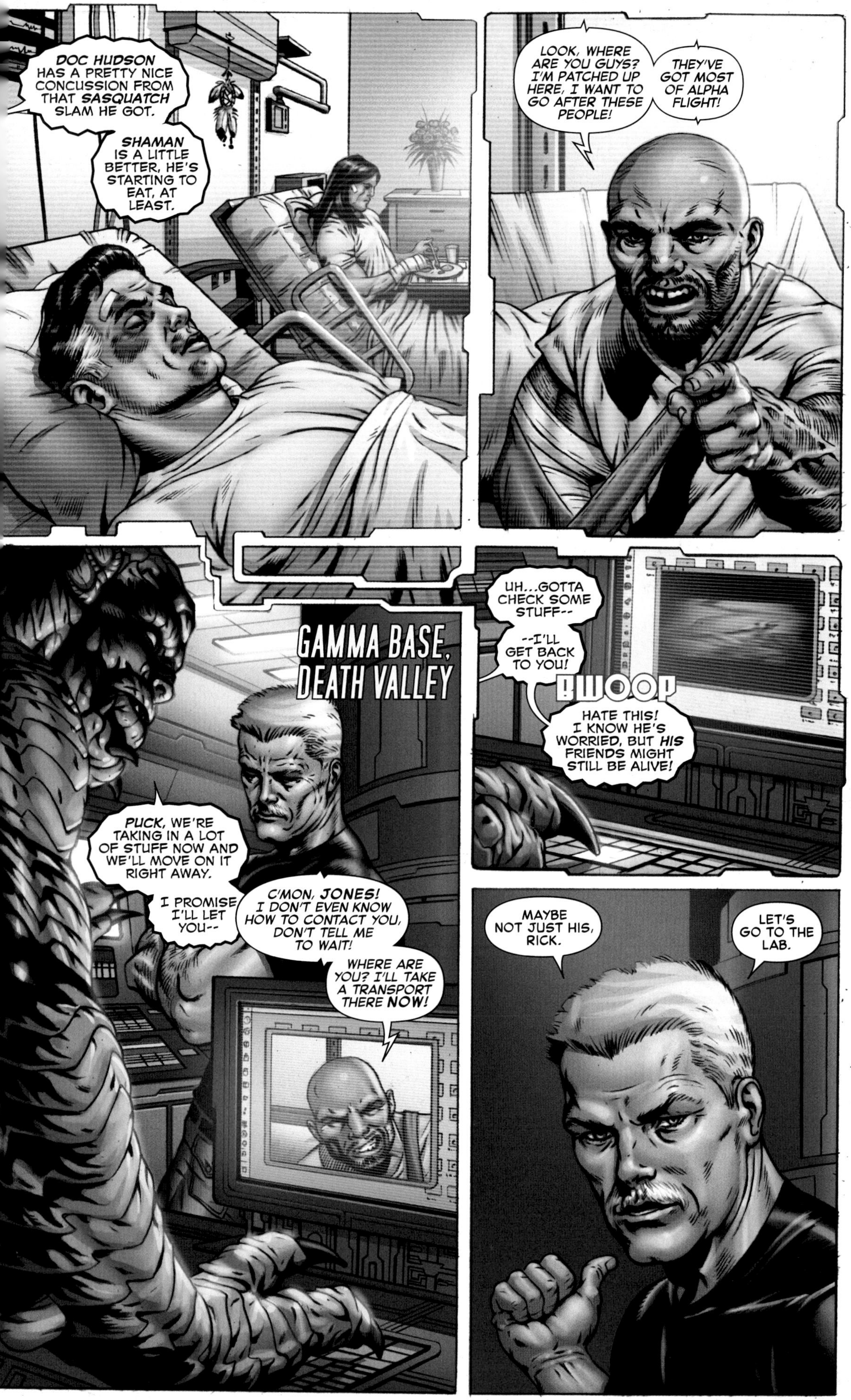
DOC HUDSON HAS A PRETTY NICE CONCUSSION FROM THAT SASQUATCH SLAM HE GOT.
SHAMAN IS A LITTLE BETTER, HE'S STARTING TO EAT, AT LEAST.
LOOK, WHERE ARE YOU GUYS? I'M PATCHED UP HERE, I WANT TO GO AFTER THESE PEOPLE!
THEY'VE GOT MOST OF ALPHA FLIGHT!
GAMMA BASE, DEATH VALLEY
PUCK, WE'RE TAKING IN A LOT OF STUFF NOW AND WE'LL MOVE ON IT RIGHT AWAY.
I PROMISE I'LL LET YOU--
C'MON, JONES! I DON'T EVEN KNOW HOW TO CONTACT YOU, DON'T TELL ME TO WAIT!
WHERE ARE YOU? I'LL TAKE A TRANSPORT THERE NOW!
UH...GOTTA CHECK SOME STUFF--
--I'LL GET BACK TO YOU!
BWOOP
HATE THIS! I KNOW HE'S WORRIED, BUT HIS FRIENDS MIGHT STILL BE ALIVE!
MAYBE NOT JUST HIS, RICK.
LET'S GO TO THE LAB.

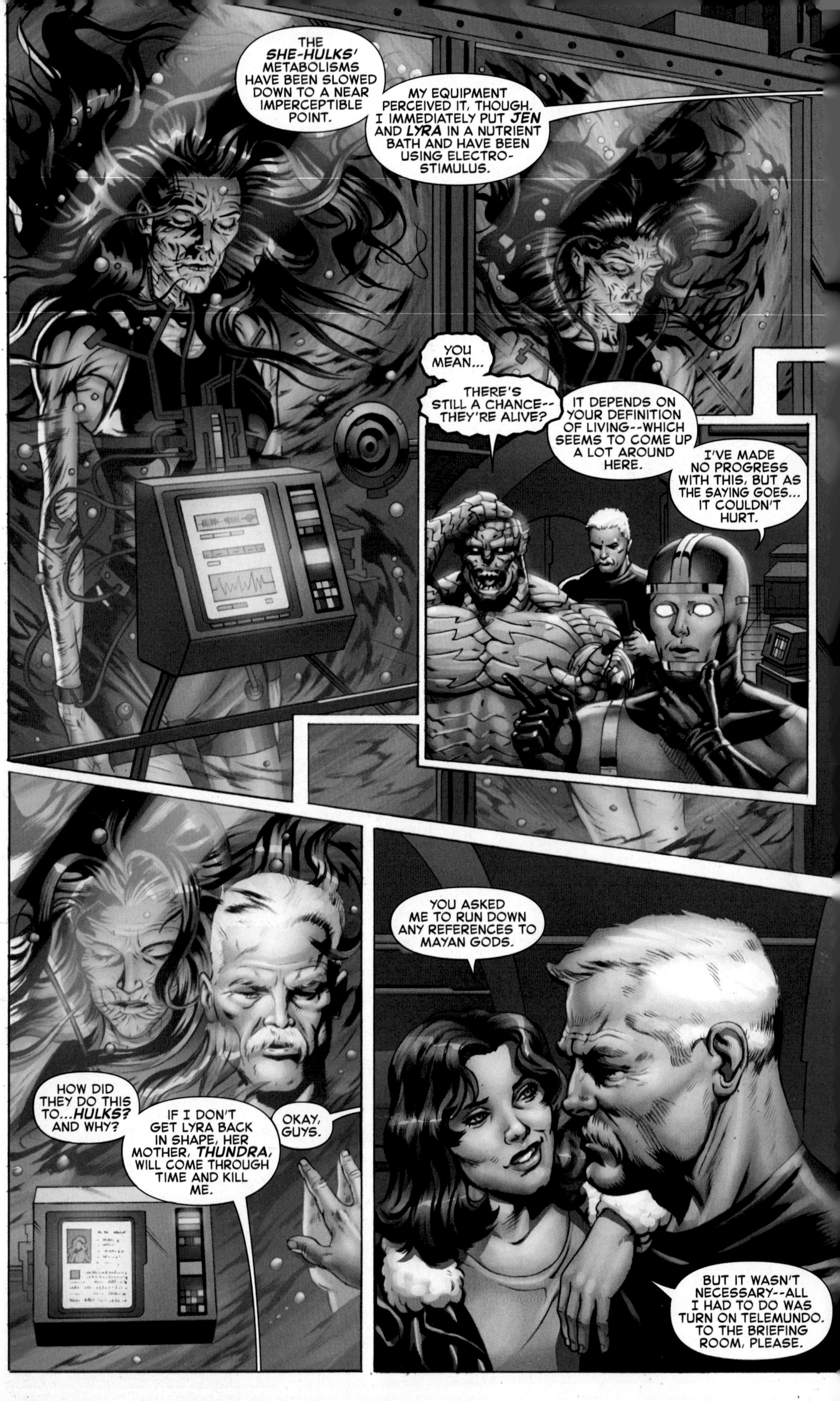
THE SHE-HULKS' METABOLISMS HAVE BEEN SLOWED DOWN TO A NEAR IMPERCEPTIBLE POINT.
MY EQUIPMENT PERCEIVED IT, THOUGH. I IMMEDIATELY PUT JEN AND LYRA IN A NUTRIENT BATH AND HAVE BEEN USING ELECTRO-STIMULUS.
YOU MEAN...
THERE'S STILL A CHANCE-- THEY'RE ALIVE?
IT DEPENDS ON YOUR DEFINITION OF LIVING--WHICH SEEMS TO COME UP A LOT AROUND HERE.
I'VE MADE NO PROGRESS WITH THIS, BUT AS THE SAYING GOES... IT COULDN'T HURT.
HOW DID THEY DO THIS TO...HULKS? AND WHY?
IF I DON'T GET LYRA BACK IN SHAPE, HER MOTHER, THUNDRA, WILL COME THROUGH TIME AND KILL ME.
OKAY, GUYS.
YOU ASKED ME TO RUN DOWN ANY REFERENCES TO MAYAN GODS.
BUT IT WASN'T NECESSARY--ALL I HAD TO DO WAS TURN ON TELEMUNDO. TO THE BRIEFING ROOM, PLEASE.

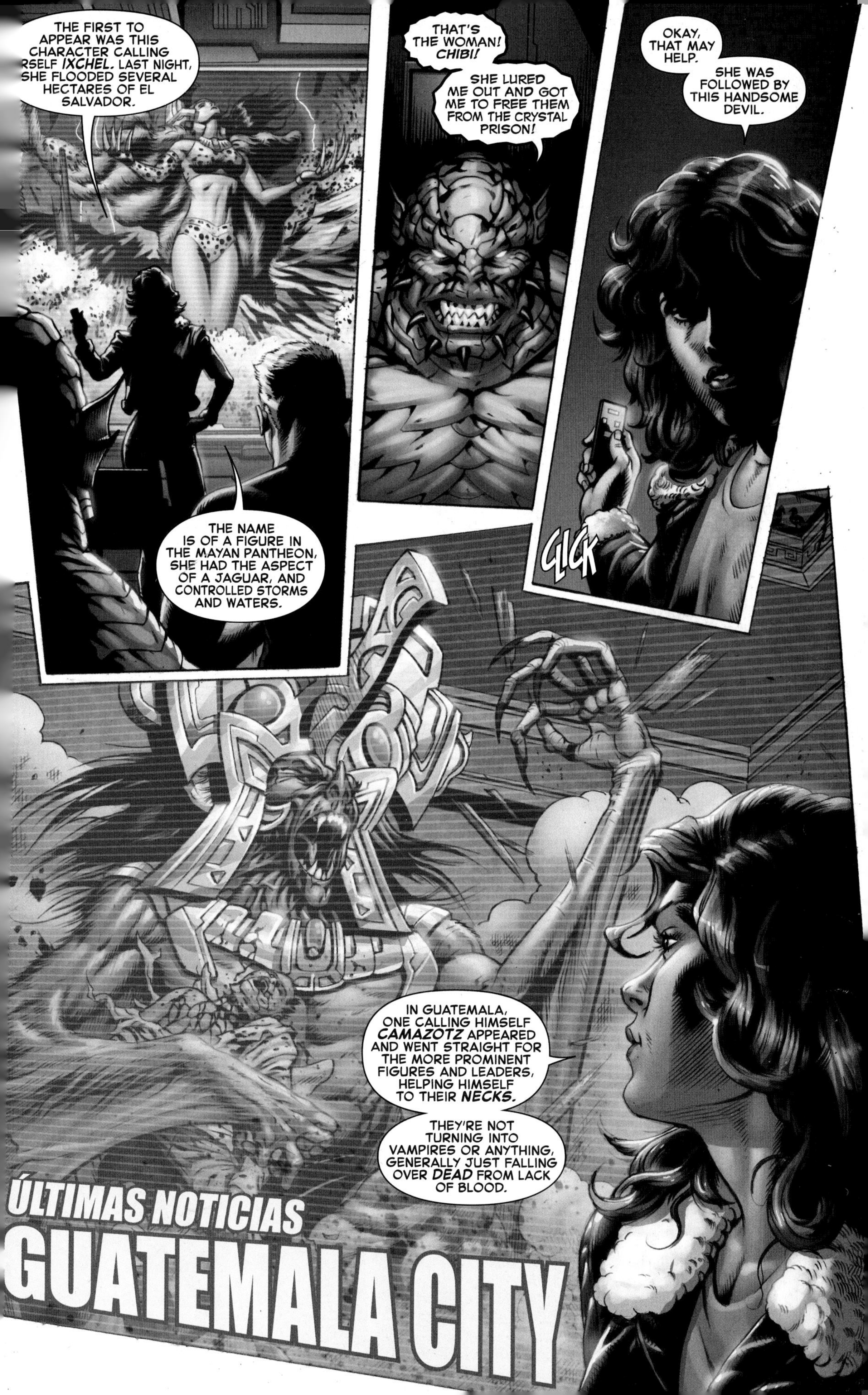
THE FIRST TO APPEAR WAS THIS CHARACTER CALLING RSELF IXCHEL. LAST NIGHT, SHE FLOODED SEVERAL HECTARES OF EL SALVADOR.
THE NAME IS OF A FIGURE IN THE MAYAN PANTHEON, SHE HAD THE ASPECT OF A JAGUAR, AND CONTROLLED STORMS AND WATERS.
THAT'S THE WOMAN! CHIBI!
SHE LURED ME OUT AND GOT ME TO FREE THEM FROM THE CRYSTAL PRISON!
OKAY, THAT MAY HELP.
SHE WAS FOLLOWED BY THIS HANDSOME DEVIL.
CLICK
IN GUATEMALA, ONE CALLING HIMSELF CAMAZOTZ APPEARED AND WENT STRAIGHT FOR THE MORE PROMINENT FIGURES AND LEADERS, HELPING HIMSELF TO THEIR NECKS.
THEY'RE NOT TURNING INTO VAMPIRES OR ANYTHING, GENERALLY JUST FALLING OVER DEAD FROM LACK OF BLOOD.
ÚLTIMAS NOTICIAS
GUATEMALA CITY

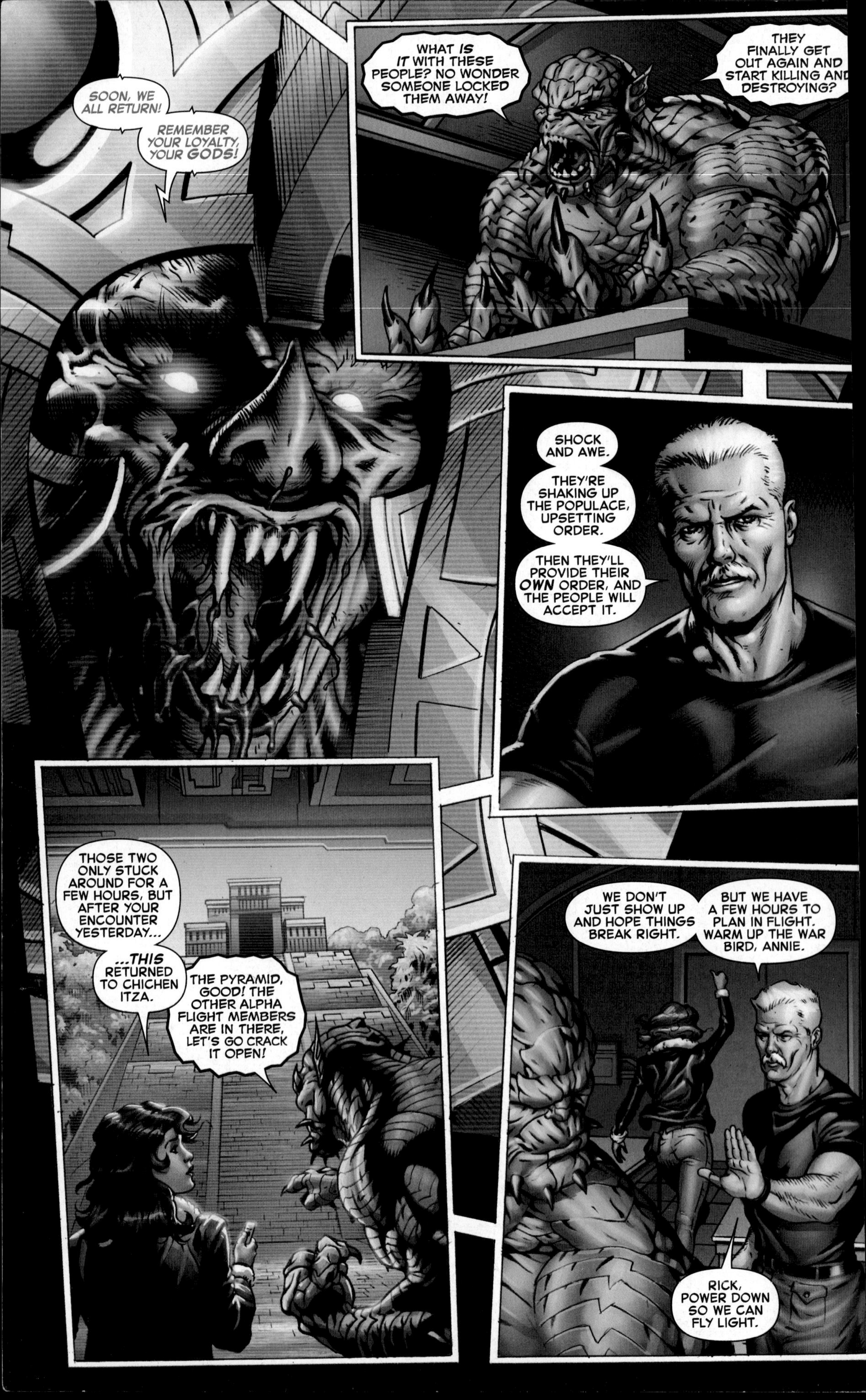
SOON, WE ALL RETURN!
REMEMBER YOUR LOYALTY, YOUR GODS!
WHAT IS IT WITH THESE PEOPLE? NO WONDER SOMEONE LOCKED THEM AWAY!
THEY FINALLY GET OUT AGAIN AND START KILLING AND DESTROYING?
SHOCK AND AWE.
THEY'RE SHAKING UP THE POPULACE, UPSETTING ORDER.
THEN THEY'LL PROVIDE THEIR OWN ORDER, AND THE PEOPLE WILL ACCEPT IT.
THOSE TWO ONLY STUCK AROUND FOR A FEW HOURS, BUT AFTER YOUR ENCOUNTER YESTERDAY...
...THIS RETURNED TO CHICHEN ITZA.
THE PYRAMID, GOOD! THE OTHER ALPHA FLIGHT MEMBERS ARE IN THERE, LET'S GO CRACK IT OPEN!
WE DON'T JUST SHOW UP AND HOPE THINGS BREAK RIGHT.
BUT WE HAVE A FEW HOURS TO PLAN IN FLIGHT. WARM UP THE WAR BIRD, ANNIE.
RICK, POWER DOWN SO WE CAN FLY LIGHT.

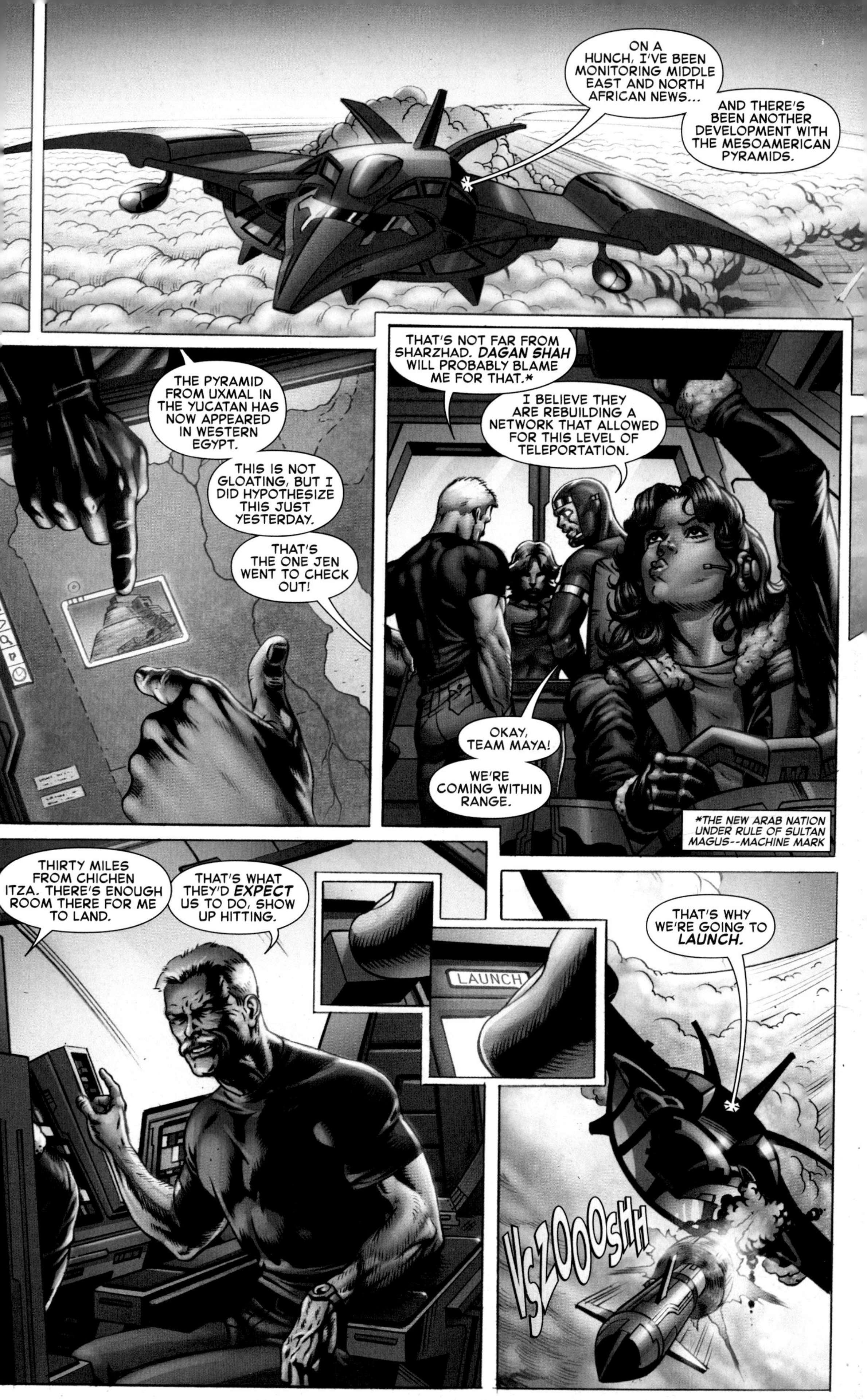
ON A HUNCH, I'VE BEEN MONITORING MIDDLE EAST AND NORTH AFRICAN NEWS...
AND THERE'S BEEN ANOTHER DEVELOPMENT WITH THE MESOAMERICAN PYRAMIDS.
THE PYRAMID FROM UXMAL IN THE YUCATAN HAS NOW APPEARED IN WESTERN EGYPT.
THIS IS NOT GLOATING, BUT I DID HYPOTHESIZE THIS JUST YESTERDAY.
THAT'S THE ONE JEN WENT TO CHECK OUT!
THAT'S NOT FAR FROM SHARZHAD. DAGAN SHAH WILL PROBABLY BLAME ME FOR THAT.*
I BELIEVE THEY ARE REBUILDING A NETWORK THAT ALLOWED FOR THIS LEVEL OF TELEPORTATION.
OKAY, TEAM MAYA!
WE'RE COMING WITHIN RANGE.
*THE NEW ARAB NATION UNDER RULE OF SULTAN MAGUS--MACHINE MARK
THIRTY MILES FROM CHICHEN ITZA. THERE'S ENOUGH ROOM THERE FOR ME TO LAND.
THAT'S WHAT THEY'D EXPECT US TO DO, SHOW UP HITTING.
LAUNCH
THAT'S WHY WE'RE GOING TO LAUNCH.
VSZOOOSHH

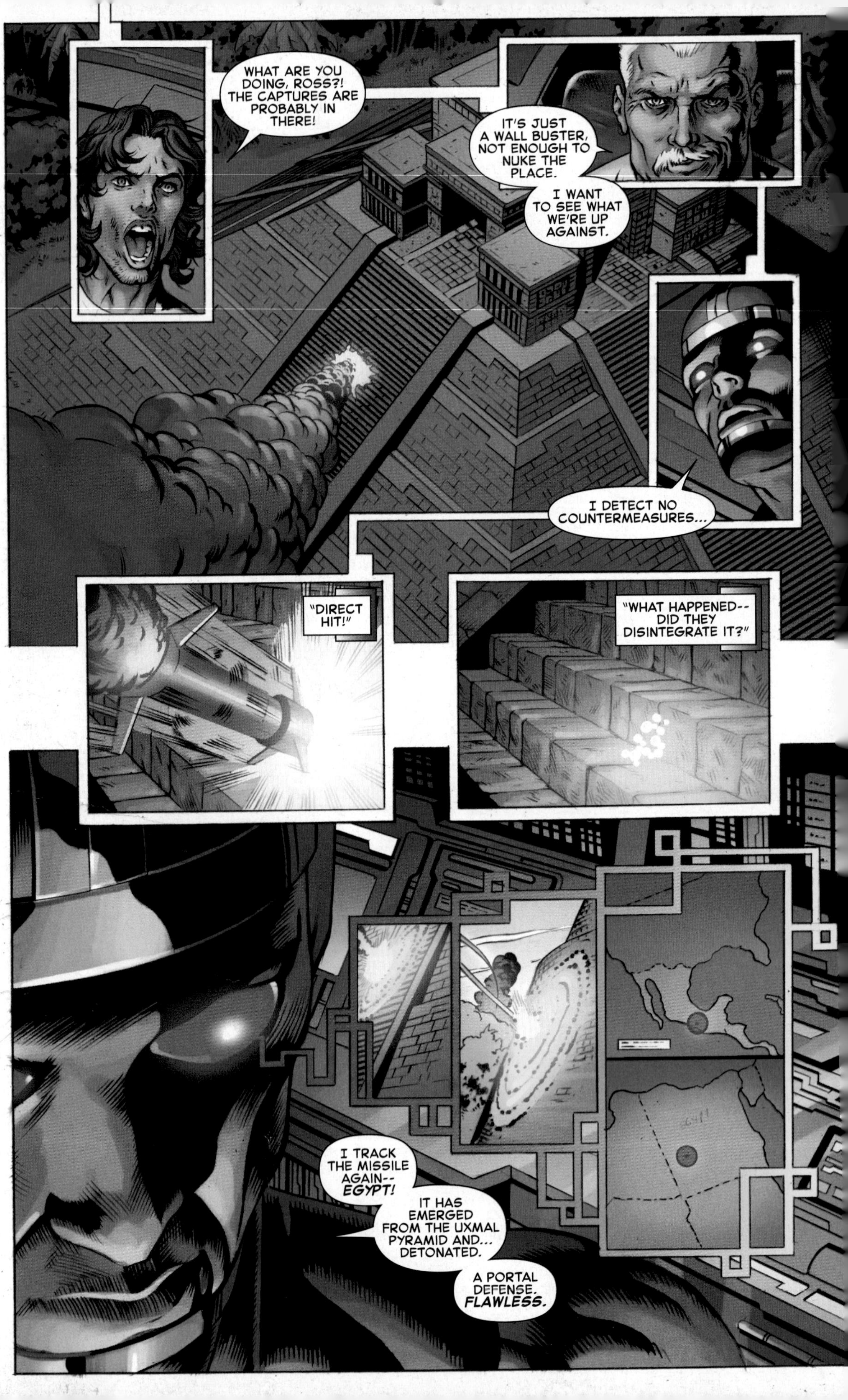
WHAT ARE YOU DOING, ROSS?! THE CAPTURES ARE PROBABLY IN THERE!
IT'S JUST A WALL BUSTER, NOT ENOUGH TO NUKE THE PLACE.
I WANT TO SEE WHAT WE'RE UP AGAINST.
I DETECT NO COUNTERMEASURES...
"DIRECT HIT!"
"WHAT HAPPENED-- DID THEY DISINTEGRATE IT?"
I TRACK THE MISSILE AGAIN-- EGYPT!
IT HAS EMERGED FROM THE UXMAL PYRAMID AND... DETONATED.
A PORTAL DEFENSE. FLAWLESS.

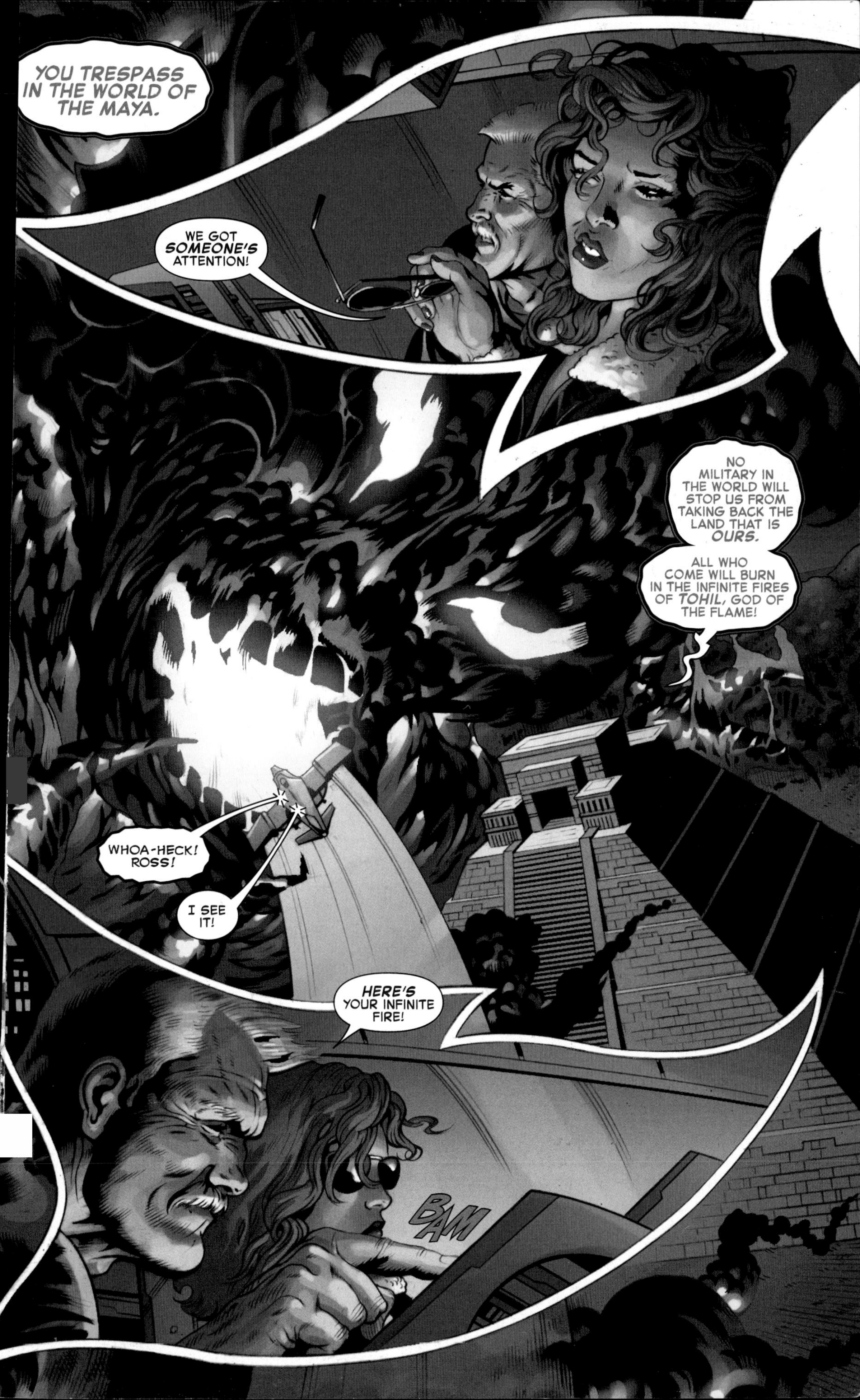
YOU TRESPASS IN THE WORLD OF THE MAYA.
WE GOT SOMEONE'S ATTENTION!
NO MILITARY IN THE WORLD WILL STOP US FROM TAKING BACK THE LAND THAT IS OURS.
ALL WHO COME WILL BURN IN THE INFINITE FIRES OF TOHIL, GOD OF THE FLAME!
WHOA-HECK! ROSS!
I SEE IT!
HERE'S YOUR INFINITE FIRE!
BAM

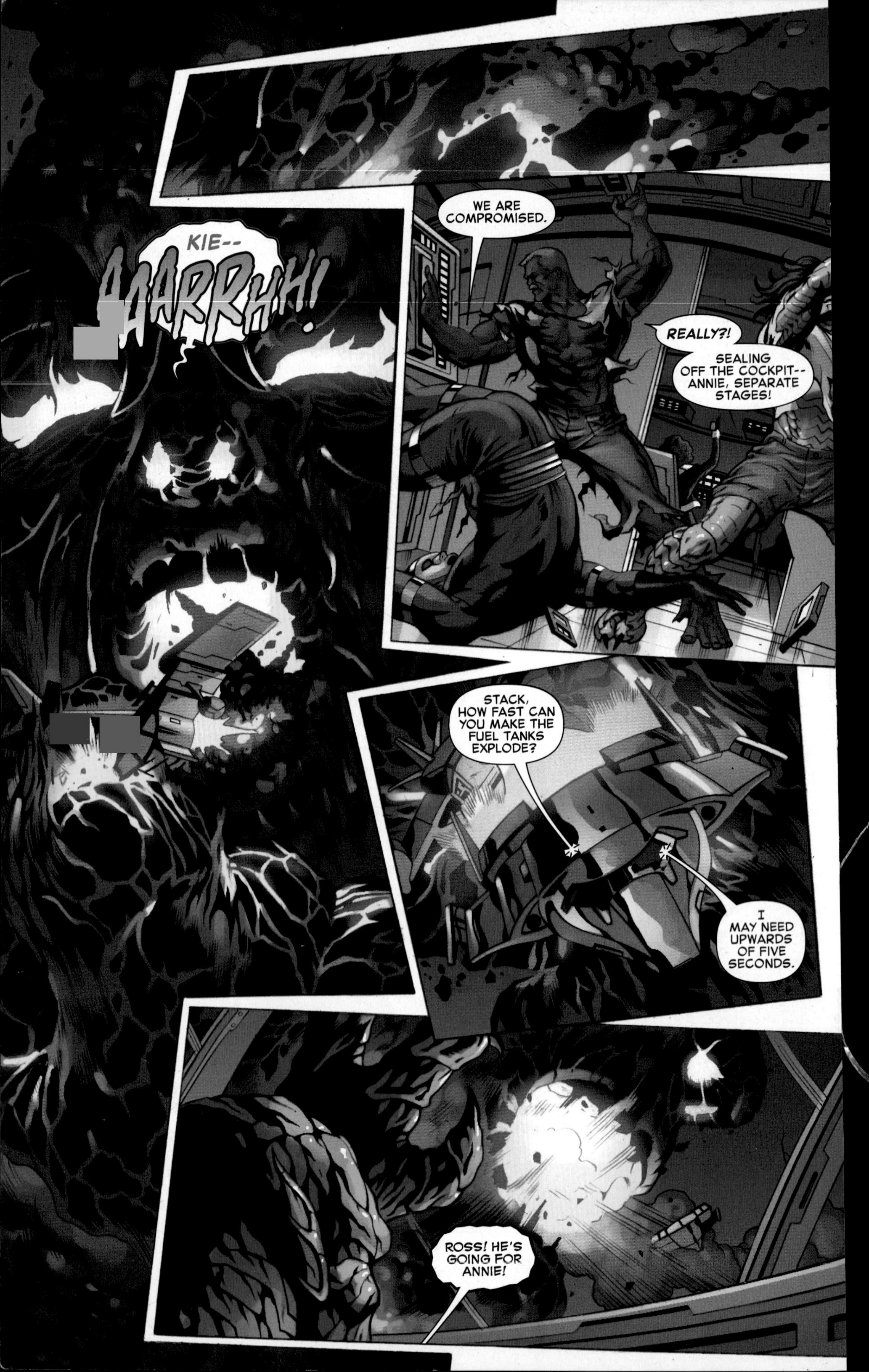
KIE--
AAARRHH!
WE ARE COMPROMISED.
REALLY?!
SEALING OFF THE COCKPIT-- ANNIE, SEPARATE STAGES!
STACK, HOW FAST CAN YOU MAKE THE FUEL TANKS EXPLODE?
I MAY NEED UPWARDS OF FIVE SECONDS.
ROSS! HE'S GOING FOR ANNIE!

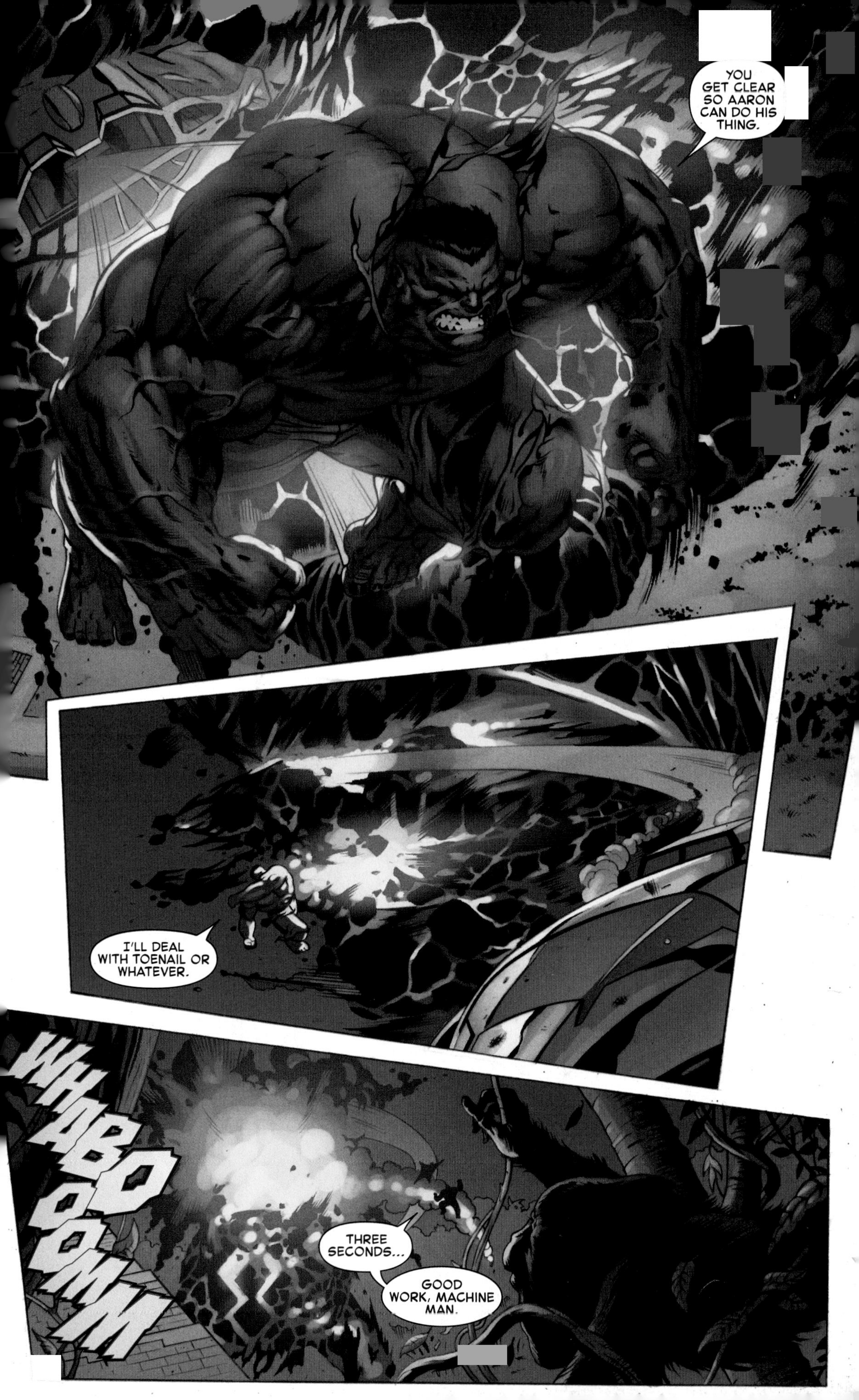
YOU GET CLEAR SO AARON CAN DO HIS THING.
I'LL DEAL WITH TOENAIL OR WHATEVER.
WHABOOOMM
THREE SECONDS...
GOOD WORK, MACHINE MAN.

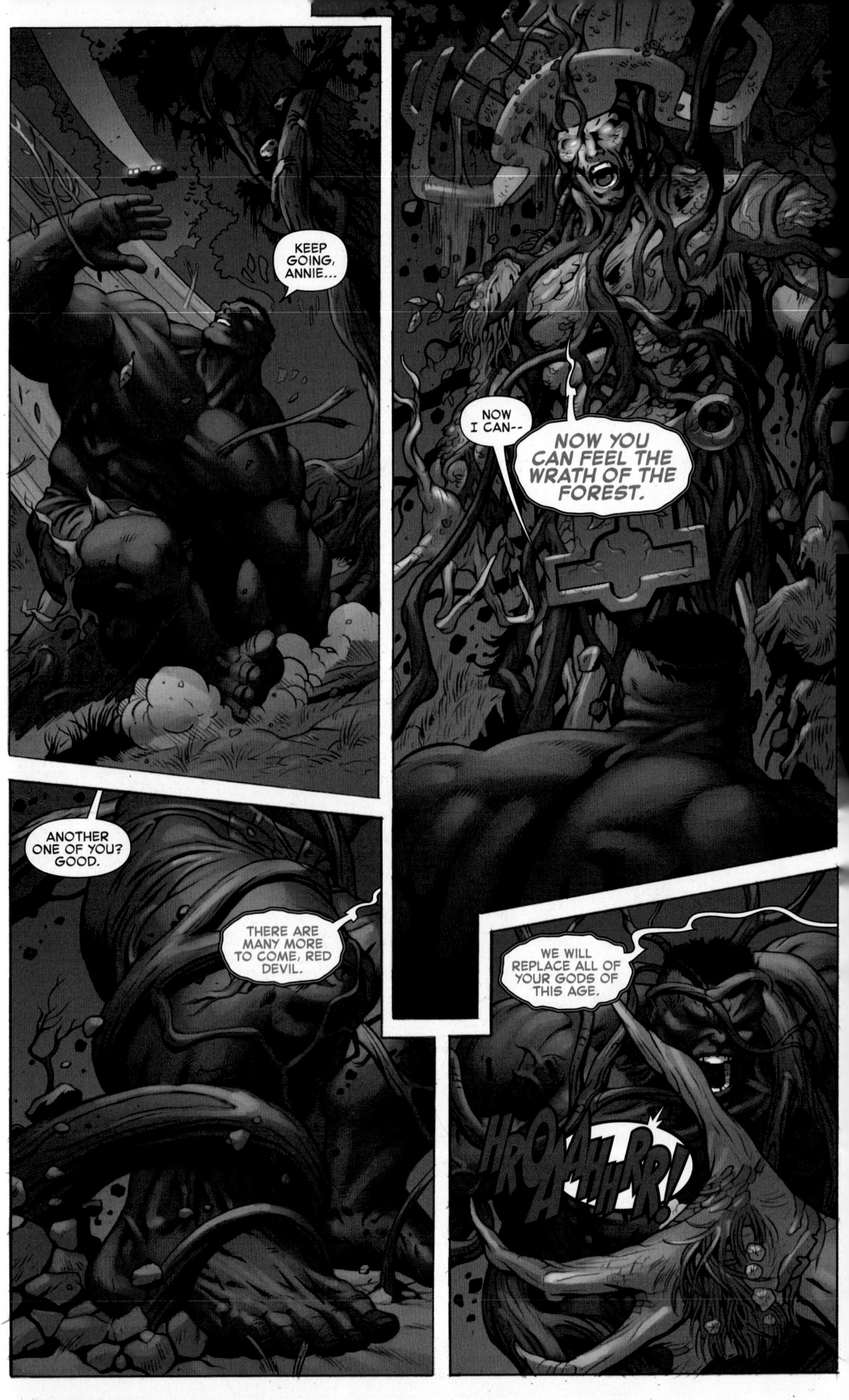
KEEP GOING, ANNIE...
NOW I CAN--
NOW YOU CAN FEEL THE WRATH OF THE FOREST.
ANOTHER ONE OF YOU? GOOD.
THERE ARE MANY MORE TO COME, RED DEVIL.
WE WILL REPLACE ALL OF YOUR GODS OF THIS AGE.
HROAAHHRR!

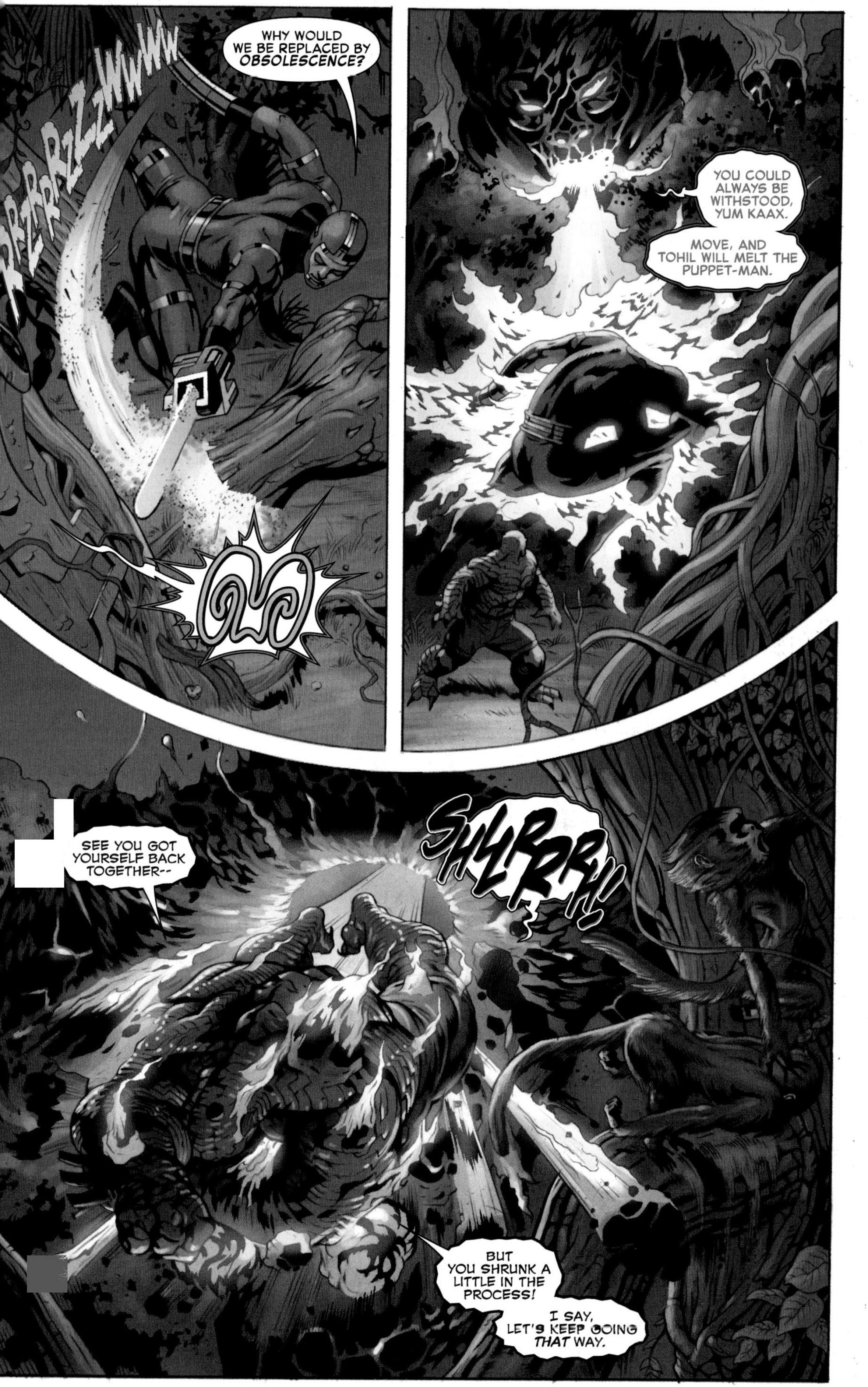
WHY WOULD WE BE REPLACED BY OBSOLESCENCE?
RRZRRZZZWWWW
YOU COULD ALWAYS BE WITHSTOOD, YUM KAAX.
MOVE, AND TOHIL WILL MELT THE PUPPET-MAN.
SEE YOU GOT YOURSELF BACK TOGETHER--
SHLURRRH!
BUT YOU SHRUNK A LITTLE IN THE PROCESS!
I SAY, LET'S KEEP GOING THAT WAY.

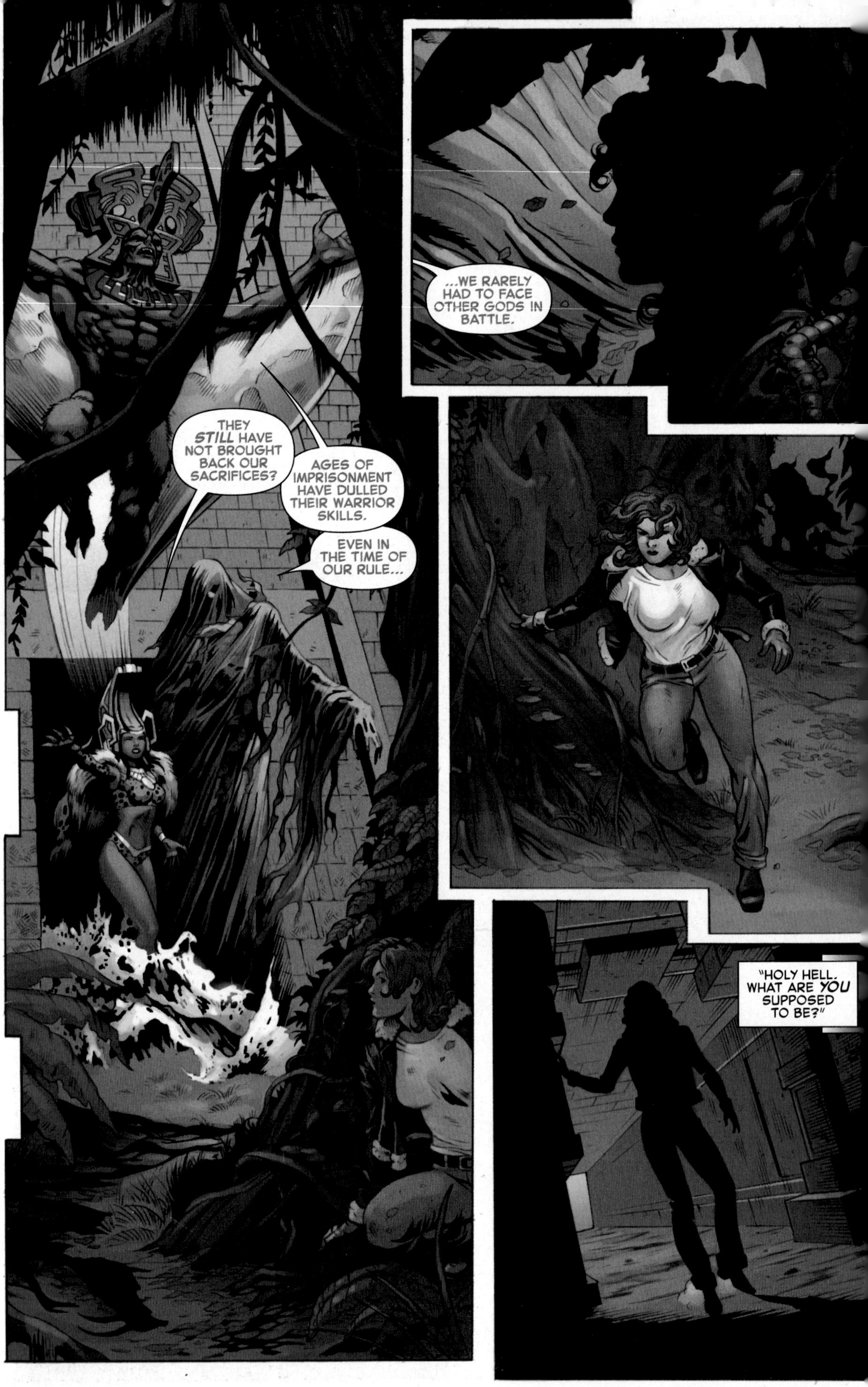
THEY *STILL* HAVE NOT BROUGHT BACK OUR SACRIFICES?
AGES OF IMPRISONMENT HAVE DULLED THEIR WARRIOR SKILLS.
EVEN IN THE TIME OF OUR RULE...
...WE RARELY HAD TO FACE OTHER GODS IN BATTLE.
"HOLY HELL. WHAT ARE *YOU* SUPPOSED TO BE?"

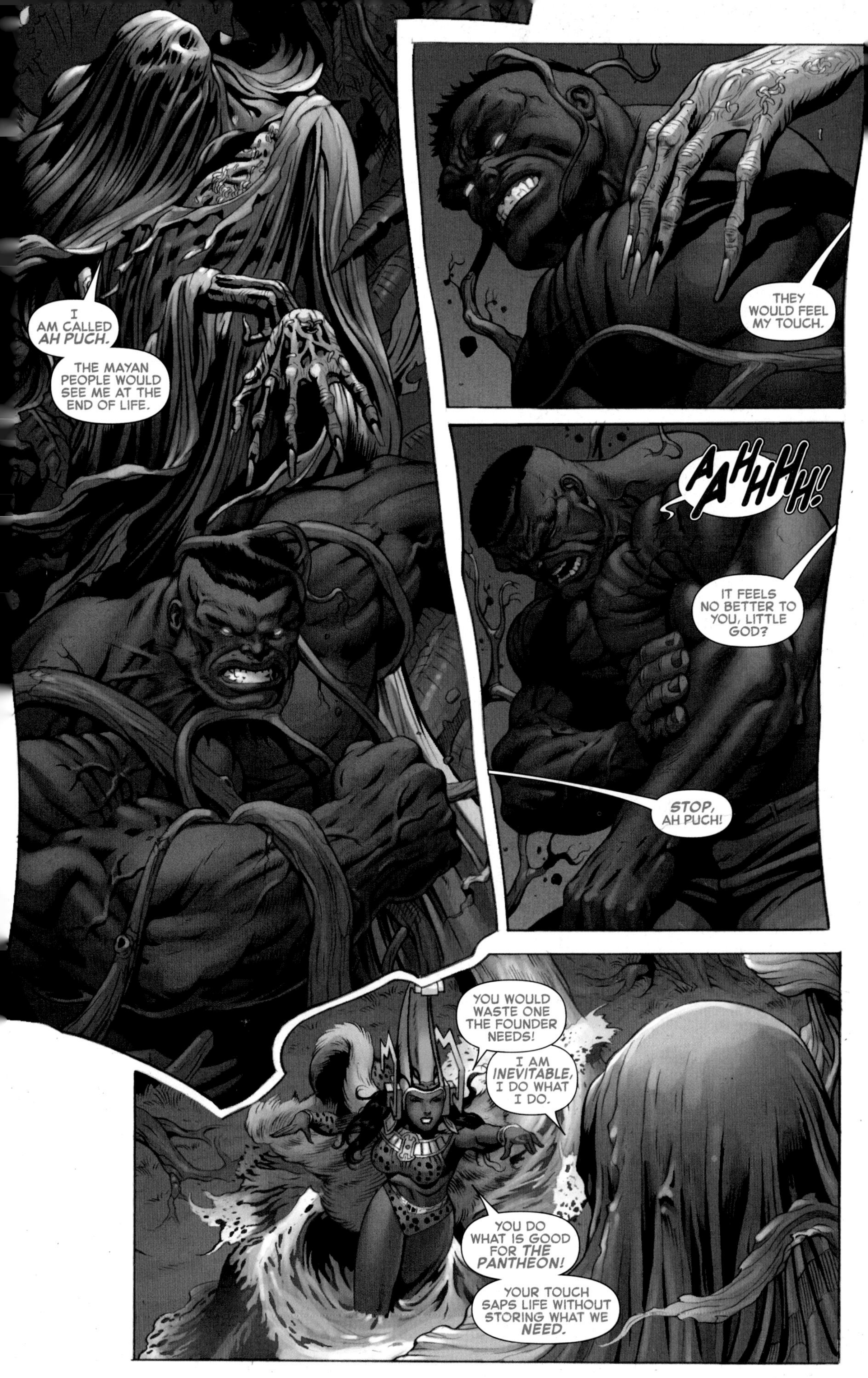

I AM CALLED AH PUCH.
THE MAYAN PEOPLE WOULD SEE ME AT THE END OF LIFE.
THEY WOULD FEEL MY TOUCH.
AAHHHH!
IT FEELS NO BETTER TO YOU, LITTLE GOD?
STOP, AH PUCH!
YOU WOULD WASTE ONE THE FOUNDER NEEDS!
I AM INEVITABLE, I DO WHAT I DO.
YOU DO WHAT IS GOOD FOR THE PANTHEON!
YOUR TOUCH SAPS LIFE WITHOUT STORING WHAT WE NEED.

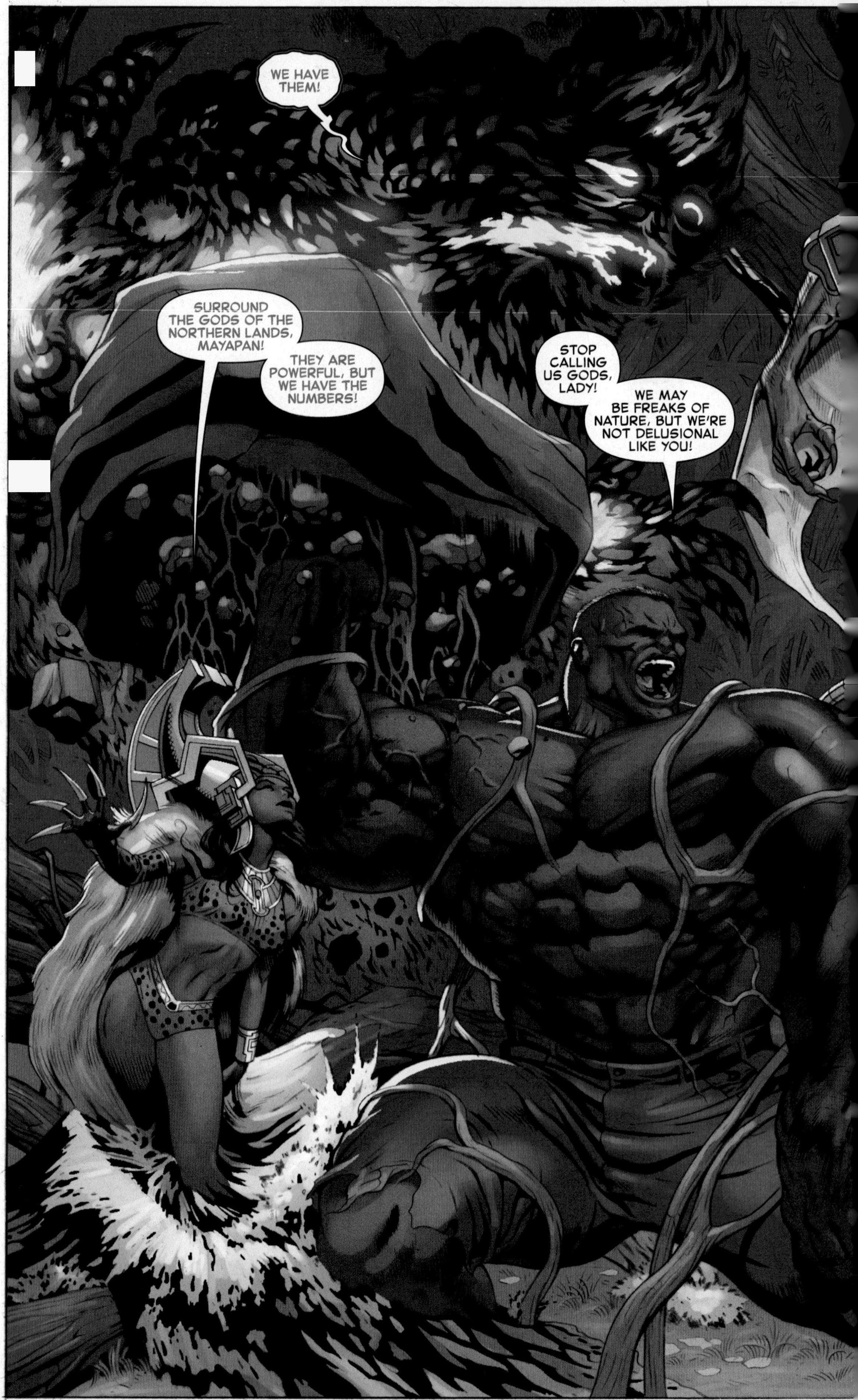
WE HAVE THEM!
SURROUND THE GODS OF THE NORTHERN LANDS, MAYAPAN!
THEY ARE POWERFUL, BUT WE HAVE THE NUMBERS!
STOP CALLING US GODS, LADY!
WE MAY BE FREAKS OF NATURE, BUT WE'RE NOT DELUSIONAL LIKE YOU!

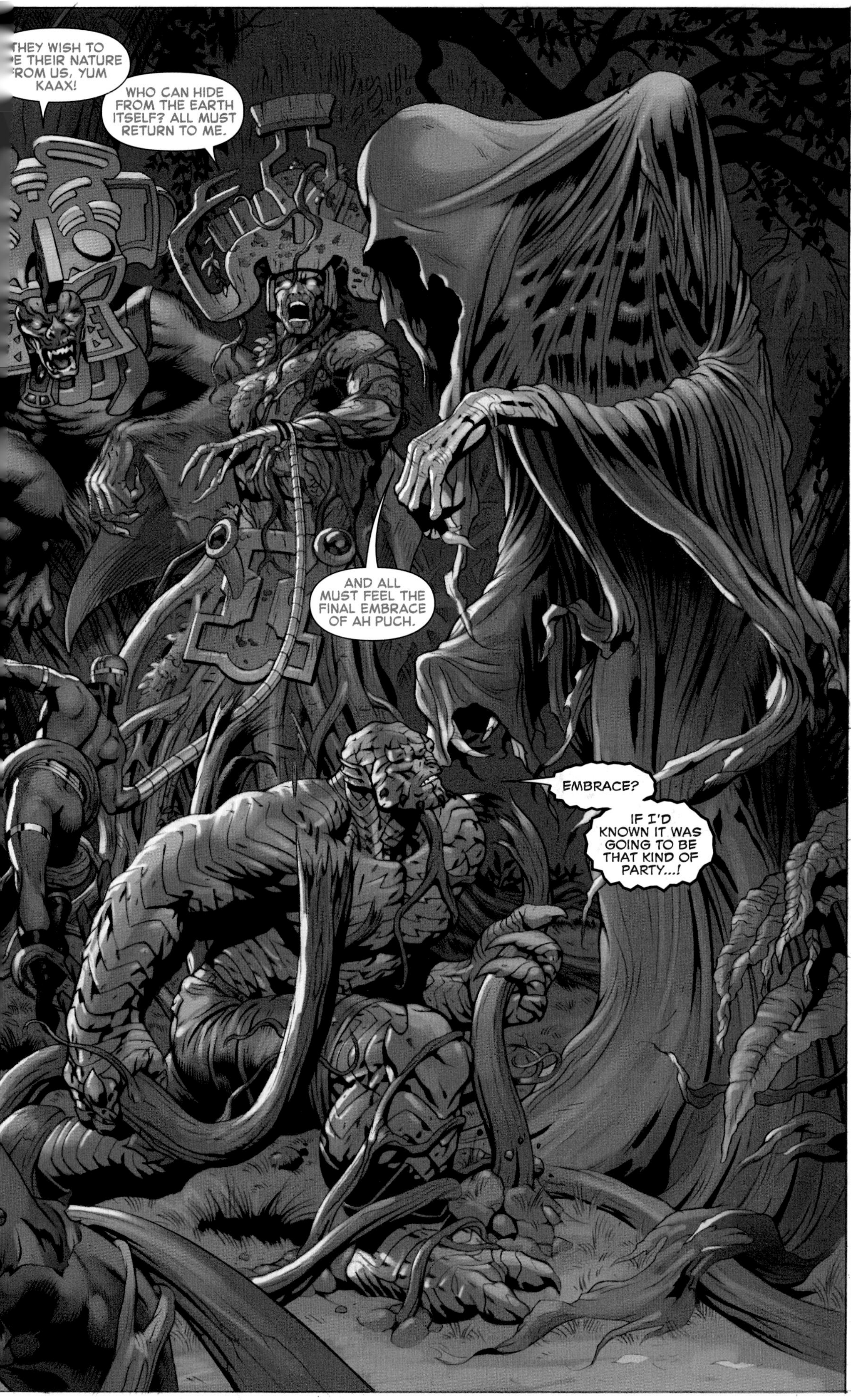

THEY WISH TO E THEIR NATURE FROM US, YUM KAAX!
WHO CAN HIDE FROM THE EARTH ITSELF? ALL MUST RETURN TO ME.
AND ALL MUST FEEL THE FINAL EMBRACE OF AH PUCH.
EMBRACE?
IF I'D KNOWN IT WAS GOING TO BE THAT KIND OF PARTY...!

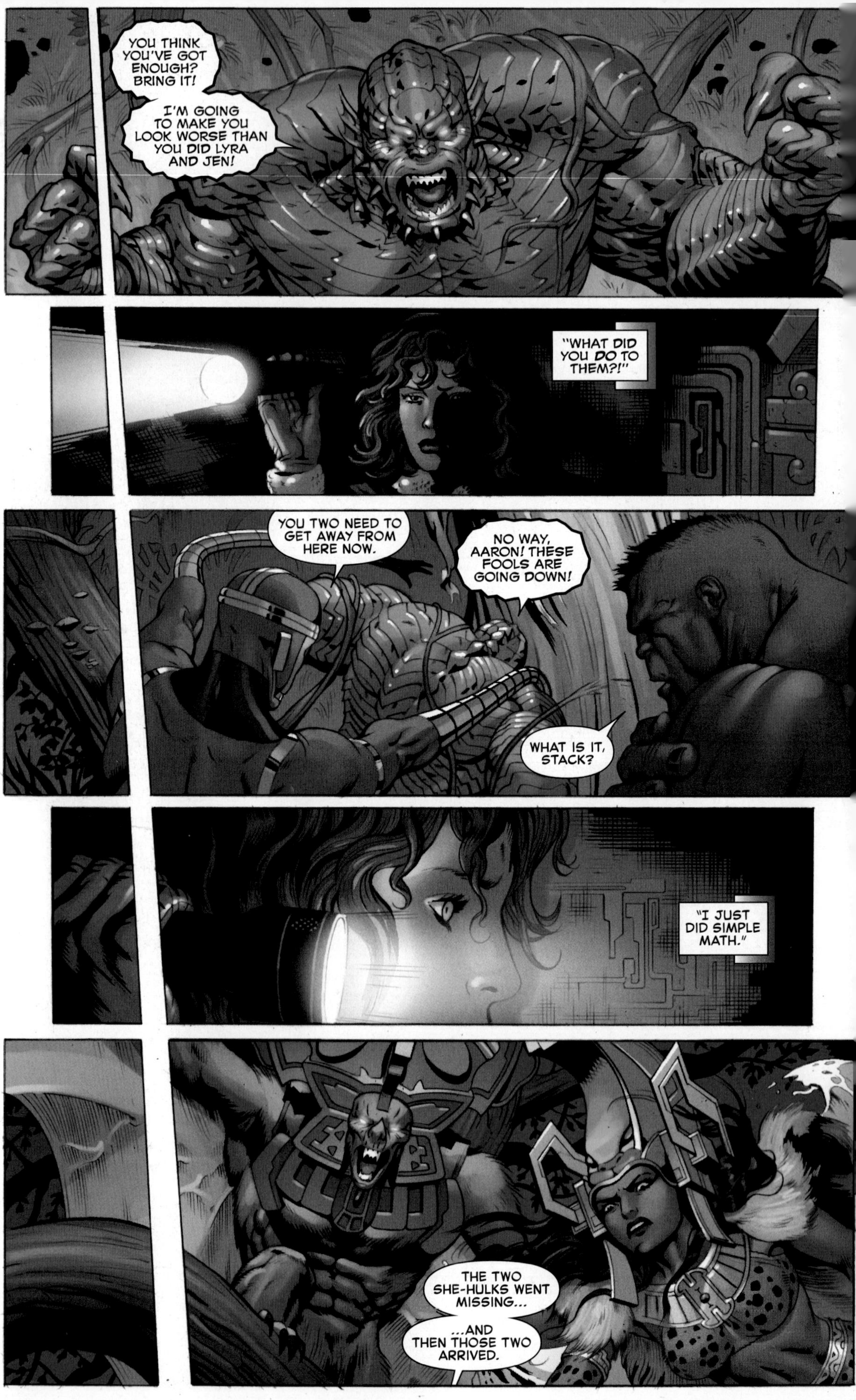
YOU THINK YOU'VE GOT ENOUGH? BRING IT!
I'M GOING TO MAKE YOU LOOK WORSE THAN YOU DID LYRA AND JEN!
"WHAT DID YOU DO TO THEM?!"
YOU TWO NEED TO GET AWAY FROM HERE NOW.
NO WAY, AARON! THESE FOOLS ARE GOING DOWN!
WHAT IS IT, STACK?
"I JUST DID SIMPLE MATH."
THE TWO SHE-HULKS WENT MISSING...
...AND THEN THOSE TWO ARRIVED.

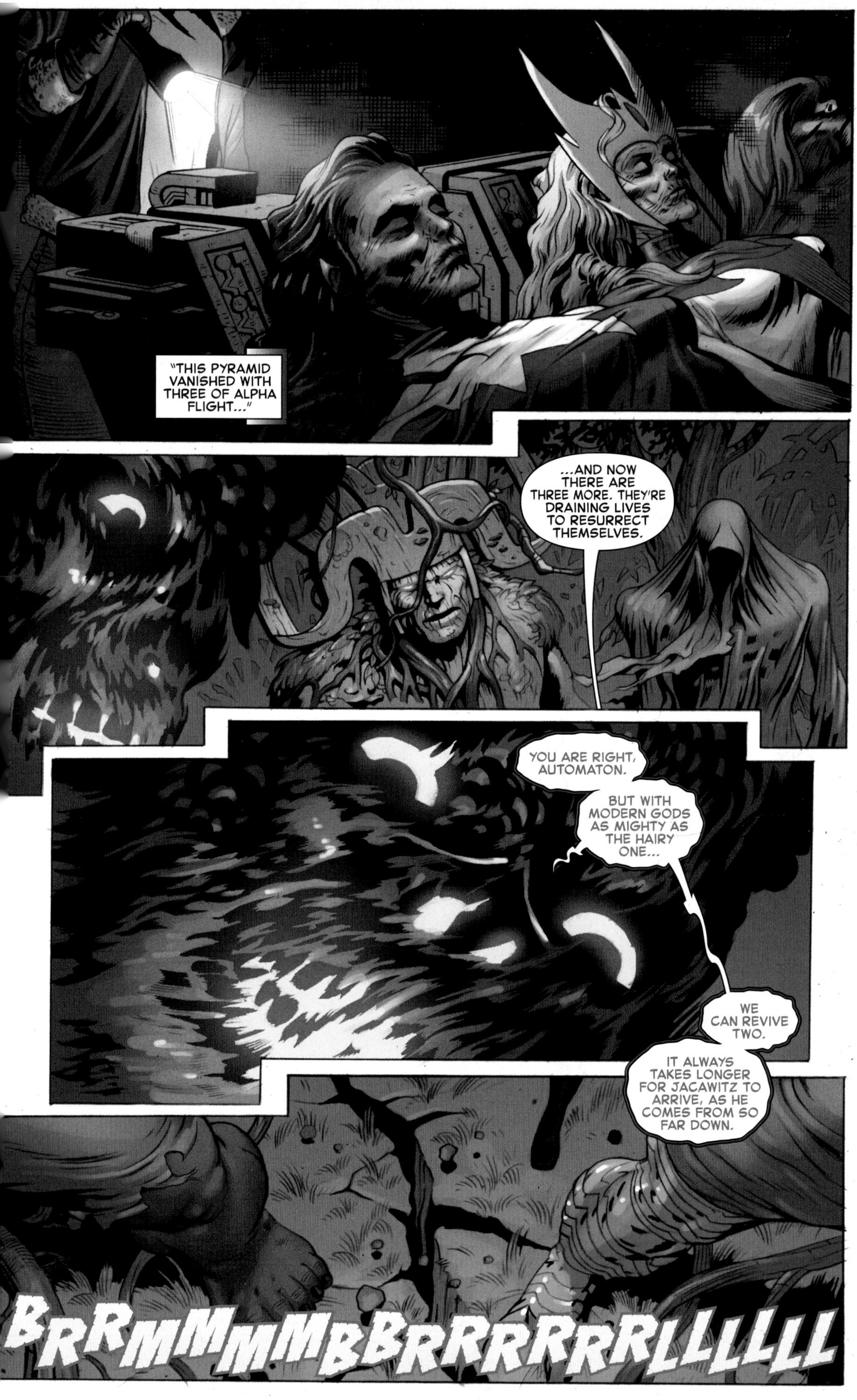
"THIS PYRAMID VANISHED WITH THREE OF ALPHA FLIGHT..."
...AND NOW THERE ARE THREE MORE. THEY'RE DRAINING LIVES TO RESURRECT THEMSELVES.
YOU ARE RIGHT, AUTOMATON.
BUT WITH MODERN GODS AS MIGHTY AS THE HAIRY ONE...
WE CAN REVIVE TWO.
IT ALWAYS TAKES LONGER FOR JACAWITZ TO ARRIVE, AS HE COMES FROM SO FAR DOWN.
BRRMMMMMBBRRRRRRRLLLLLL

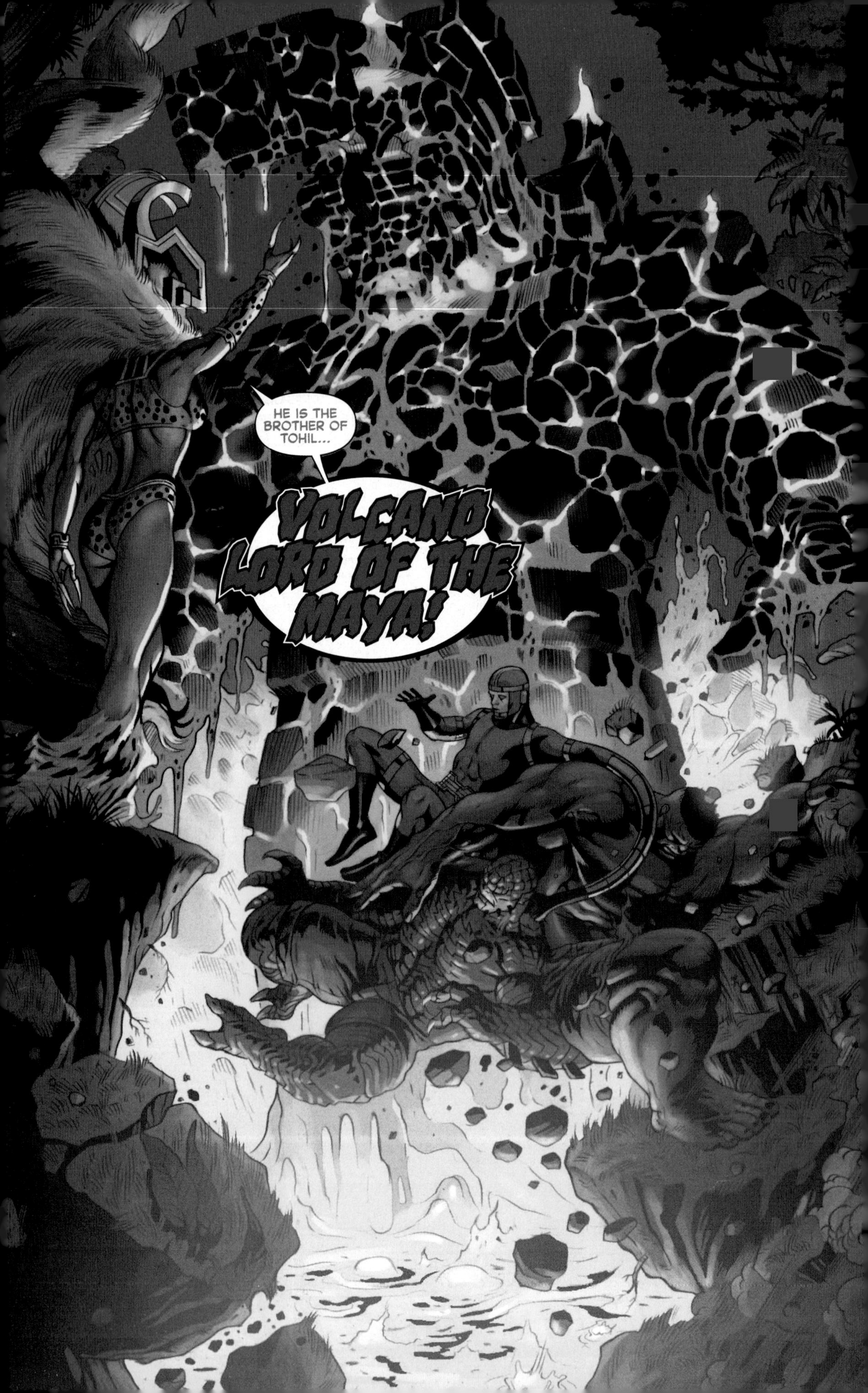
HE IS THE BROTHER OF TOHIL...
VOLCANO LORD OF THE MAYA!

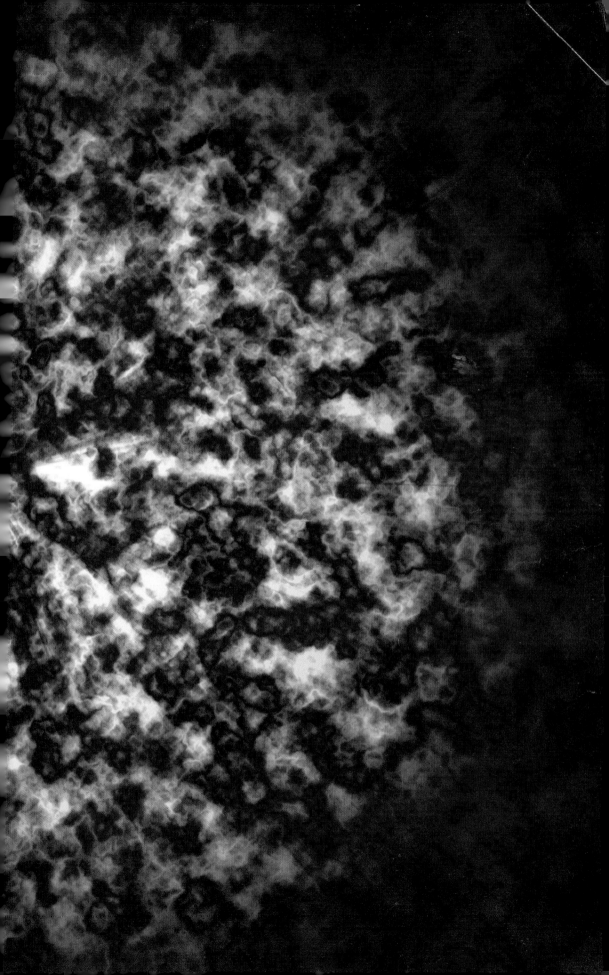

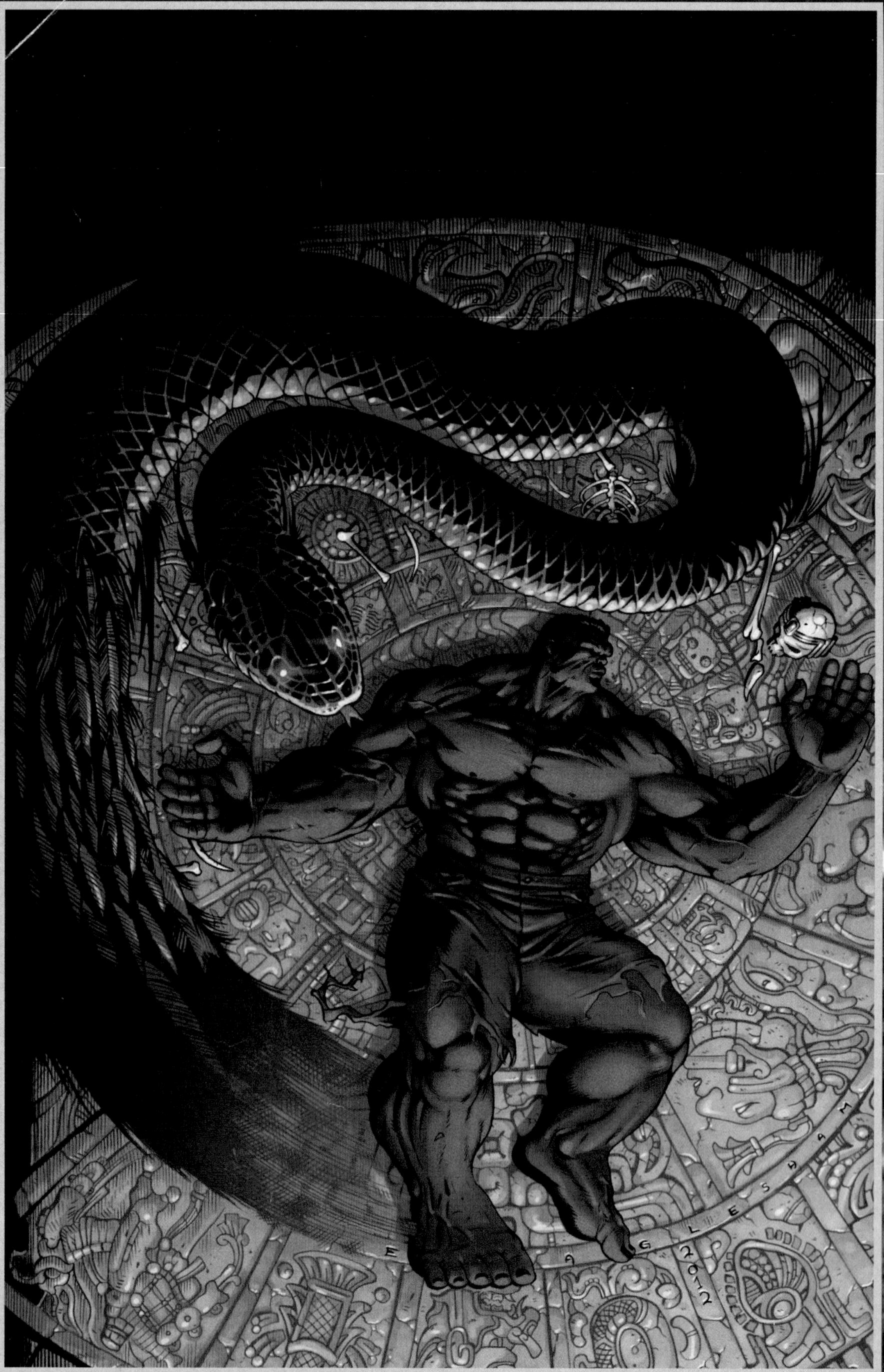
EAGLESHAM
2012

HULK #55

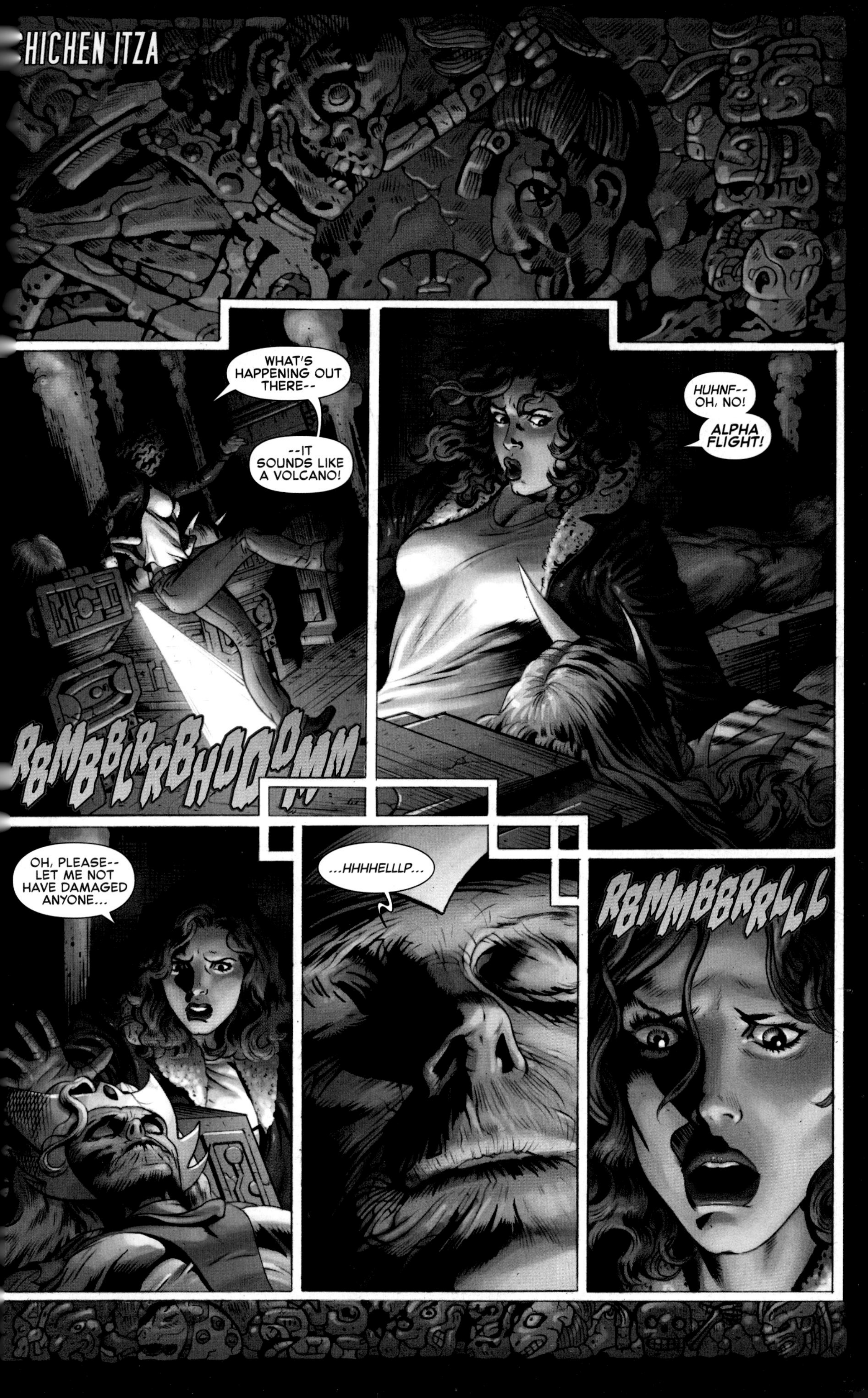
CHICHEN ITZA
WHAT'S HAPPENING OUT THERE--
--IT SOUNDS LIKE A VOLCANO!
RBMBBLRRBHOOOMM
HUHNF-- OH, NO!
ALPHA FLIGHT!
OH, PLEASE-- LET ME NOT HAVE DAMAGED ANYONE...
...HHHHELLLP...
RBMMBBRRLLL

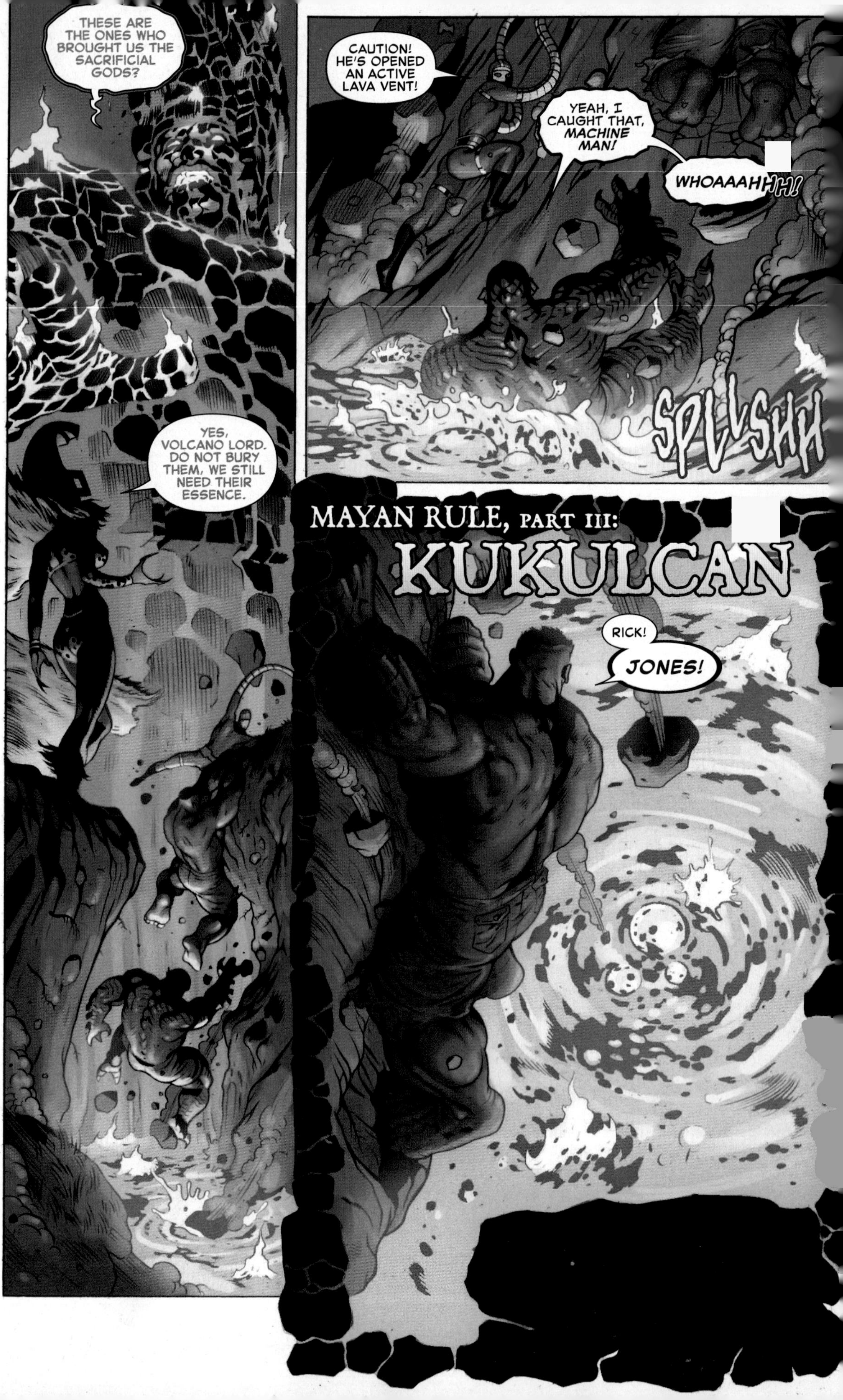
THESE ARE THE ONES WHO BROUGHT US THE SACRIFICIAL GODS?
CAUTION! HE'S OPENED AN ACTIVE LAVA VENT!
YEAH, I CAUGHT THAT, MACHINE MAN!
WHOAAAHHH!
SPLLSHH
YES, VOLCANO LORD. DO NOT BURY THEM, WE STILL NEED THEIR ESSENCE.
MAYAN RULE, PART III:
KUKULCAN
RICK!
JONES!

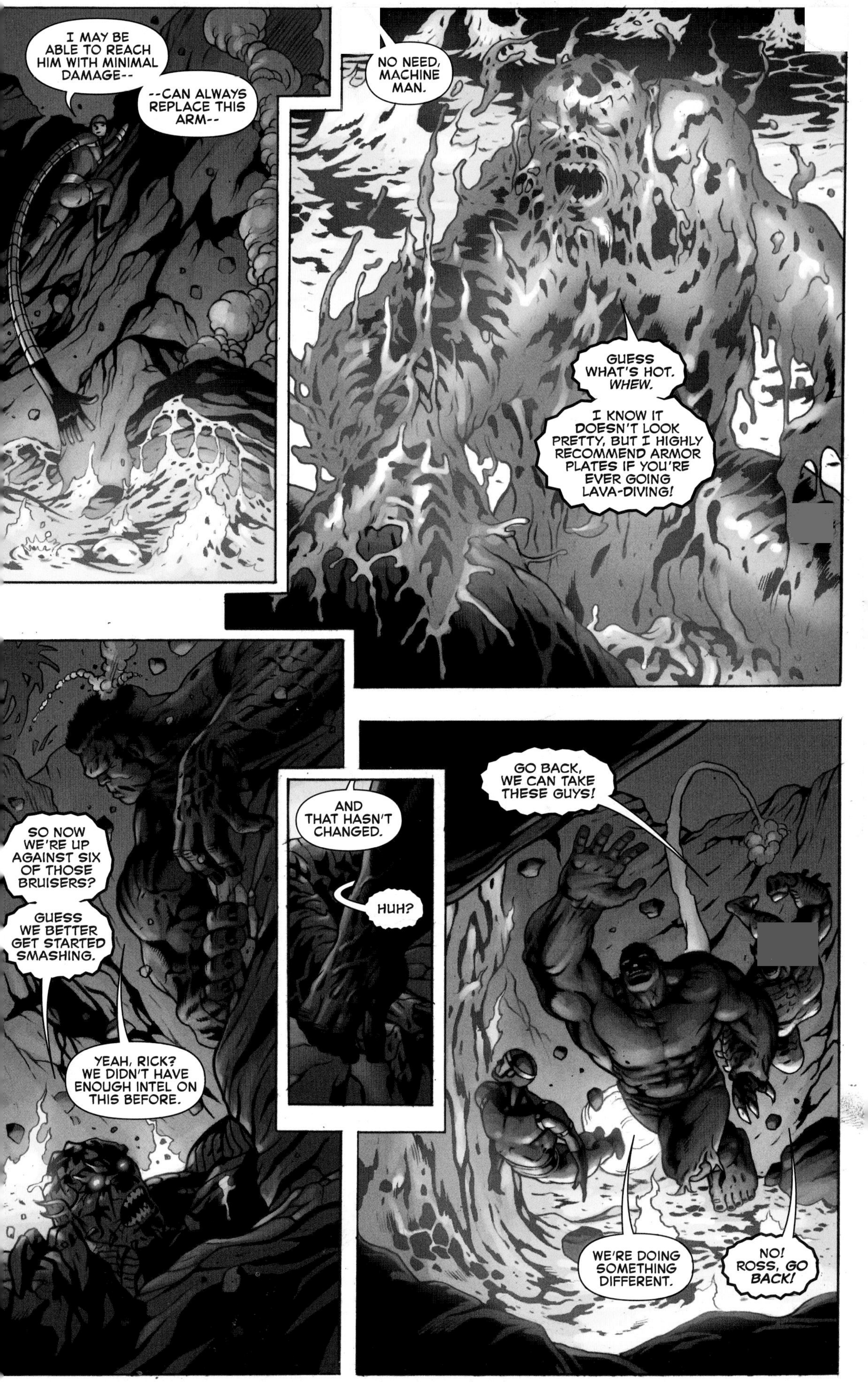
I MAY BE ABLE TO REACH HIM WITH MINIMAL DAMAGE--
--CAN ALWAYS REPLACE THIS ARM--
NO NEED, MACHINE MAN.
GUESS WHAT'S HOT. *WHEW.*
I KNOW IT DOESN'T LOOK PRETTY, BUT I HIGHLY RECOMMEND ARMOR PLATES IF YOU'RE EVER GOING LAVA-DIVING!
SO NOW WE'RE UP AGAINST SIX OF THOSE BRUISERS?
GUESS WE BETTER GET STARTED SMASHING.
YEAH, RICK? WE DIDN'T HAVE ENOUGH INTEL ON THIS BEFORE.
AND THAT HASN'T CHANGED.
HUH?
GO BACK, WE CAN TAKE THESE GUYS!
WE'RE DOING SOMETHING DIFFERENT.
NO! ROSS, GO BACK!

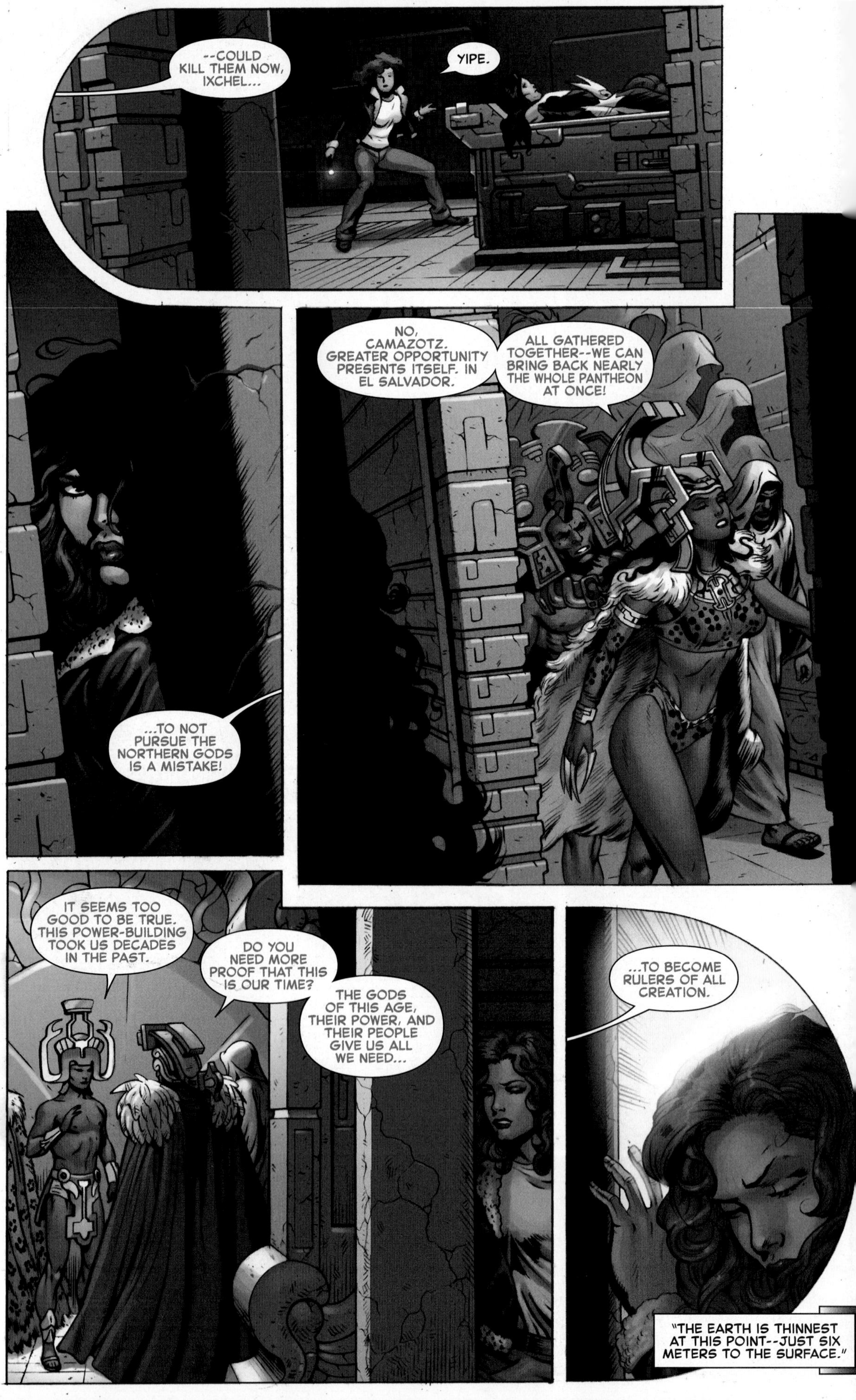
--COULD KILL THEM NOW, IXCHEL...
YIPE.
...TO NOT PURSUE THE NORTHERN GODS IS A MISTAKE!
NO, CAMAZOTZ. GREATER OPPORTUNITY PRESENTS ITSELF. IN EL SALVADOR.
ALL GATHERED TOGETHER--WE CAN BRING BACK NEARLY THE WHOLE PANTHEON AT ONCE!
IT SEEMS TOO GOOD TO BE TRUE. THIS POWER-BUILDING TOOK US DECADES IN THE PAST.
DO YOU NEED MORE PROOF THAT THIS IS OUR TIME?
THE GODS OF THIS AGE, THEIR POWER, AND THEIR PEOPLE GIVE US ALL WE NEED...
...TO BECOME RULERS OF ALL CREATION.
"THE EARTH IS THINNEST AT THIS POINT--JUST SIX METERS TO THE SURFACE."

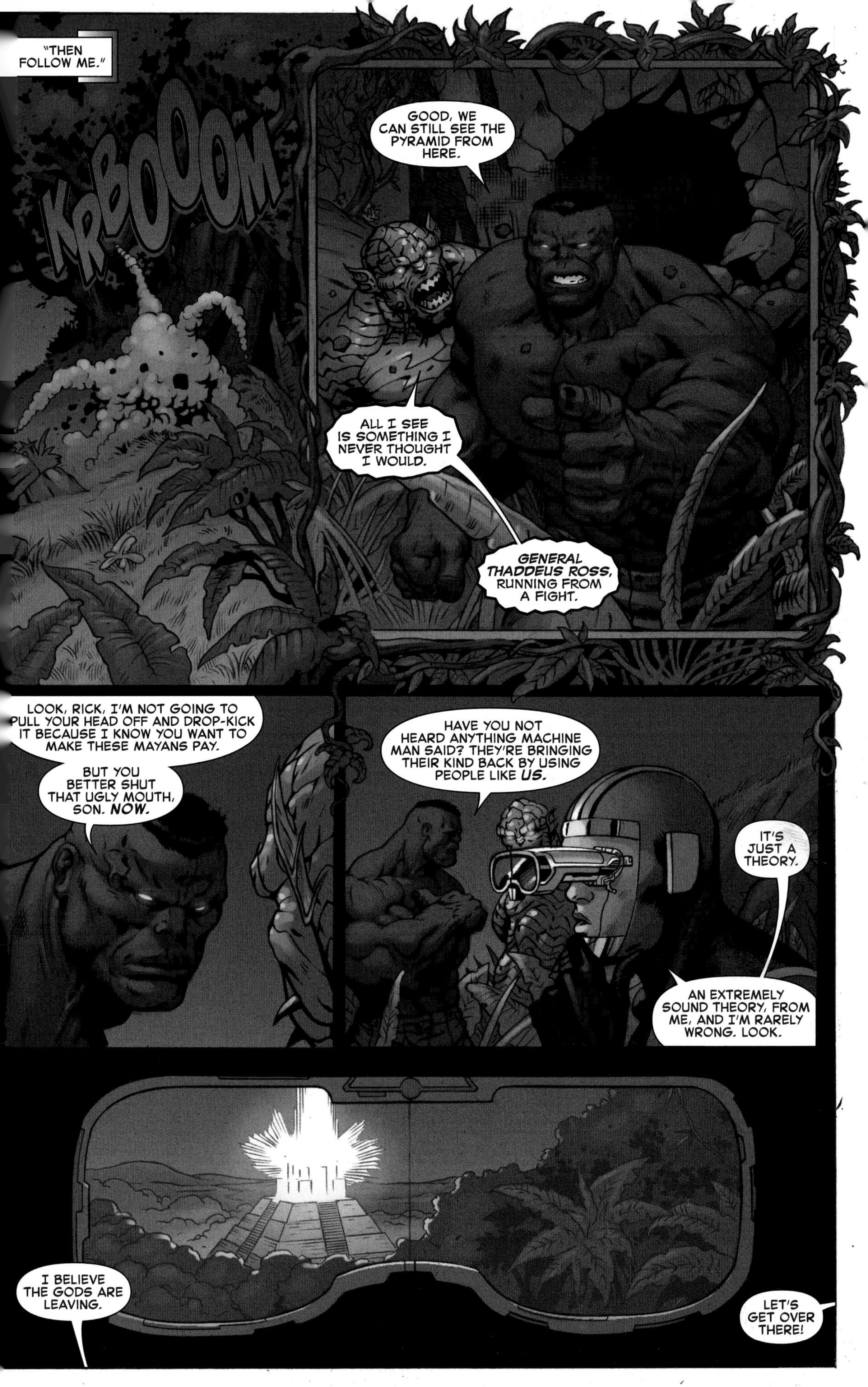
"THEN FOLLOW ME."
KRBOOOM
GOOD, WE CAN STILL SEE THE PYRAMID FROM HERE.
ALL I SEE IS SOMETHING I NEVER THOUGHT I WOULD.
GENERAL THADDEUS ROSS, RUNNING FROM A FIGHT.
LOOK, RICK, I'M NOT GOING TO PULL YOUR HEAD OFF AND DROP-KICK IT BECAUSE I KNOW YOU WANT TO MAKE THESE MAYANS PAY.
BUT YOU BETTER SHUT THAT UGLY MOUTH, SON. NOW.
HAVE YOU NOT HEARD ANYTHING MACHINE MAN SAID? THEY'RE BRINGING THEIR KIND BACK BY USING PEOPLE LIKE US.
IT'S JUST A THEORY.
AN EXTREMELY SOUND THEORY, FROM ME, AND I'M RARELY WRONG. LOOK.
I BELIEVE THE GODS ARE LEAVING.
LET'S GET OVER THERE!

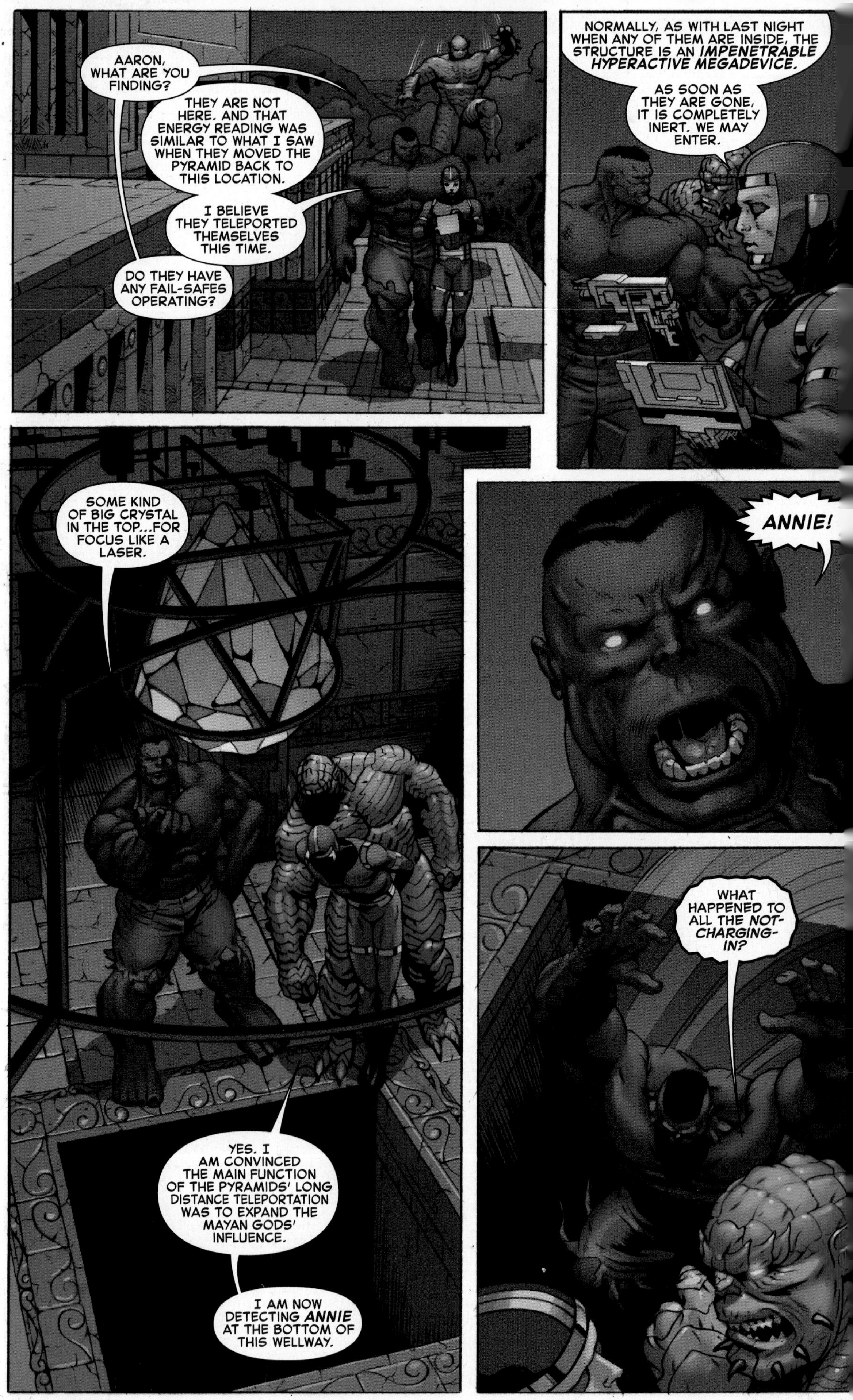
AARON, WHAT ARE YOU FINDING?
THEY ARE NOT HERE. AND THAT ENERGY READING WAS SIMILAR TO WHAT I SAW WHEN THEY MOVED THE PYRAMID BACK TO THIS LOCATION.
I BELIEVE THEY TELEPORTED THEMSELVES THIS TIME.
DO THEY HAVE ANY FAIL-SAFES OPERATING?
NORMALLY, AS WITH LAST NIGHT WHEN ANY OF THEM ARE INSIDE, THE STRUCTURE IS AN *IMPENETRABLE HYPERACTIVE MEGADEVICE.*
AS SOON AS THEY ARE GONE, IT IS COMPLETELY INERT. WE MAY ENTER.
SOME KIND OF BIG CRYSTAL IN THE TOP...FOR FOCUS LIKE A LASER.
YES. I AM CONVINCED THE MAIN FUNCTION OF THE PYRAMIDS' LONG DISTANCE TELEPORTATION WAS TO EXPAND THE MAYAN GODS' INFLUENCE.
I AM NOW DETECTING *ANNIE* AT THE BOTTOM OF THIS WELLWAY.
ANNIE!
WHAT HAPPENED TO ALL THE *NOT-CHARGING-IN?*

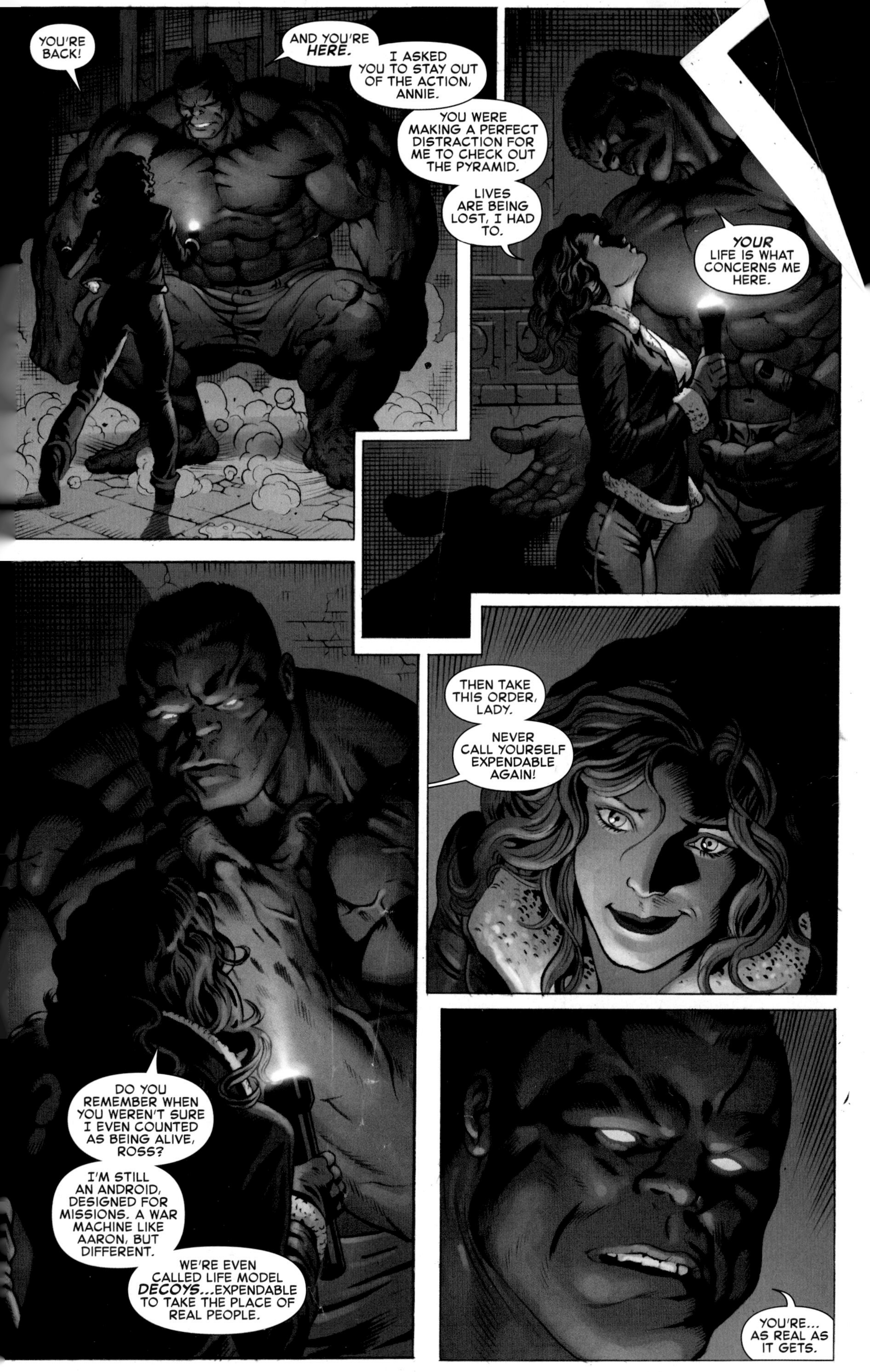
YOU'RE BACK!
AND YOU'RE *HERE.*
I ASKED YOU TO STAY OUT OF THE ACTION, ANNIE.
YOU WERE MAKING A PERFECT DISTRACTION FOR ME TO CHECK OUT THE PYRAMID.
LIVES ARE BEING LOST, I HAD TO.
YOUR LIFE IS WHAT CONCERNS ME HERE.
DO YOU REMEMBER WHEN YOU WEREN'T SURE I EVEN COUNTED AS BEING ALIVE, ROSS?
I'M STILL AN ANDROID, DESIGNED FOR MISSIONS. A WAR MACHINE LIKE AARON, BUT DIFFERENT.
WE'RE EVEN CALLED LIFE MODEL *DECOYS...*EXPENDABLE TO TAKE THE PLACE OF REAL PEOPLE.
THEN TAKE THIS ORDER, LADY.
NEVER CALL YOURSELF EXPENDABLE AGAIN!
YOU'RE... AS REAL AS IT GETS.

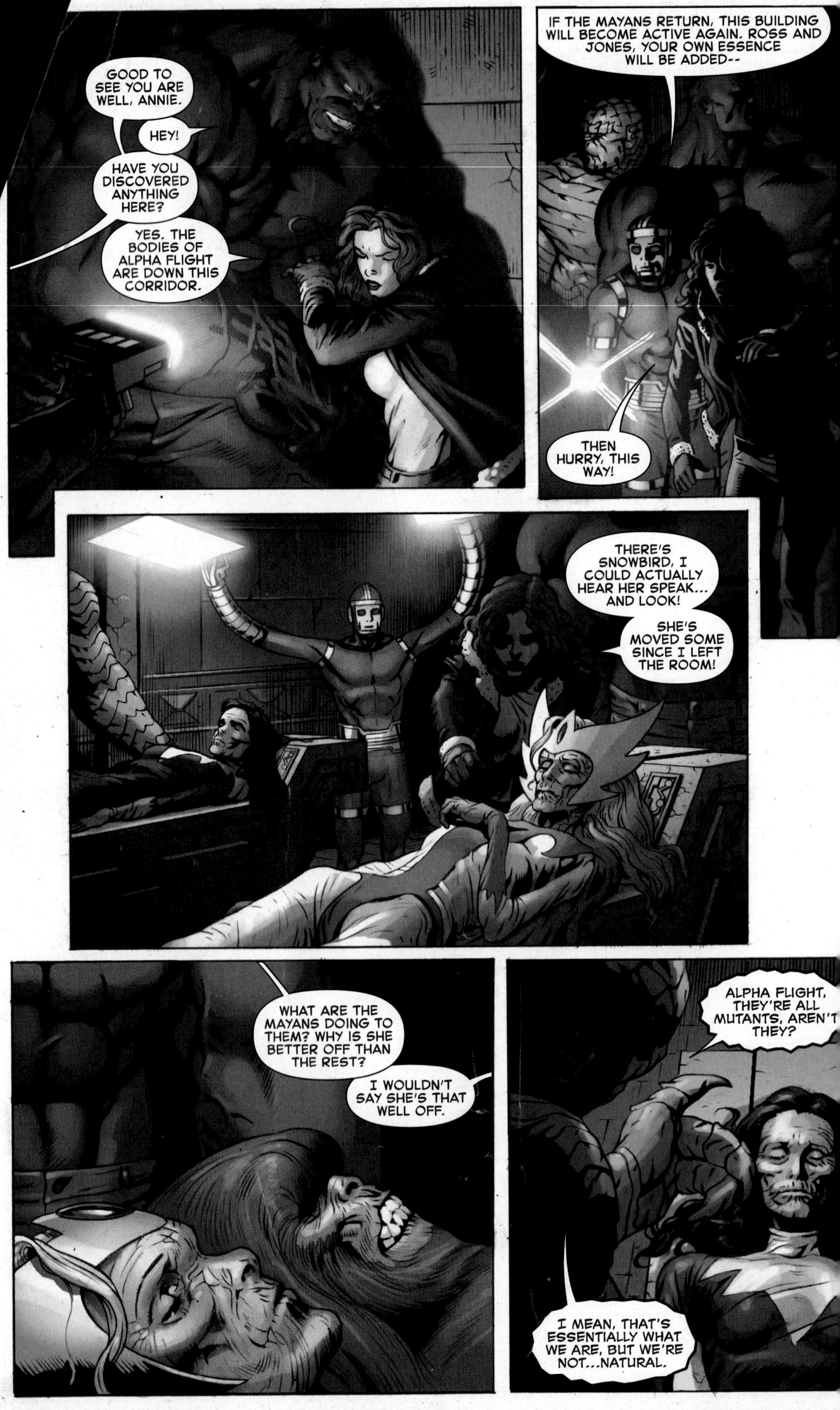
GOOD TO SEE YOU ARE WELL, ANNIE.
HEY!
HAVE YOU DISCOVERED ANYTHING HERE?
YES. THE BODIES OF ALPHA FLIGHT ARE DOWN THIS CORRIDOR.
IF THE MAYANS RETURN, THIS BUILDING WILL BECOME ACTIVE AGAIN. ROSS AND JONES, YOUR OWN ESSENCE WILL BE ADDED--
THEN HURRY, THIS WAY!
THERE'S SNOWBIRD, I COULD ACTUALLY HEAR HER SPEAK... AND LOOK!
SHE'S MOVED SOME SINCE I LEFT THE ROOM!
WHAT ARE THE MAYANS DOING TO THEM? WHY IS SHE BETTER OFF THAN THE REST?
I WOULDN'T SAY SHE'S THAT WELL OFF.
ALPHA FLIGHT, THEY'RE ALL MUTANTS, AREN'T THEY?
I MEAN, THAT'S ESSENTIALLY WHAT WE ARE, BUT WE'RE NOT...NATURAL.

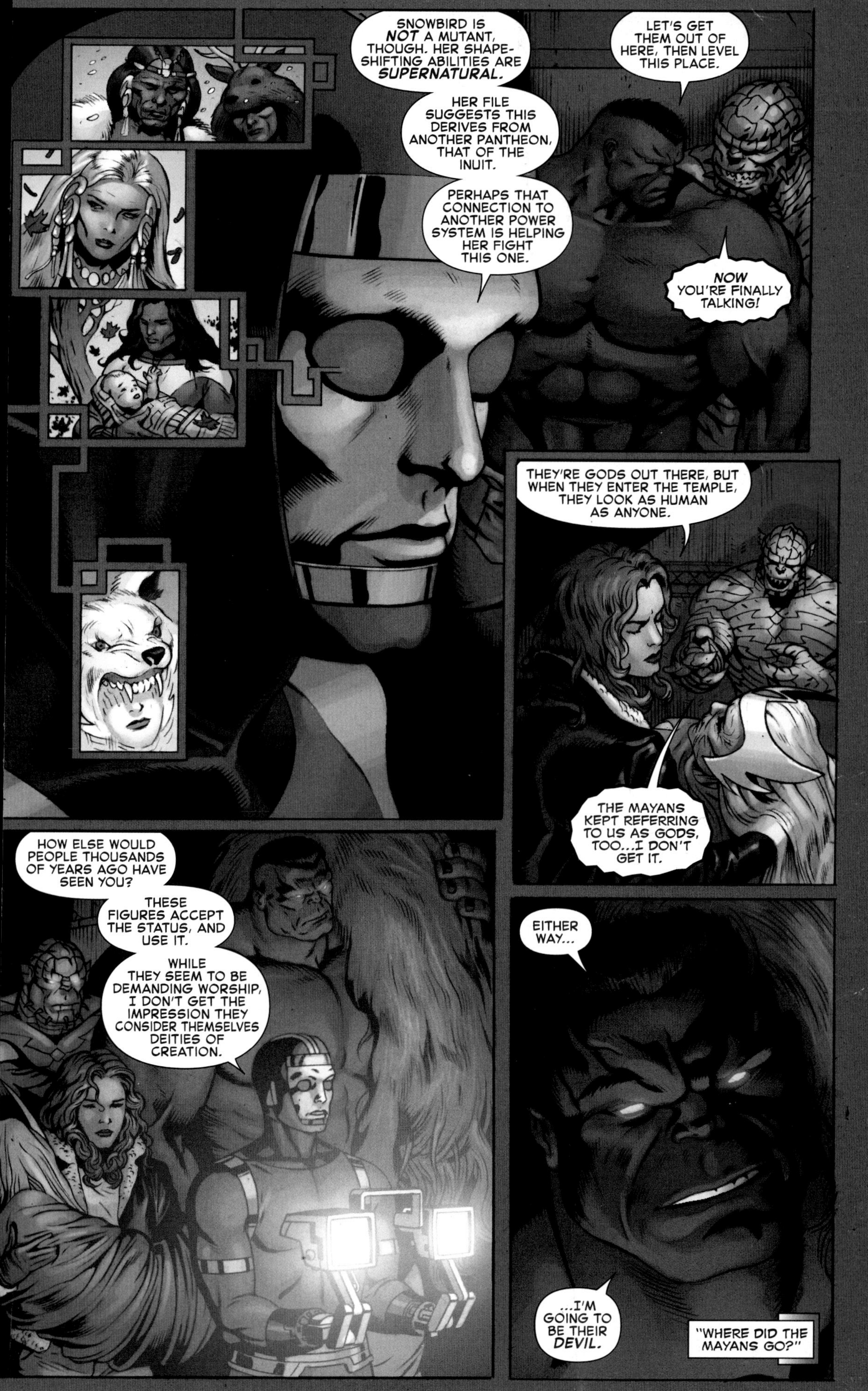

SNOWBIRD IS NOT A MUTANT, THOUGH. HER SHAPE-SHIFTING ABILITIES ARE SUPERNATURAL.
HER FILE SUGGESTS THIS DERIVES FROM ANOTHER PANTHEON, THAT OF THE INUIT.
PERHAPS THAT CONNECTION TO ANOTHER POWER SYSTEM IS HELPING HER FIGHT THIS ONE.
LET'S GET THEM OUT OF HERE, THEN LEVEL THIS PLACE.
NOW YOU'RE FINALLY TALKING!
THEY'RE GODS OUT THERE, BUT WHEN THEY ENTER THE TEMPLE, THEY LOOK AS HUMAN AS ANYONE.
THE MAYANS KEPT REFERRING TO US AS GODS, TOO...I DON'T GET IT.
HOW ELSE WOULD PEOPLE THOUSANDS OF YEARS AGO HAVE SEEN YOU?
THESE FIGURES ACCEPT THE STATUS, AND USE IT.
WHILE THEY SEEM TO BE DEMANDING WORSHIP, I DON'T GET THE IMPRESSION THEY CONSIDER THEMSELVES DEITIES OF CREATION.
EITHER WAY...
...I'M GOING TO BE THEIR DEVIL.
"WHERE DID THE MAYANS GO?"

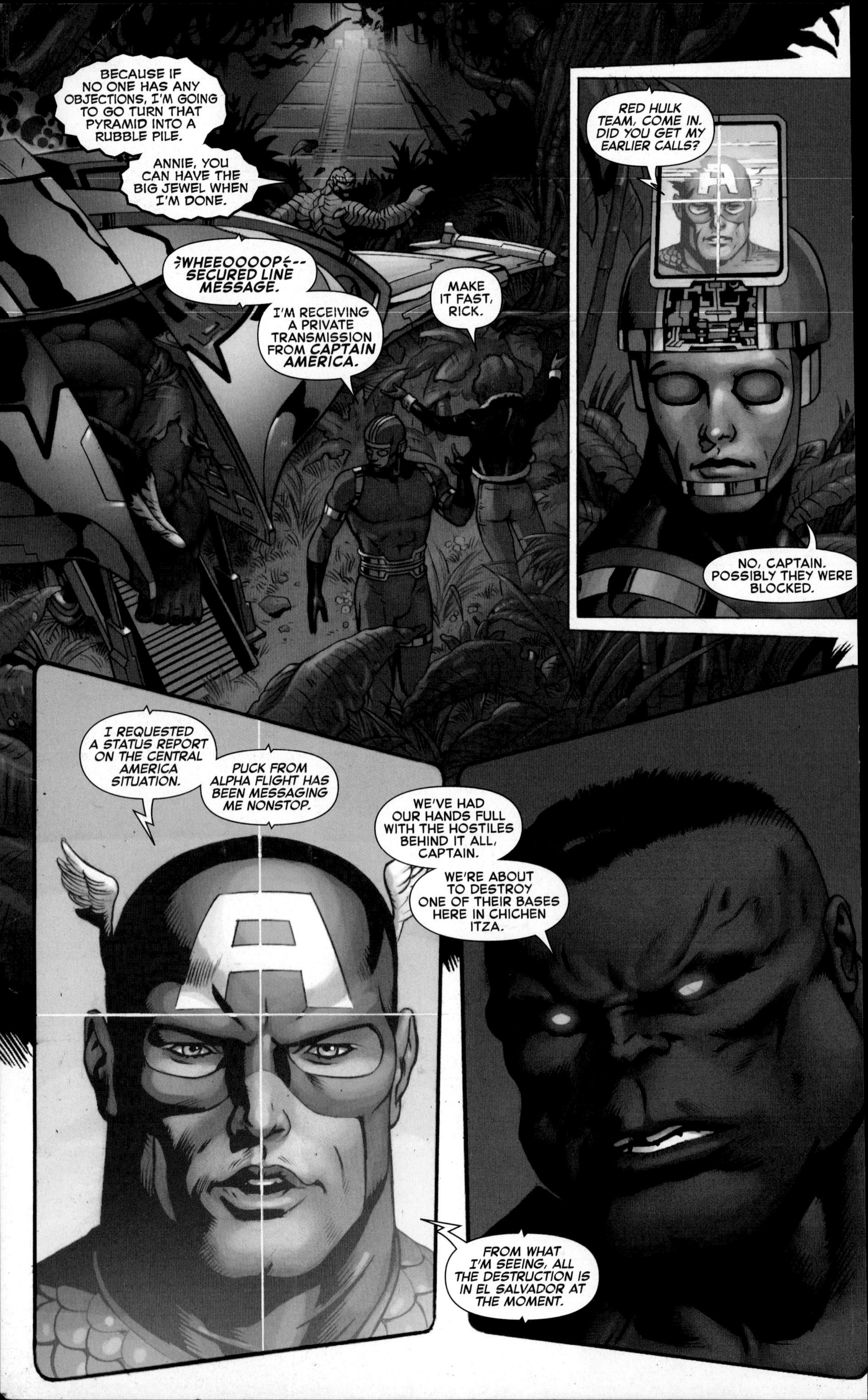
BECAUSE IF NO ONE HAS ANY OBJECTIONS, I'M GOING TO GO TURN THAT PYRAMID INTO A RUBBLE PILE.
ANNIE, YOU CAN HAVE THE BIG JEWEL WHEN I'M DONE.
RED HULK TEAM, COME IN. DID YOU GET MY EARLIER CALLS?
>WHEEOOOOP<-- SECURED LINE MESSAGE.
I'M RECEIVING A PRIVATE TRANSMISSION FROM CAPTAIN AMERICA.
MAKE IT FAST, RICK.
NO, CAPTAIN. POSSIBLY THEY WERE BLOCKED.
I REQUESTED A STATUS REPORT ON THE CENTRAL AMERICA SITUATION.
PUCK FROM ALPHA FLIGHT HAS BEEN MESSAGING ME NONSTOP.
WE'VE HAD OUR HANDS FULL WITH THE HOSTILES BEHIND IT ALL, CAPTAIN.
WE'RE ABOUT TO DESTROY ONE OF THEIR BASES HERE IN CHICHEN ITZA.
FROM WHAT I'M SEEING, ALL THE DESTRUCTION IS IN EL SALVADOR AT THE MOMENT.

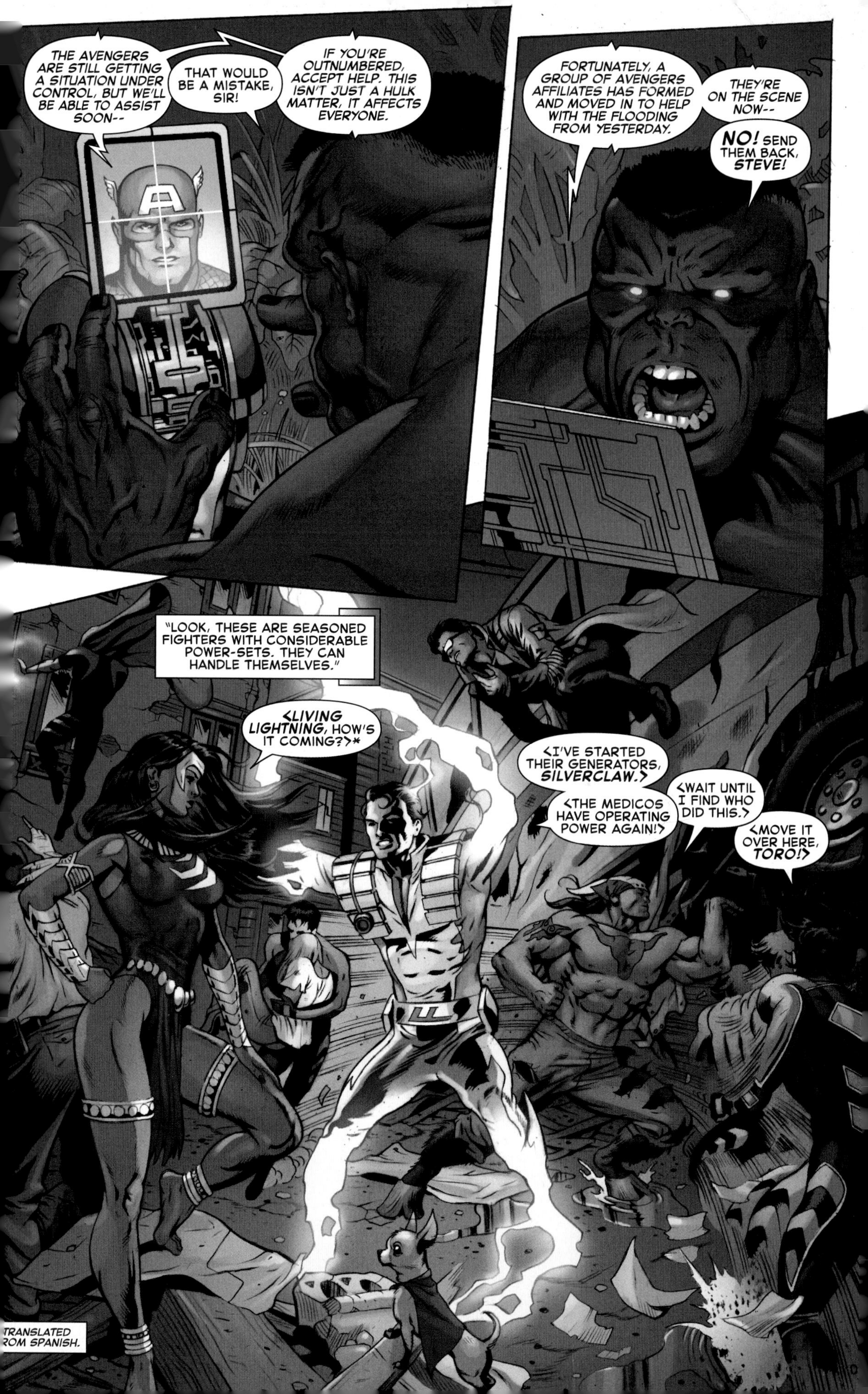
THE AVENGERS ARE STILL GETTING A SITUATION UNDER CONTROL, BUT WE'LL BE ABLE TO ASSIST SOON--
THAT WOULD BE A MISTAKE, SIR!
IF YOU'RE OUTNUMBERED, ACCEPT HELP. THIS ISN'T JUST A HULK MATTER, IT AFFECTS EVERYONE.
FORTUNATELY, A GROUP OF AVENGERS AFFILIATES HAS FORMED AND MOVED IN TO HELP WITH THE FLOODING FROM YESTERDAY.
THEY'RE ON THE SCENE NOW--
NO! SEND THEM BACK, STEVE!
"LOOK, THESE ARE SEASONED FIGHTERS WITH CONSIDERABLE POWER-SETS. THEY CAN HANDLE THEMSELVES."
<LIVING LIGHTNING, HOW'S IT COMING?>*
<I'VE STARTED THEIR GENERATORS, SILVERCLAW.>
<THE MEDICOS HAVE OPERATING POWER AGAIN!>
<WAIT UNTIL I FIND WHO DID THIS.>
<MOVE IT OVER HERE, TORO!>
*TRANSLATED FROM SPANISH.

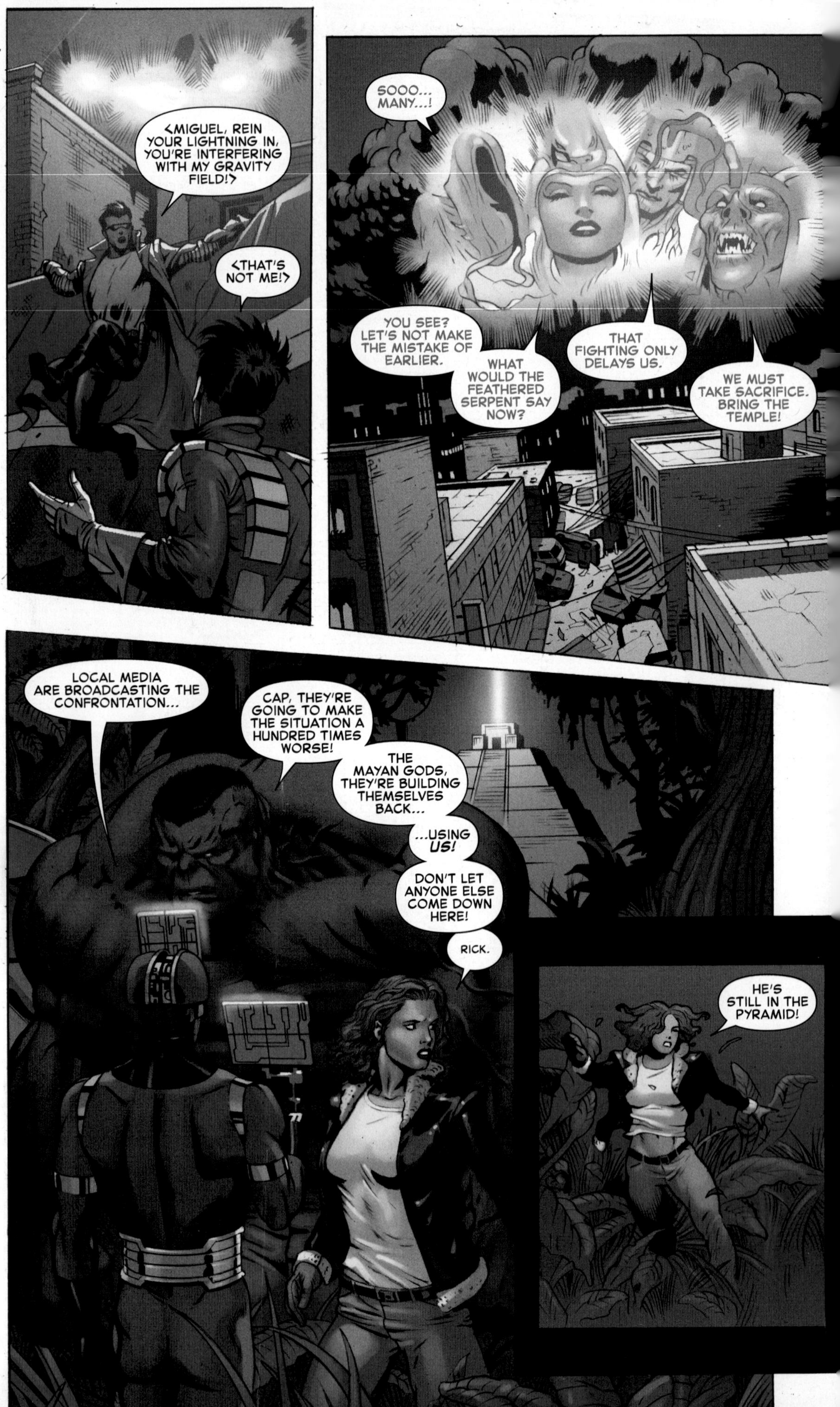

<MIGUEL, REIN YOUR LIGHTNING IN, YOU'RE INTERFERING WITH MY GRAVITY FIELD!>
<THAT'S NOT ME!>
SOOO... MANY...!
YOU SEE? LET'S NOT MAKE THE MISTAKE OF EARLIER.
WHAT WOULD THE FEATHERED SERPENT SAY NOW?
THAT FIGHTING ONLY DELAYS US.
WE MUST TAKE SACRIFICE. BRING THE TEMPLE!
LOCAL MEDIA ARE BROADCASTING THE CONFRONTATION...
CAP, THEY'RE GOING TO MAKE THE SITUATION A HUNDRED TIMES WORSE!
THE MAYAN GODS, THEY'RE BUILDING THEMSELVES BACK...
...USING US!
DON'T LET ANYONE ELSE COME DOWN HERE!
RICK.
HE'S STILL IN THE PYRAMID!

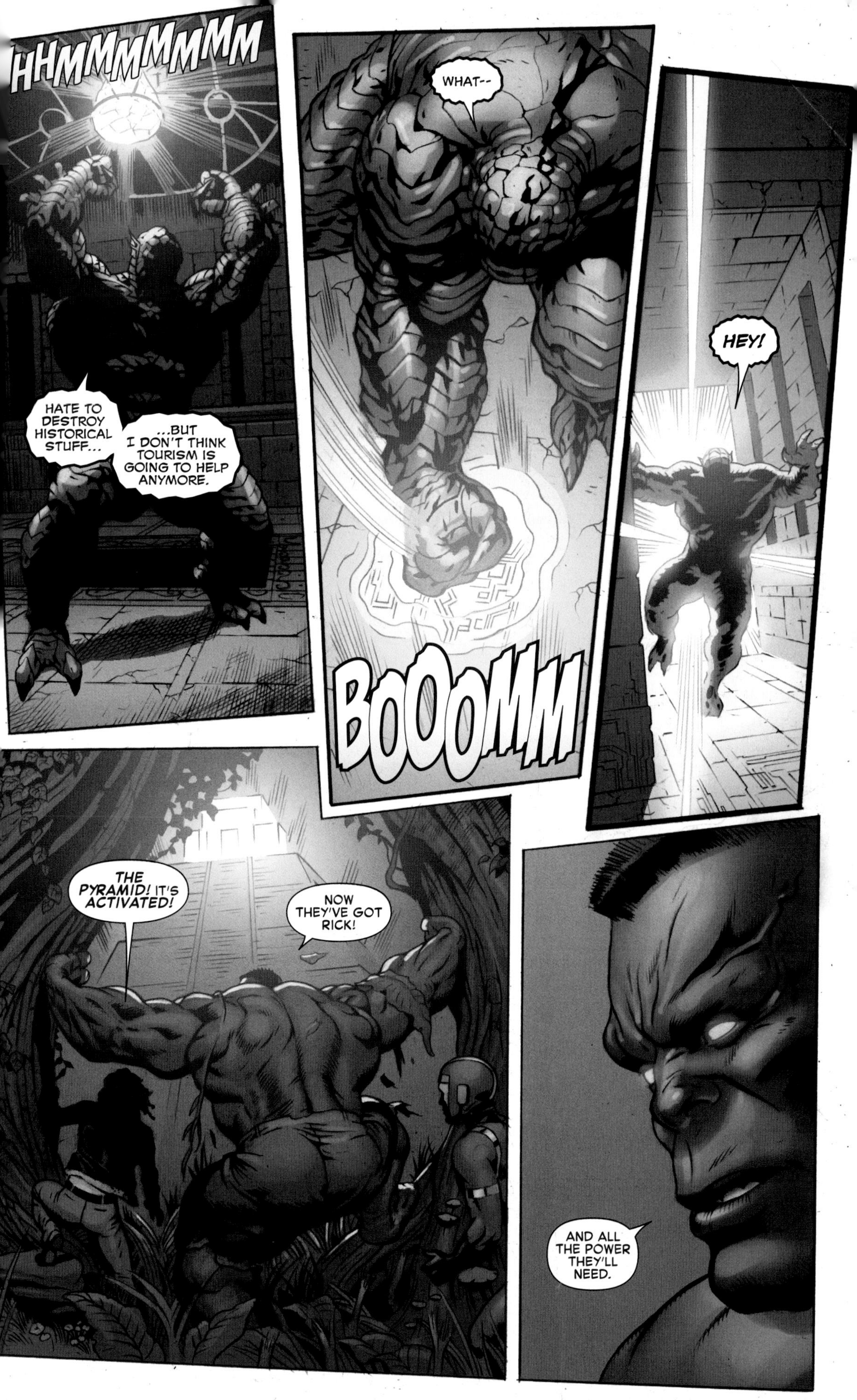
HHMMMMMMM
HATE TO DESTROY HISTORICAL STUFF...
...BUT I DON'T THINK TOURISM IS GOING TO HELP ANYMORE.
WHAT--
BOOOMM
HEY!
THE PYRAMID! IT'S ACTIVATED!
NOW THEY'VE GOT RICK!
AND ALL THE POWER THEY'LL NEED.

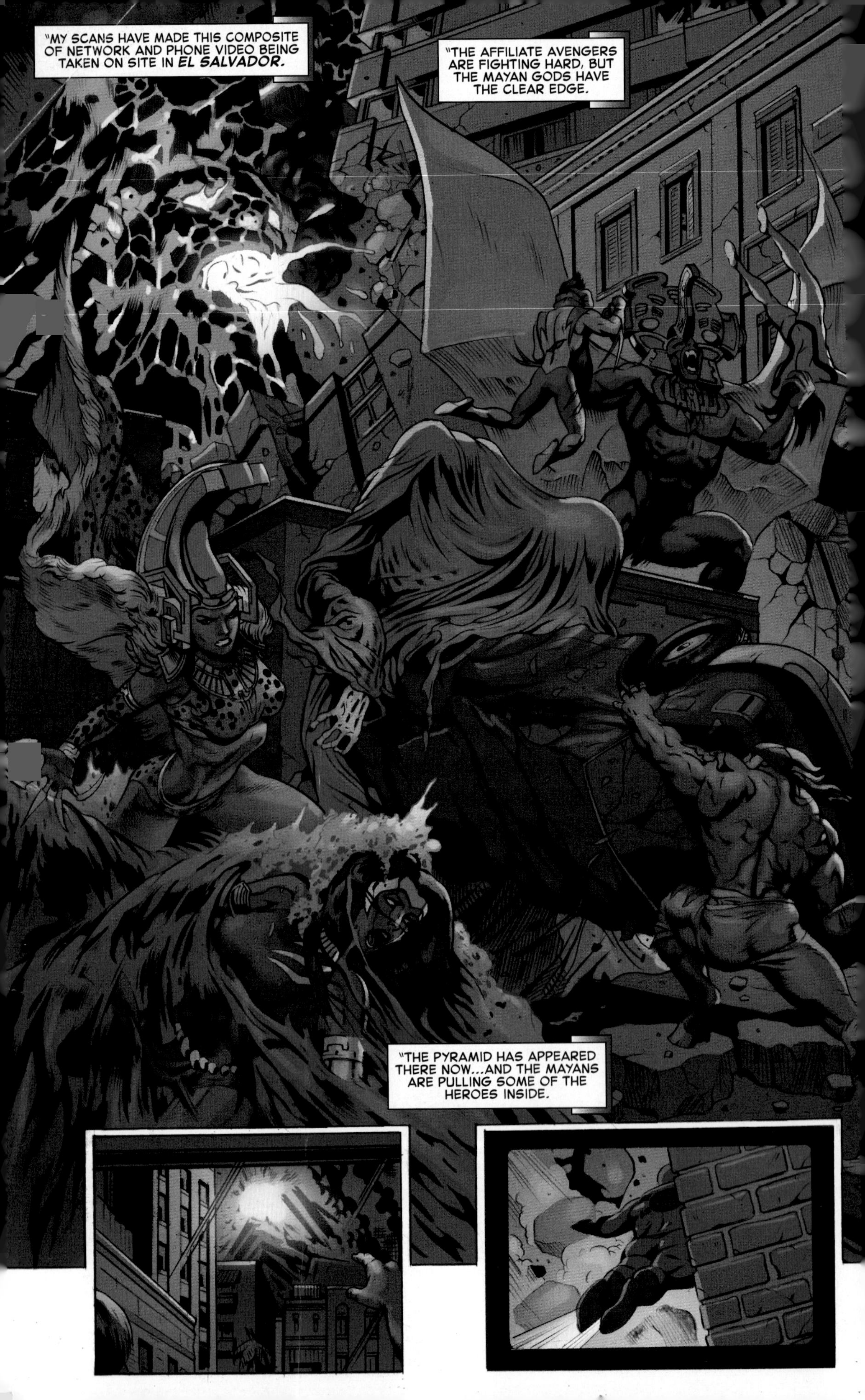
"MY SCANS HAVE MADE THIS COMPOSITE OF NETWORK AND PHONE VIDEO BEING TAKEN ON SITE IN EL SALVADOR.
"THE AFFILIATE AVENGERS ARE FIGHTING HARD, BUT THE MAYAN GODS HAVE THE CLEAR EDGE.
"THE PYRAMID HAS APPEARED THERE NOW...AND THE MAYANS ARE PULLING SOME OF THE HEROES INSIDE.

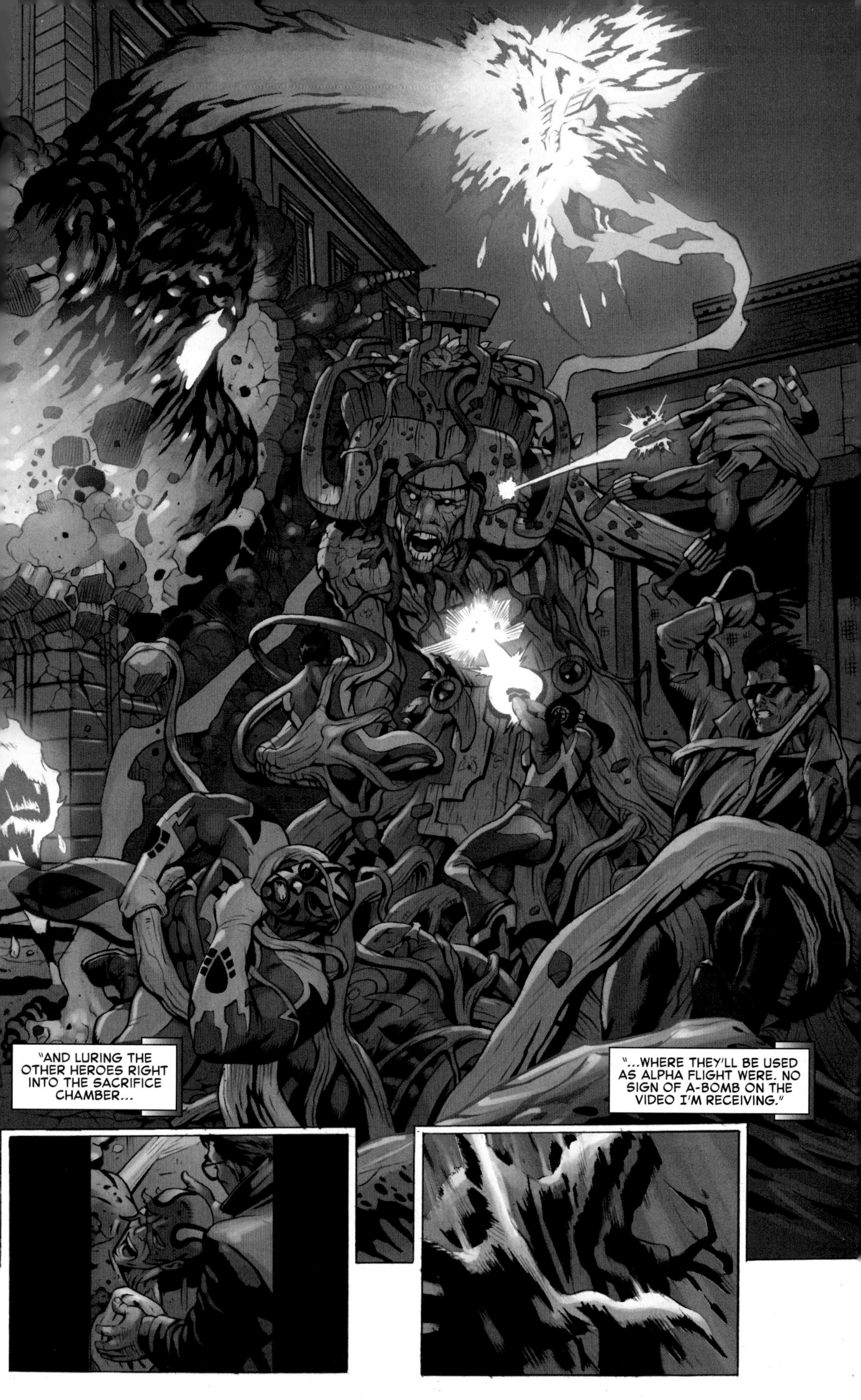
"AND LURING THE OTHER HEROES RIGHT INTO THE SACRIFICE CHAMBER...
"...WHERE THEY'LL BE USED AS ALPHA FLIGHT WERE. NO SIGN OF A-BOMB ON THE VIDEO I'M RECEIVING."

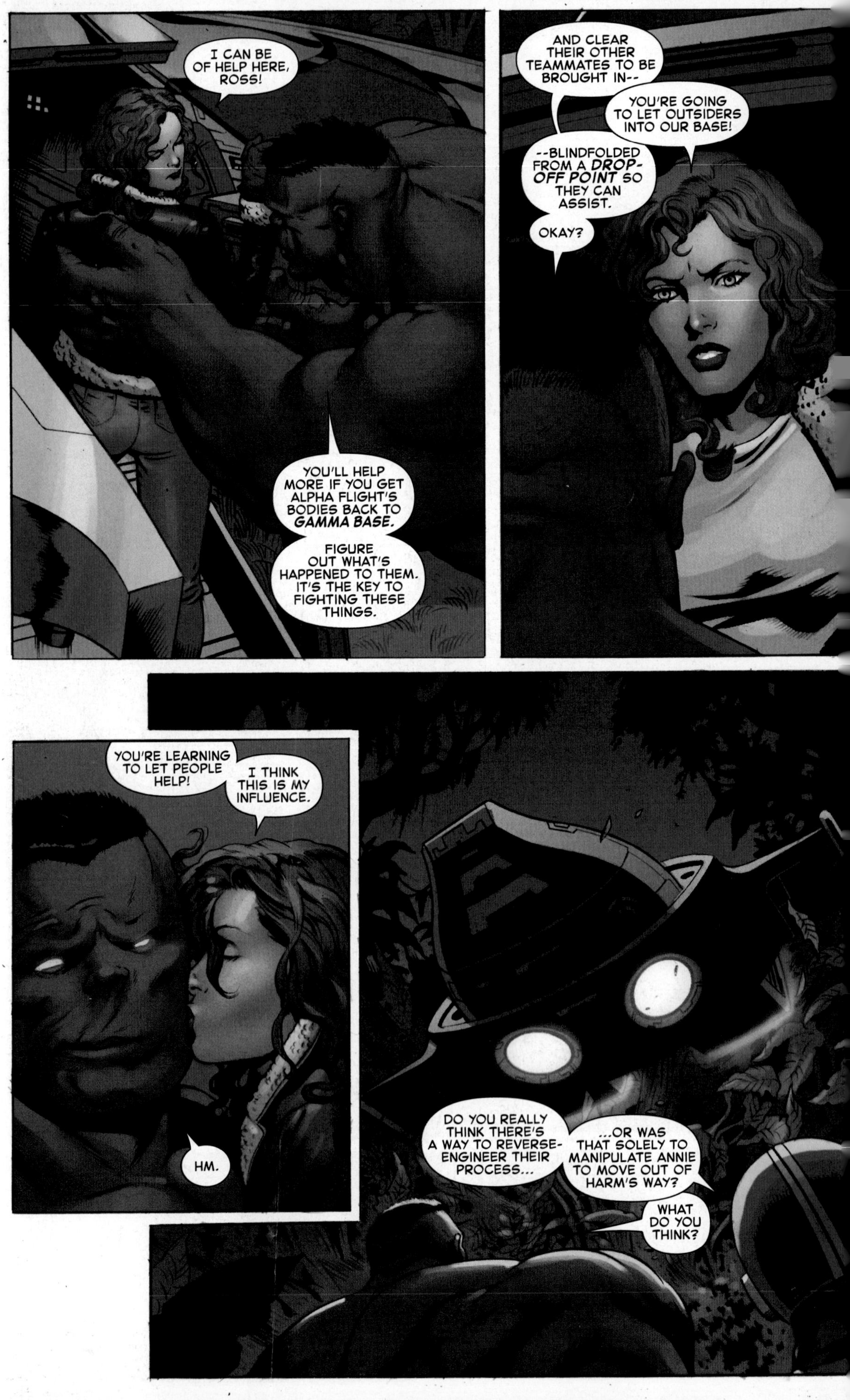
I CAN BE OF HELP HERE, ROSS!
YOU'LL HELP MORE IF YOU GET ALPHA FLIGHT'S BODIES BACK TO *GAMMA BASE.*
FIGURE OUT WHAT'S HAPPENED TO THEM. IT'S THE KEY TO FIGHTING THESE THINGS.
AND CLEAR THEIR OTHER TEAMMATES TO BE BROUGHT IN--
YOU'RE GOING TO LET OUTSIDERS INTO OUR BASE!
--BLINDFOLDED FROM A *DROP-OFF POINT* SO THEY CAN ASSIST.
OKAY?
YOU'RE LEARNING TO LET PEOPLE HELP!
I THINK THIS IS MY INFLUENCE.
HM.
DO YOU REALLY THINK THERE'S A WAY TO REVERSE-ENGINEER THEIR PROCESS...
...OR WAS THAT SOLELY TO MANIPULATE ANNIE TO MOVE OUT OF HARM'S WAY?
WHAT DO YOU THINK?

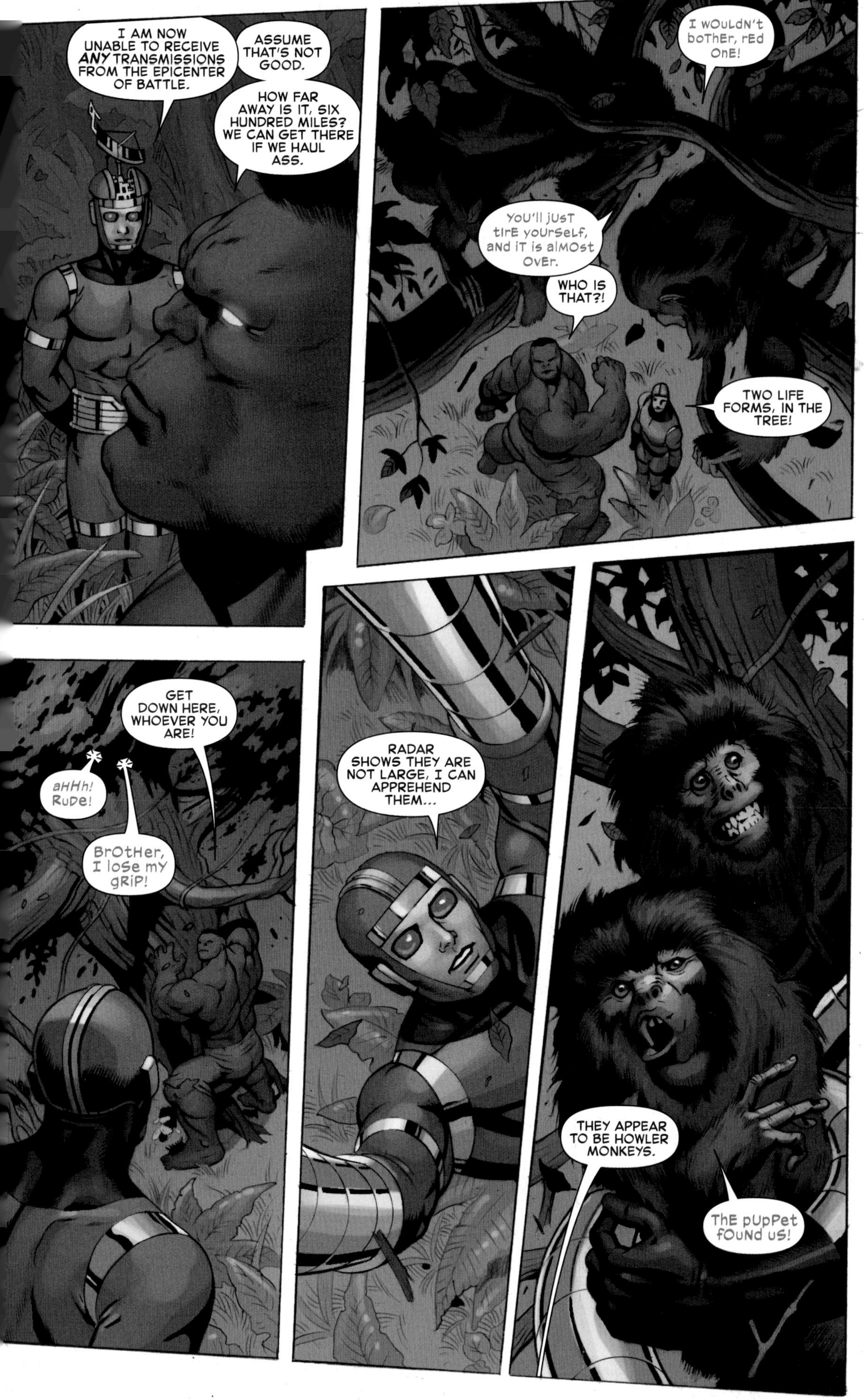
I AM NOW UNABLE TO RECEIVE ANY TRANSMISSIONS FROM THE EPICENTER OF BATTLE.
ASSUME THAT'S NOT GOOD.
HOW FAR AWAY IS IT, SIX HUNDRED MILES? WE CAN GET THERE IF WE HAUL ASS.
I WOULDN'T BOTHER, RED ONE!
YOU'LL JUST TIRE YOURSELF, AND IT IS ALMOST OVER.
WHO IS THAT?!
TWO LIFE FORMS, IN THE TREE!
GET DOWN HERE, WHOEVER YOU ARE!
AHHH! RUDE!
BROTHER, I LOSE MY GRIP!
RADAR SHOWS THEY ARE NOT LARGE, I CAN APPREHEND THEM...
THEY APPEAR TO BE HOWLER MONKEYS.
THE PUPPET FOUND US!

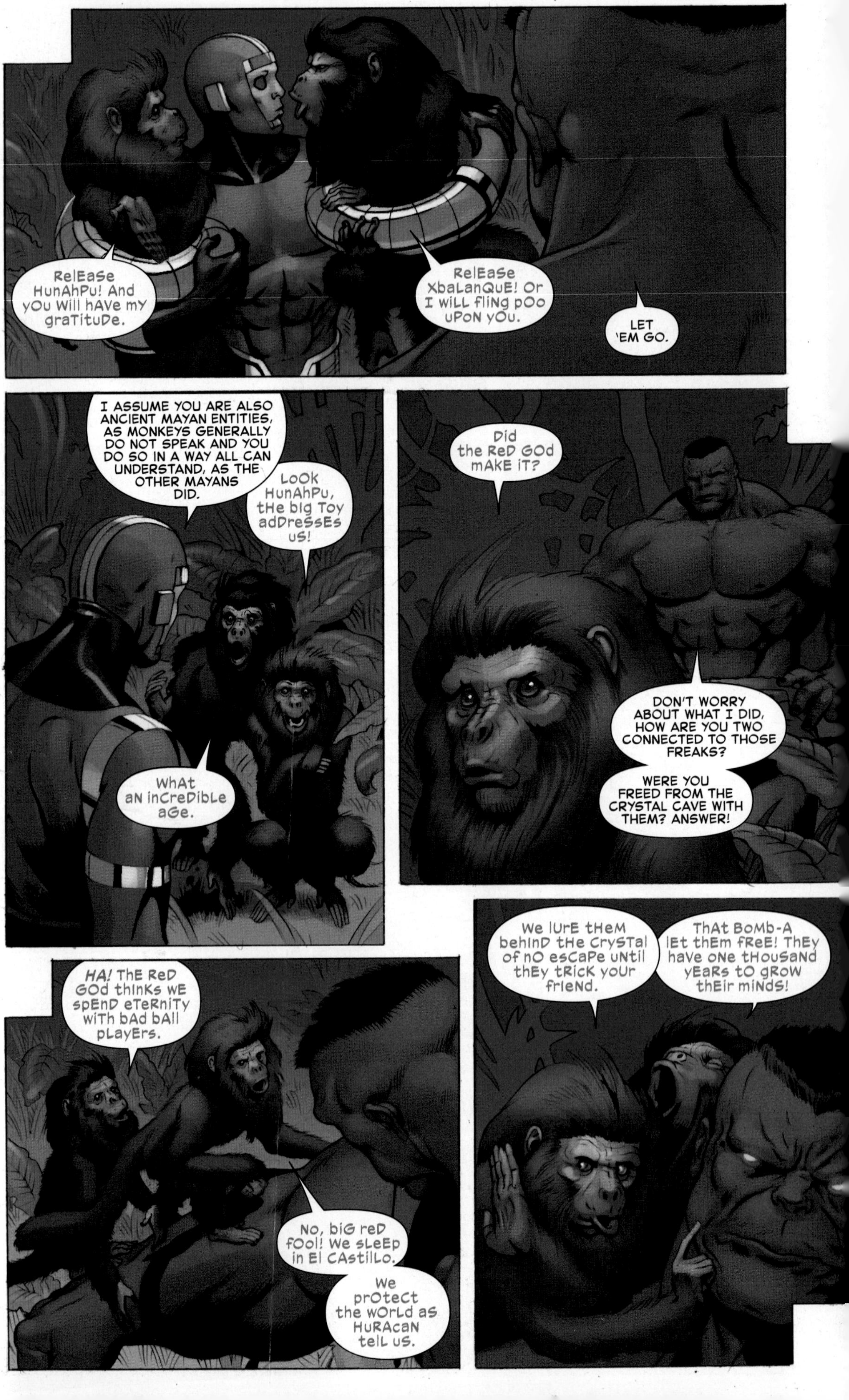

RelEaSe HunAhPu! And yOu Will hAve my graTituDe.
RelEase XbaLanQuE! Or I wiLL fling pOo uPON yOu.
LET 'EM GO.
I ASSUME YOU ARE ALSO ANCIENT MAYAN ENTITIES, AS MONKEYS GENERALLY DO NOT SPEAK AND YOU DO SO IN A WAY ALL CAN UNDERSTAND, AS THE OTHER MAYANS DID.
LoOK HunAhPu, tHe big Toy addresses uS!
WhAt an increDible aGe.
Did the ReD GOd mAKE iT?
DON'T WORRY ABOUT WHAT I DID, HOW ARE YOU TWO CONNECTED TO THOSE FREAKS?
WERE YOU FREED FROM THE CRYSTAL CAVE WITH THEM? ANSWER!
HA! ThE ReD GOd thinks WE spEnD eTErnity with bad baLL pLayErs.
No, biG reD fOol! We sLeEp in El CAstiLLo.
We prOtect the wOrld as HuRAcAN teLL uS.
We lure tHeM behinD the CrySTal of nO escape unTil tHey tRick your friend.
ThAt BOMB-A lEt tHem frEE! They have one tHousand yEars to grow theIr minds!

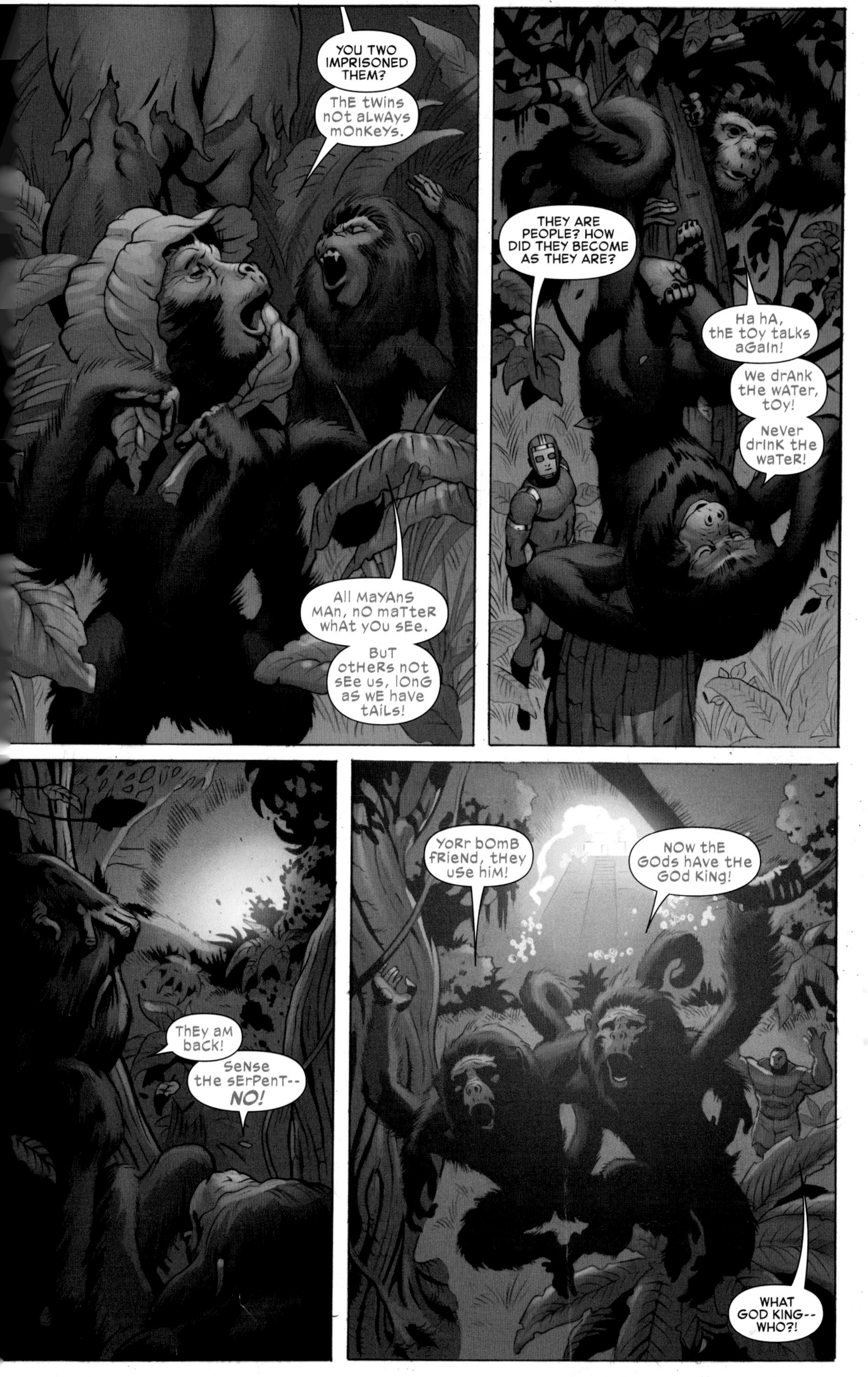
YOU TWO IMPRISONED THEM?
ThE tWins nOt aLWAys mOnKeys.
All MAYAnS MAn, nO maTTeR wHAt yOu sEe.
BuT otHeRs nOt sEe us, lOnG as WE have tAiLs!
THEY ARE PEOPLE? HOW DID THEY BECOME AS THEY ARE?
Ha hA, thE tOy taLks aGaIn!
We drAnk tHe wATer, tOy!
Never drink tHe waTeR!
ThEy aM back!
SeNse tHe sErPenT-- NO!
YoRr bOmB fRiend, tHey uSe hiM!
NOw thE GOds hAve tHe GOd King!
WHAT GOD KING-- WHO?!

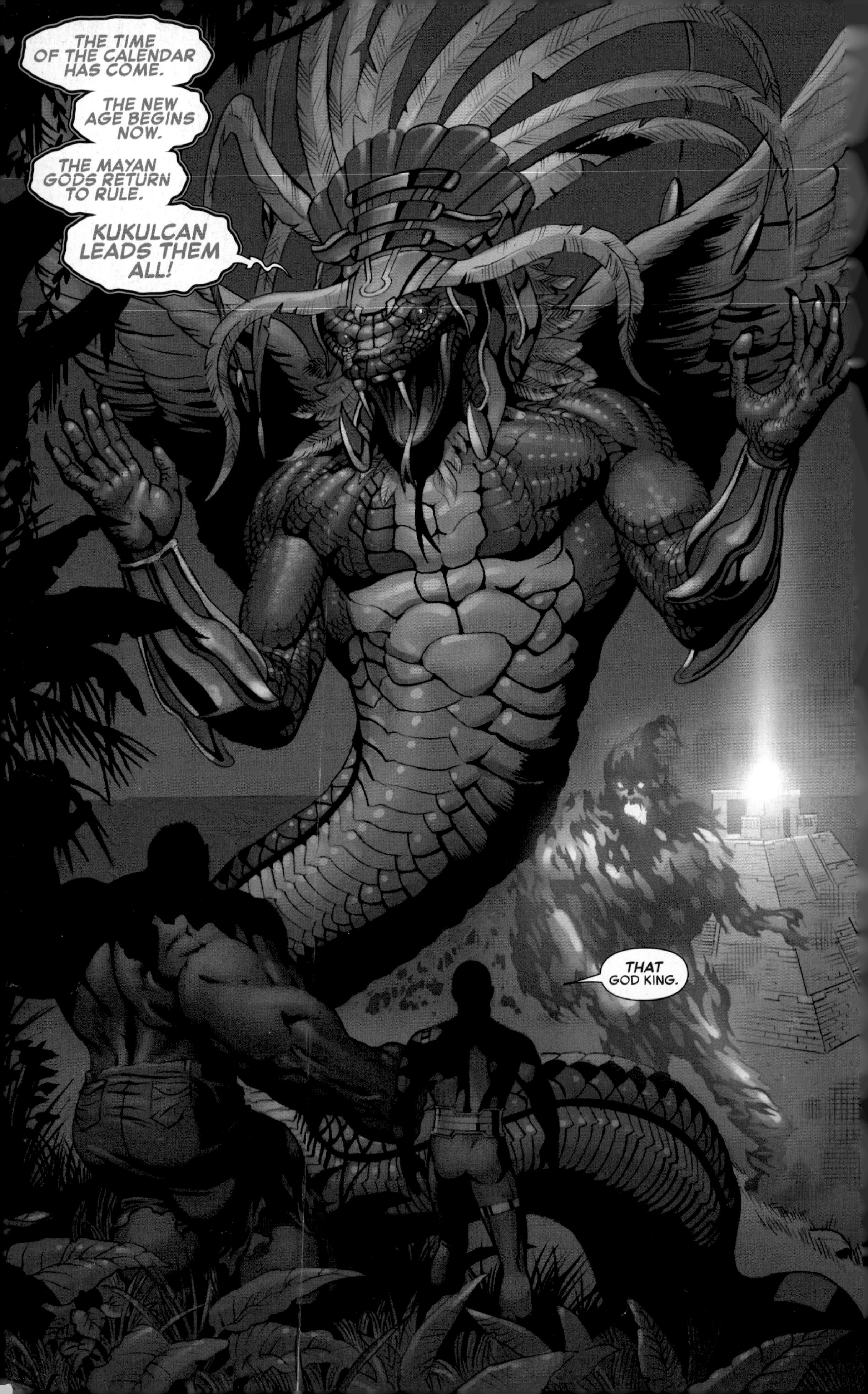
THE TIME OF THE CALENDAR HAS COME.
THE NEW AGE BEGINS NOW.
THE MAYAN GODS RETURN TO RULE.
KUKULCAN LEADS THEM ALL!
THAT GOD KING.

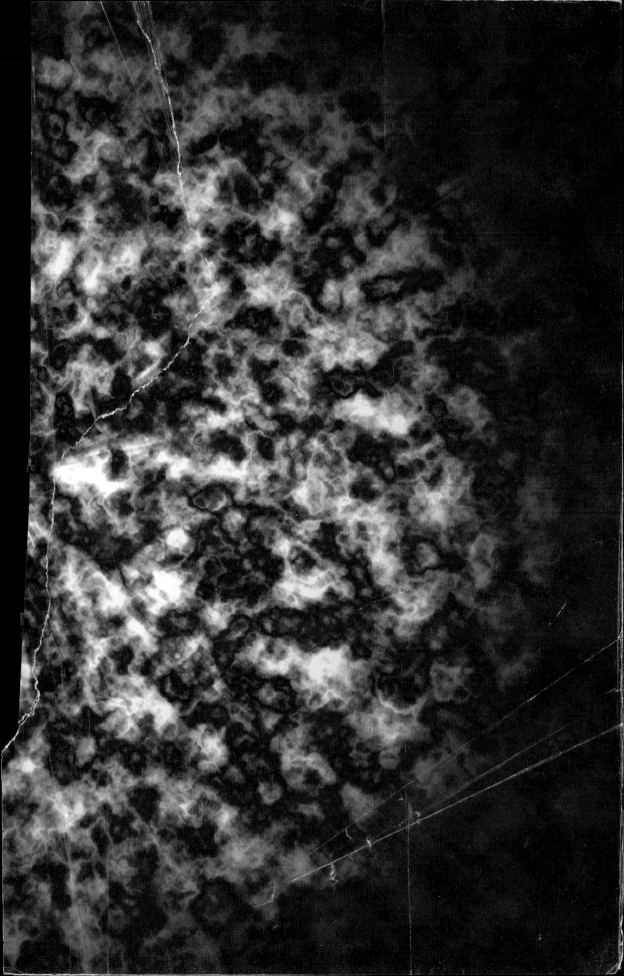

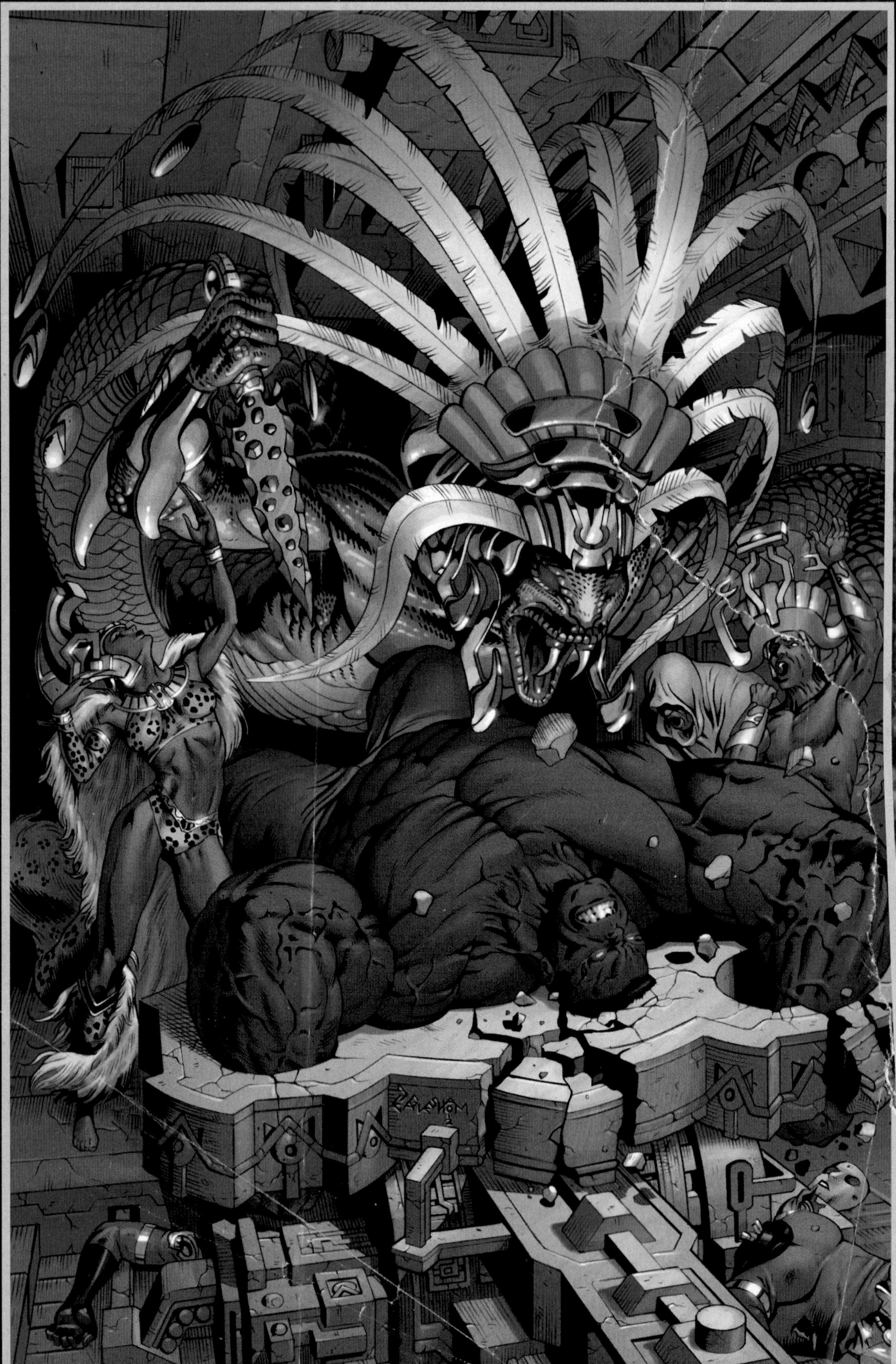

HULK #56

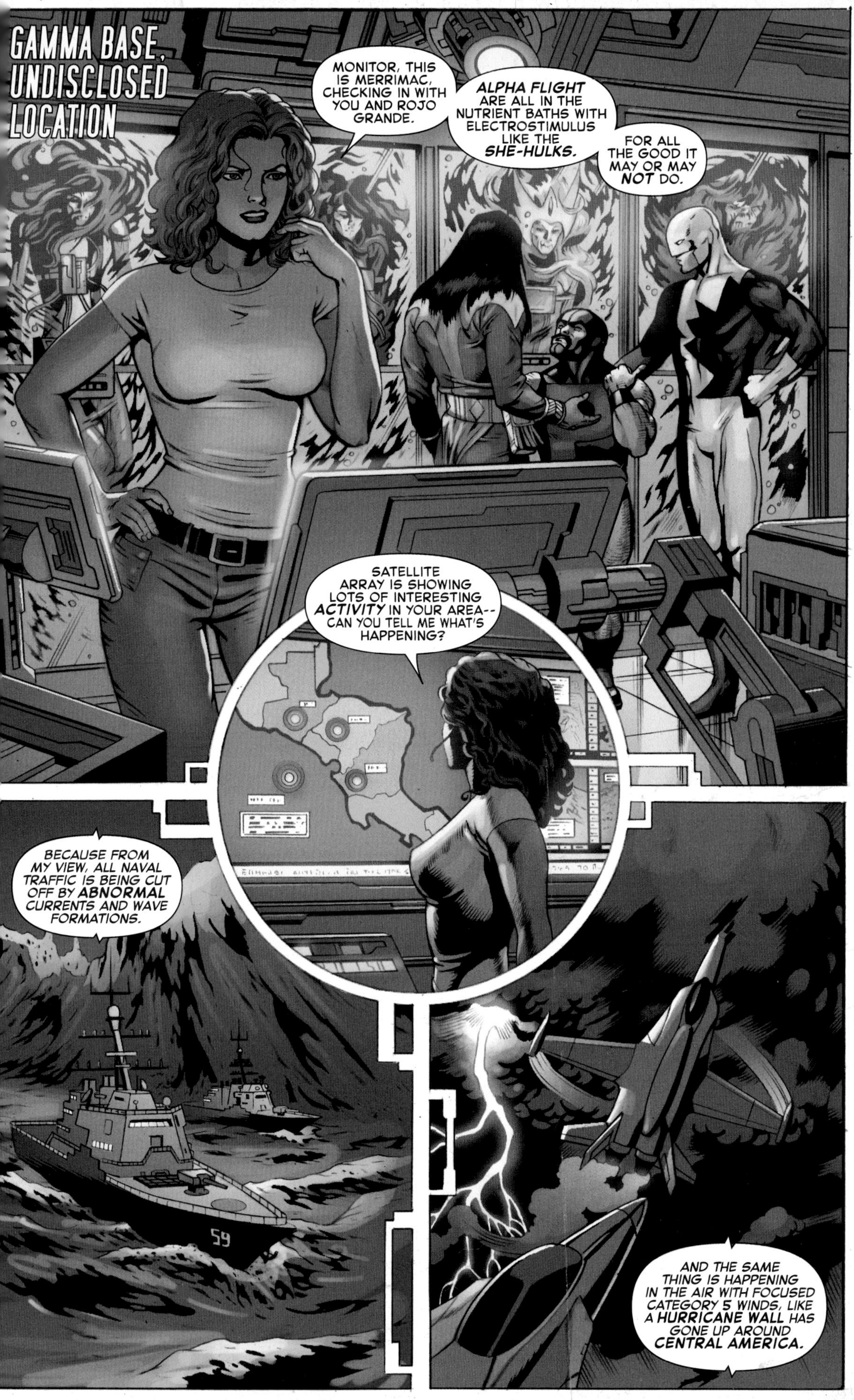
GAMMA BASE, UNDISCLOSED LOCATION
MONITOR, THIS IS MERRIMAC, CHECKING IN WITH YOU AND ROJO GRANDE.
ALPHA FLIGHT ARE ALL IN THE NUTRIENT BATHS WITH ELECTROSTIMULUS LIKE THE SHE-HULKS.
FOR ALL THE GOOD IT MAY OR MAY NOT DO.
SATELLITE ARRAY IS SHOWING LOTS OF INTERESTING ACTIVITY IN YOUR AREA-- CAN YOU TELL ME WHAT'S HAPPENING?
BECAUSE FROM MY VIEW, ALL NAVAL TRAFFIC IS BEING CUT OFF BY ABNORMAL CURRENTS AND WAVE FORMATIONS.
59
AND THE SAME THING IS HAPPENING IN THE AIR WITH FOCUSED CATEGORY 5 WINDS, LIKE A HURRICANE WALL HAS GONE UP AROUND CENTRAL AMERICA.

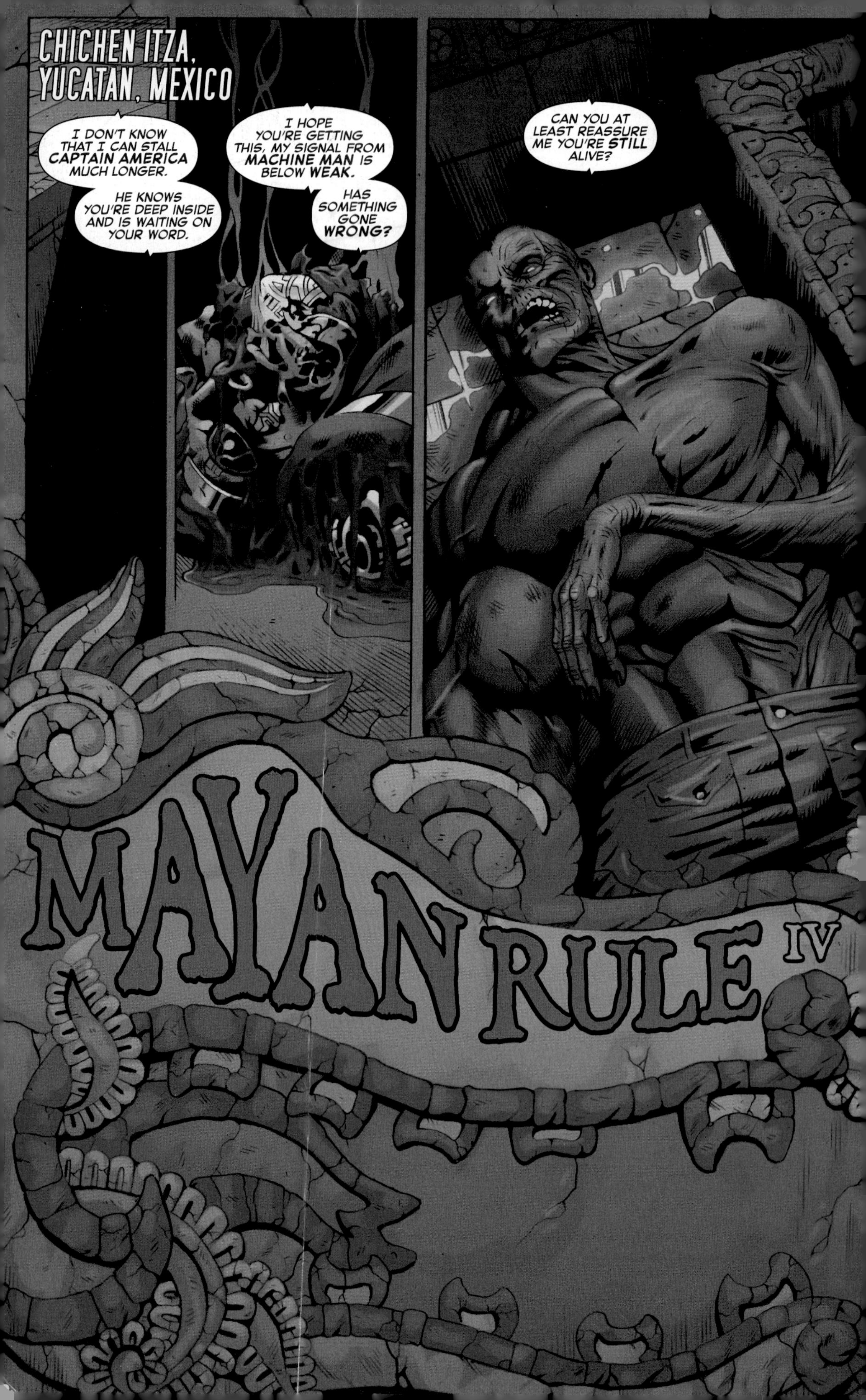
CHICHEN ITZA, YUCATAN, MEXICO
I DON'T KNOW THAT I CAN STALL CAPTAIN AMERICA MUCH LONGER.
HE KNOWS YOU'RE DEEP INSIDE AND IS WAITING ON YOUR WORD.
I HOPE YOU'RE GETTING THIS, MY SIGNAL FROM MACHINE MAN IS BELOW WEAK.
HAS SOMETHING GONE WRONG?
CAN YOU AT LEAST REASSURE ME YOU'RE STILL ALIVE?
MAYAN RULE IV

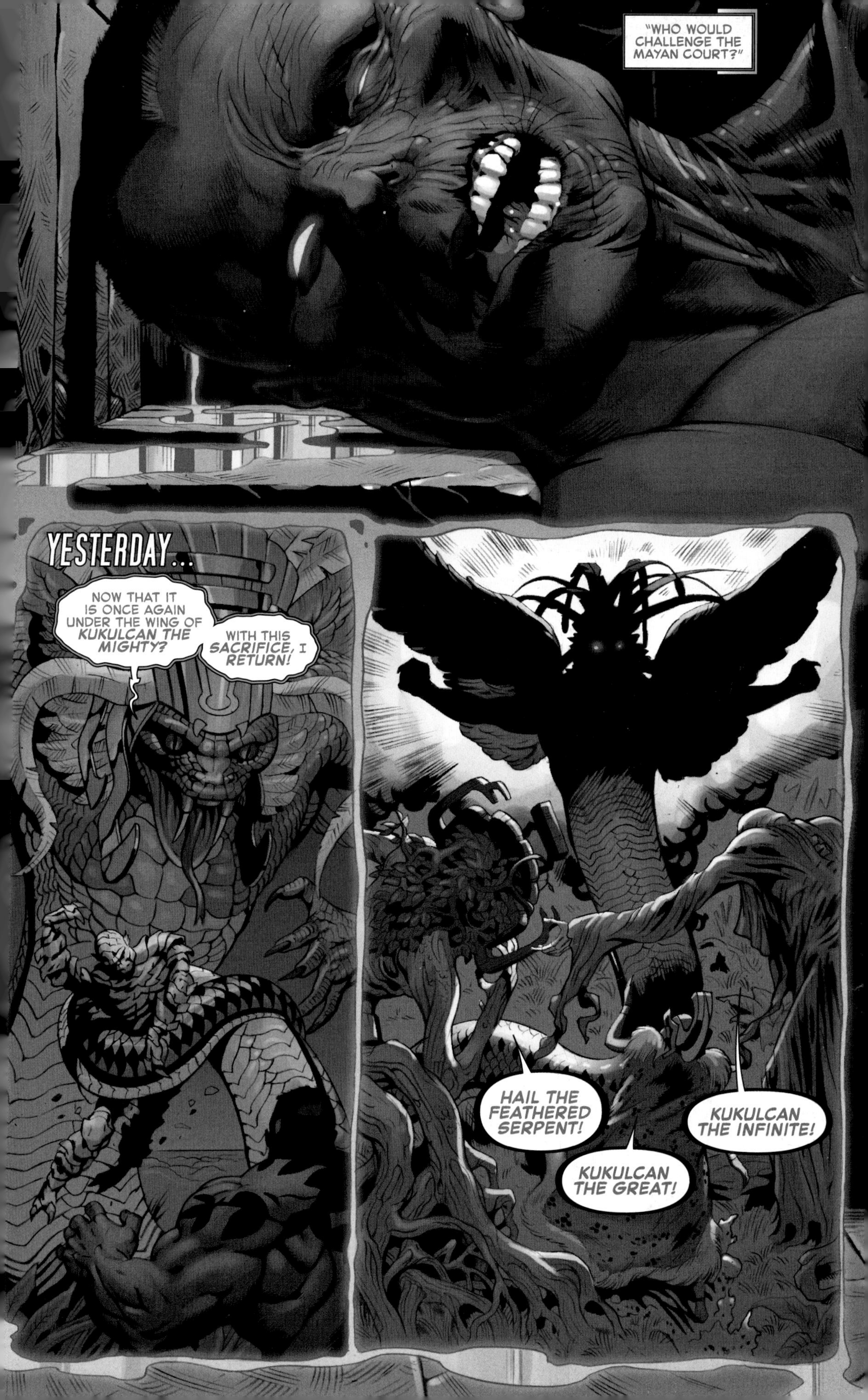
"WHO WOULD CHALLENGE THE MAYAN COURT?"
YESTERDAY...
NOW THAT IT IS ONCE AGAIN UNDER THE WING OF *KUKULCAN THE MIGHTY?*
WITH THIS *SACRIFICE*, I *RETURN!*
HAIL THE FEATHERED SERPENT!
KUKULCAN THE GREAT!
KUKULCAN THE INFINITE!

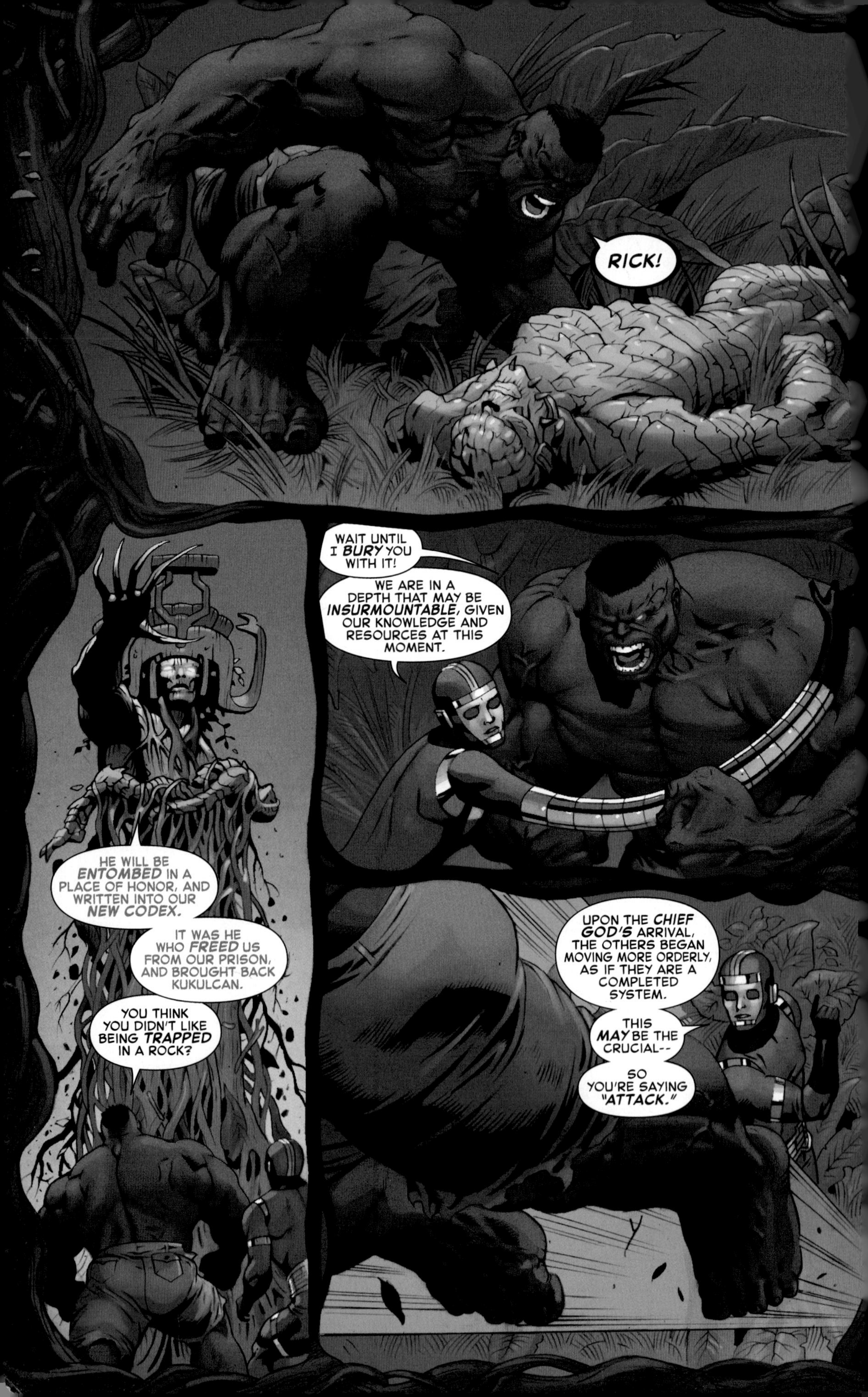
RICK!
WAIT UNTIL I BURY YOU WITH IT!
WE ARE IN A DEPTH THAT MAY BE INSURMOUNTABLE, GIVEN OUR KNOWLEDGE AND RESOURCES AT THIS MOMENT.
HE WILL BE ENTOMBED IN A PLACE OF HONOR, AND WRITTEN INTO OUR NEW CODEX.
IT WAS HE WHO FREED US FROM OUR PRISON, AND BROUGHT BACK KUKULCAN.
YOU THINK YOU DIDN'T LIKE BEING TRAPPED IN A ROCK?
UPON THE CHIEF GOD'S ARRIVAL, THE OTHERS BEGAN MOVING MORE ORDERLY, AS IF THEY ARE A COMPLETED SYSTEM.
THIS MAY BE THE CRUCIAL--
SO YOU'RE SAYING "ATTACK."

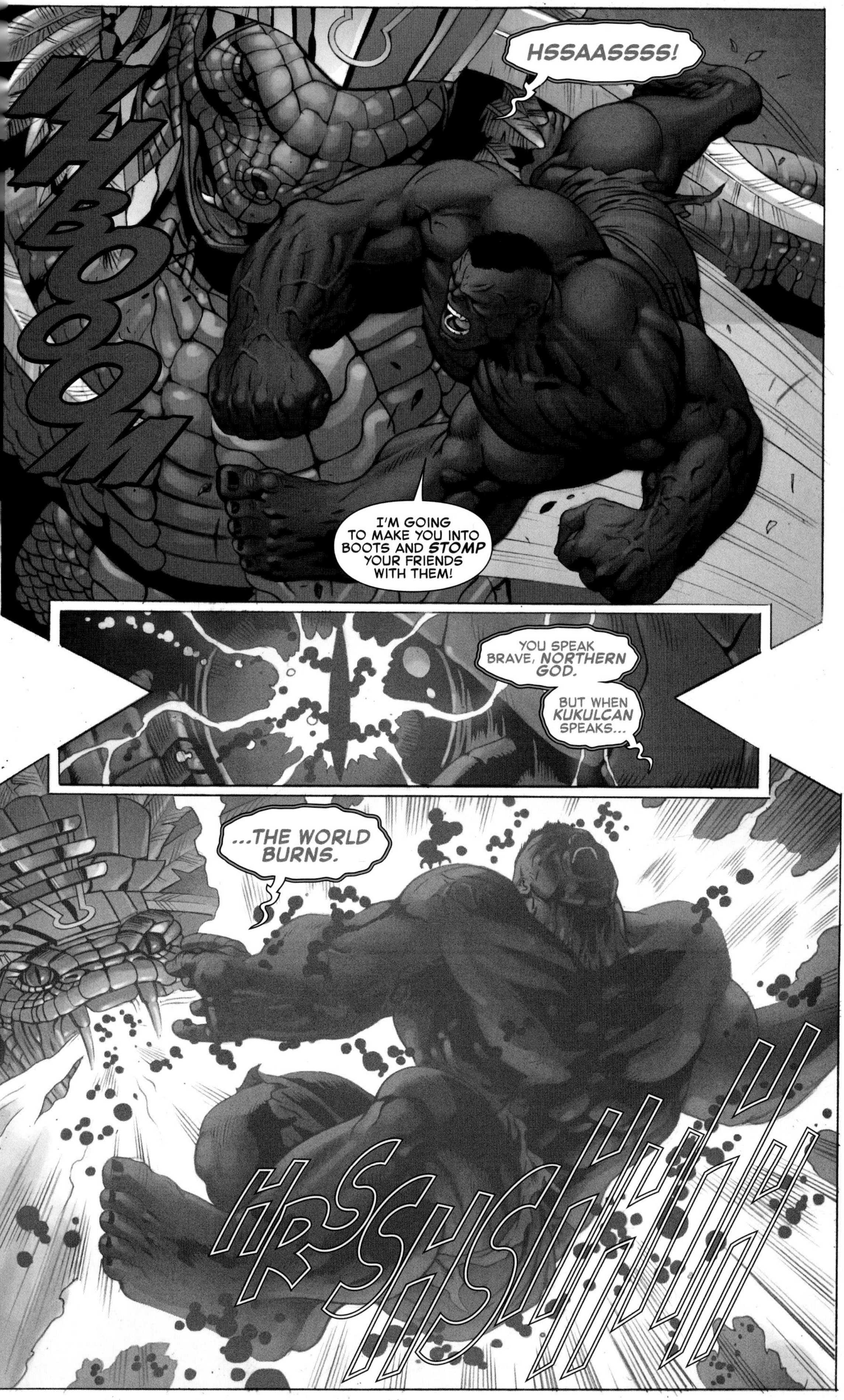
WHBOOOM
HSSAASSSS!
I'M GOING TO MAKE YOU INTO BOOTS AND STOMP YOUR FRIENDS WITH THEM!
YOU SPEAK BRAVE, NORTHERN GOD.
BUT WHEN KUKULCAN SPEAKS...
...THE WORLD BURNS.

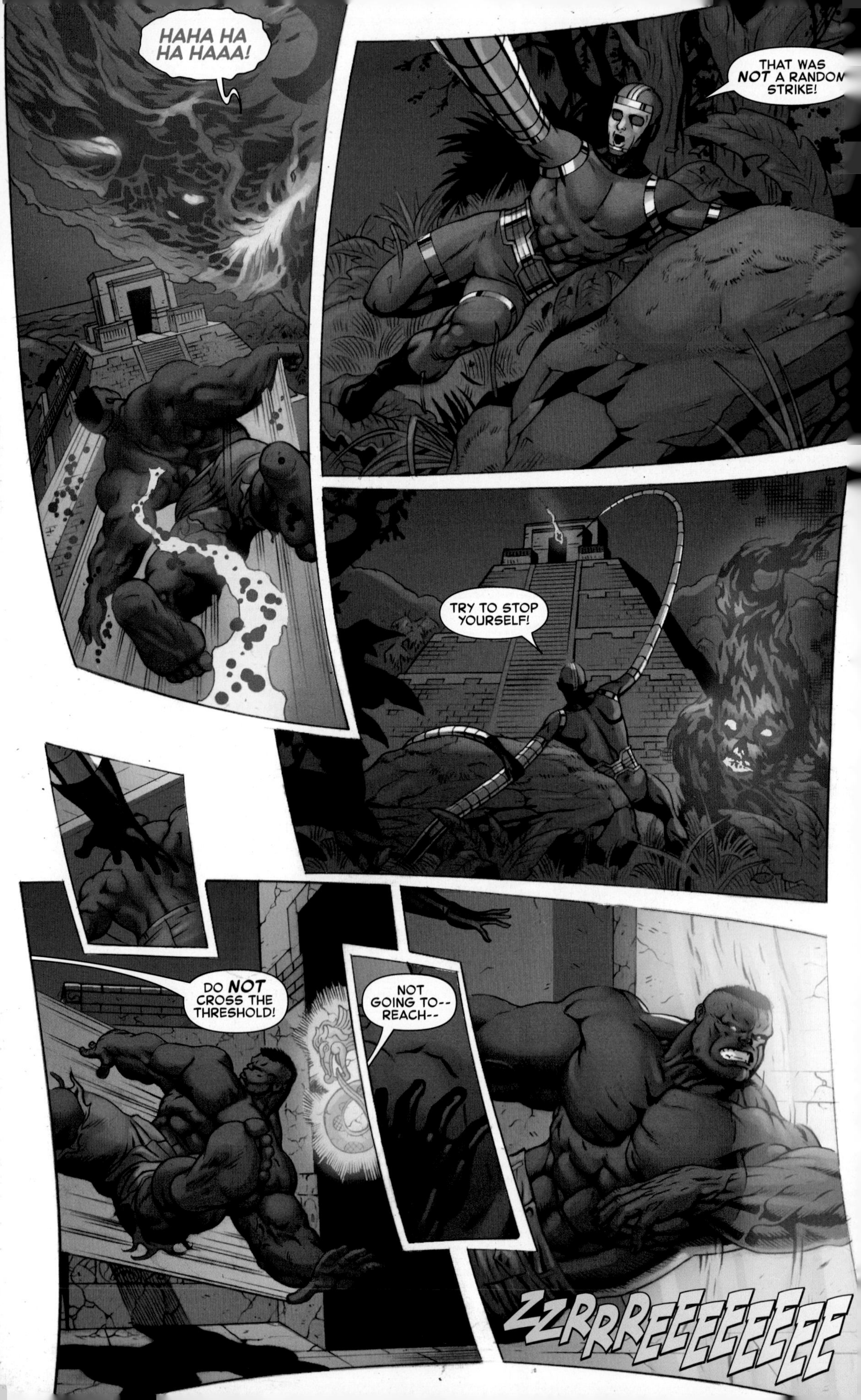
HAHA HA HA HAAA!
THAT WAS NOT A RANDOM STRIKE!
TRY TO STOP YOURSELF!
DO NOT CROSS THE THRESHOLD!
NOT GOING TO-- REACH--
ZZRRREEEEEEEEE

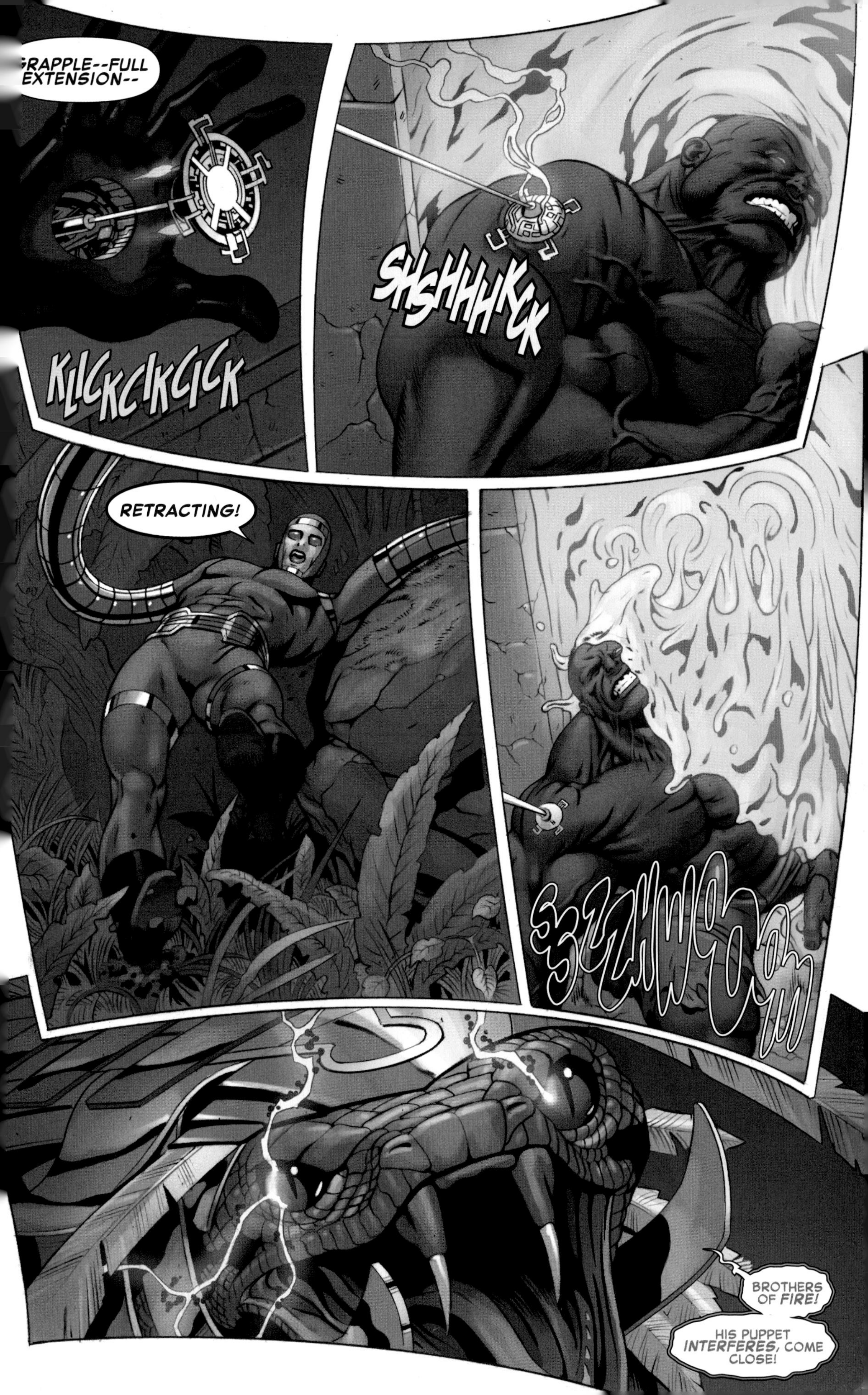

GRAPPLE--FULL EXTENSION--
KLICKCIKCICK
SHSHHHKCK
RETRACTING!
BROTHERS OF FIRE!
HIS PUPPET INTERFERES, COME CLOSE!

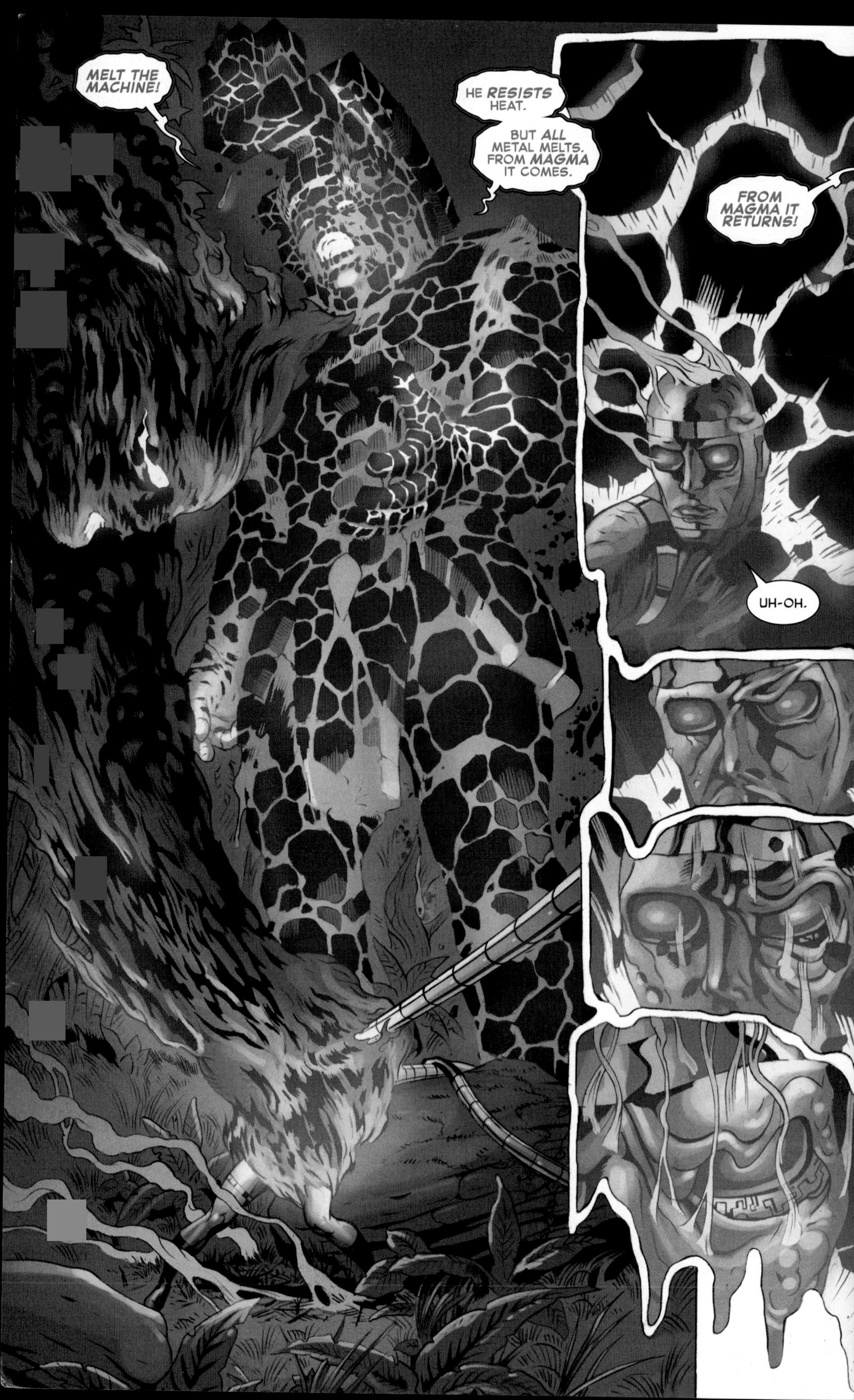
MELT THE MACHINE!
HE RESISTS HEAT.
BUT ALL METAL MELTS. FROM MAGMA IT COMES.
FROM MAGMA IT RETURNS!
UH-OH.

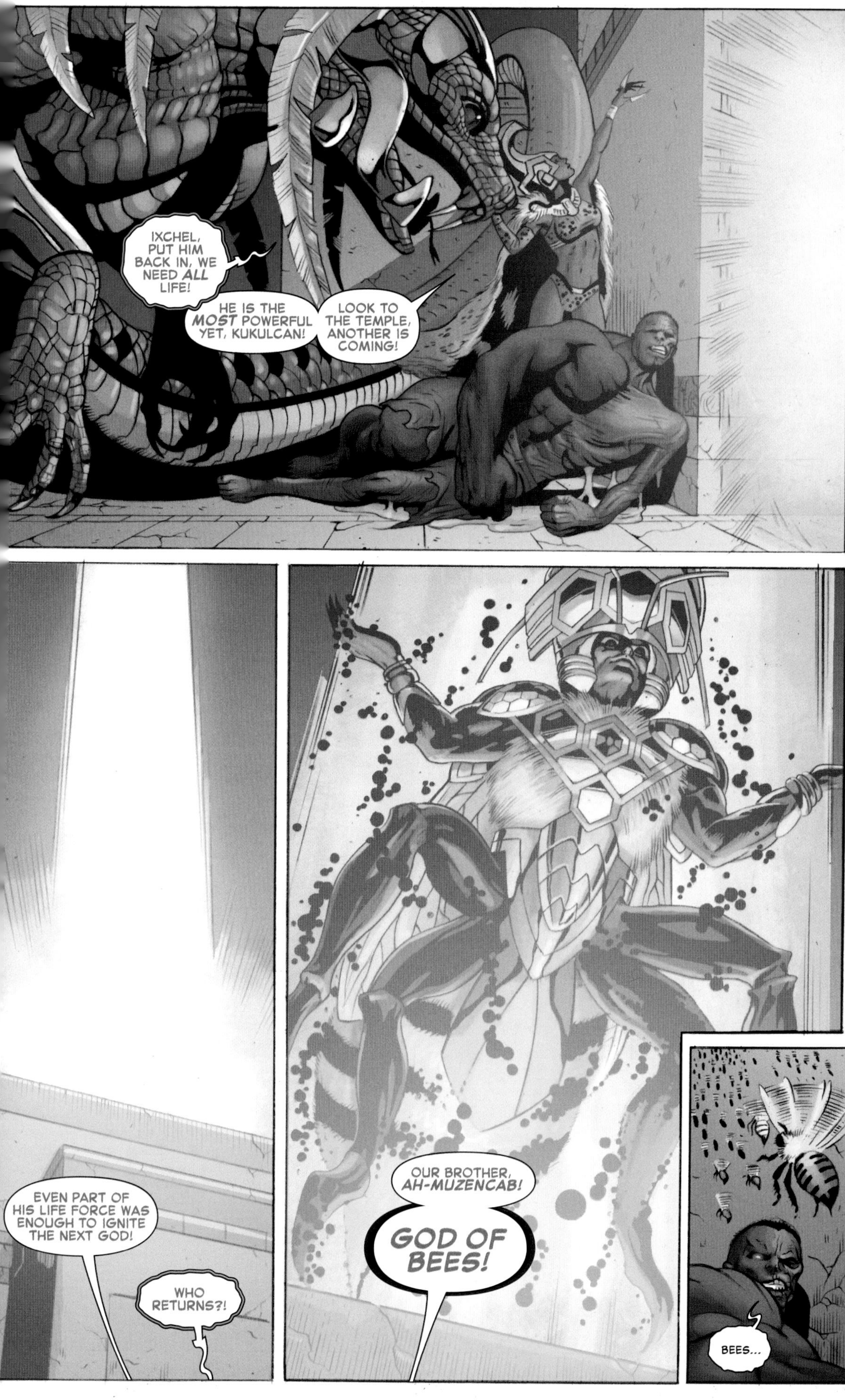
IXCHEL, PUT HIM BACK IN, WE NEED ALL LIFE!
HE IS THE MOST POWERFUL YET, KUKULCAN!
LOOK TO THE TEMPLE, ANOTHER IS COMING!
EVEN PART OF HIS LIFE FORCE WAS ENOUGH TO IGNITE THE NEXT GOD!
WHO RETURNS?!
OUR BROTHER, AH-MUZENCAB!
GOD OF BEES!
BEES...

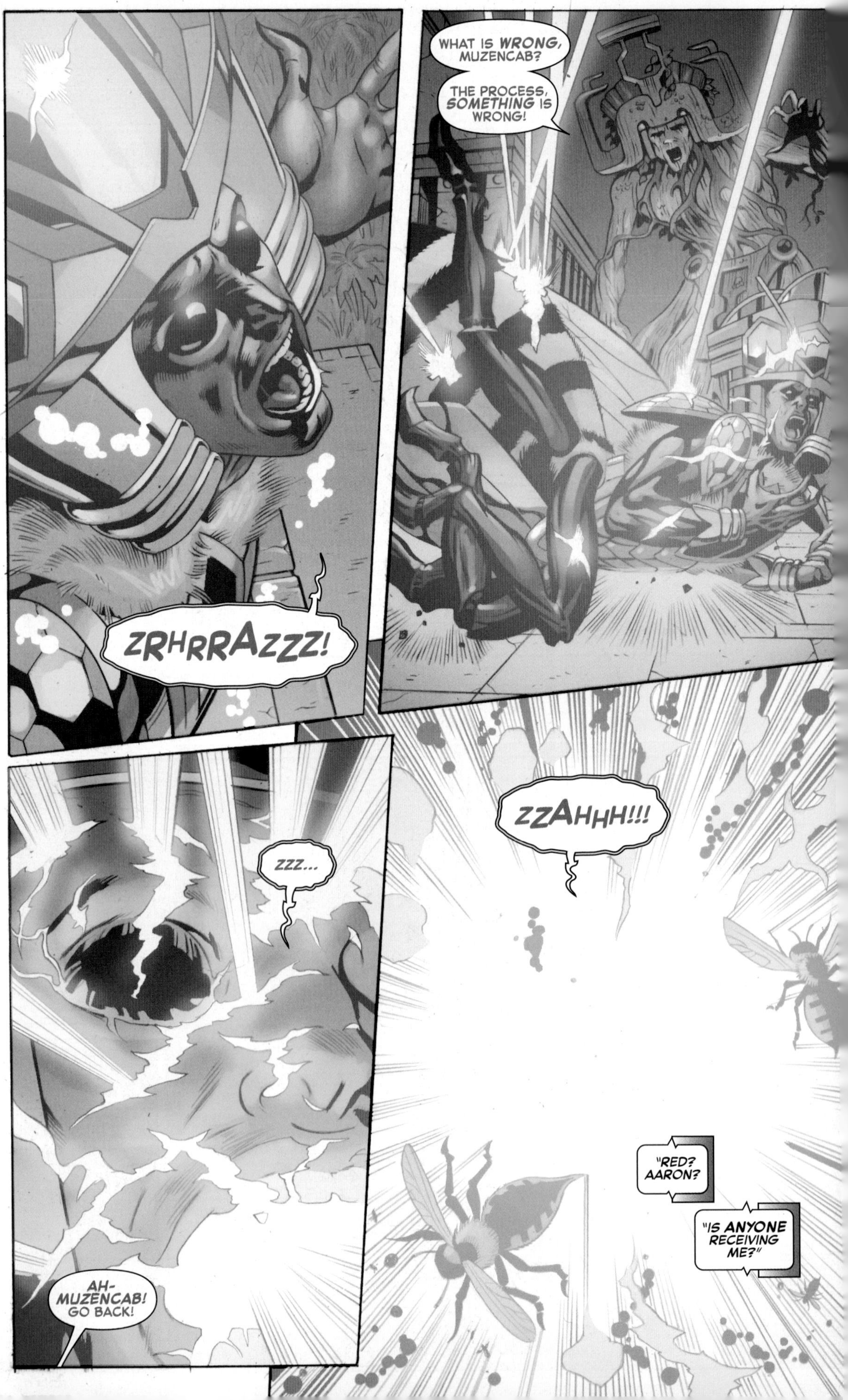
ZRHRRAZZZ!
WHAT IS WRONG, MUZENCAB?
THE PROCESS, SOMETHING IS WRONG!
ZZZ...
AH-MUZENCAB! GO BACK!
ZZAHHH!!!
"RED? AARON?
"IS ANYONE RECEIVING ME?"

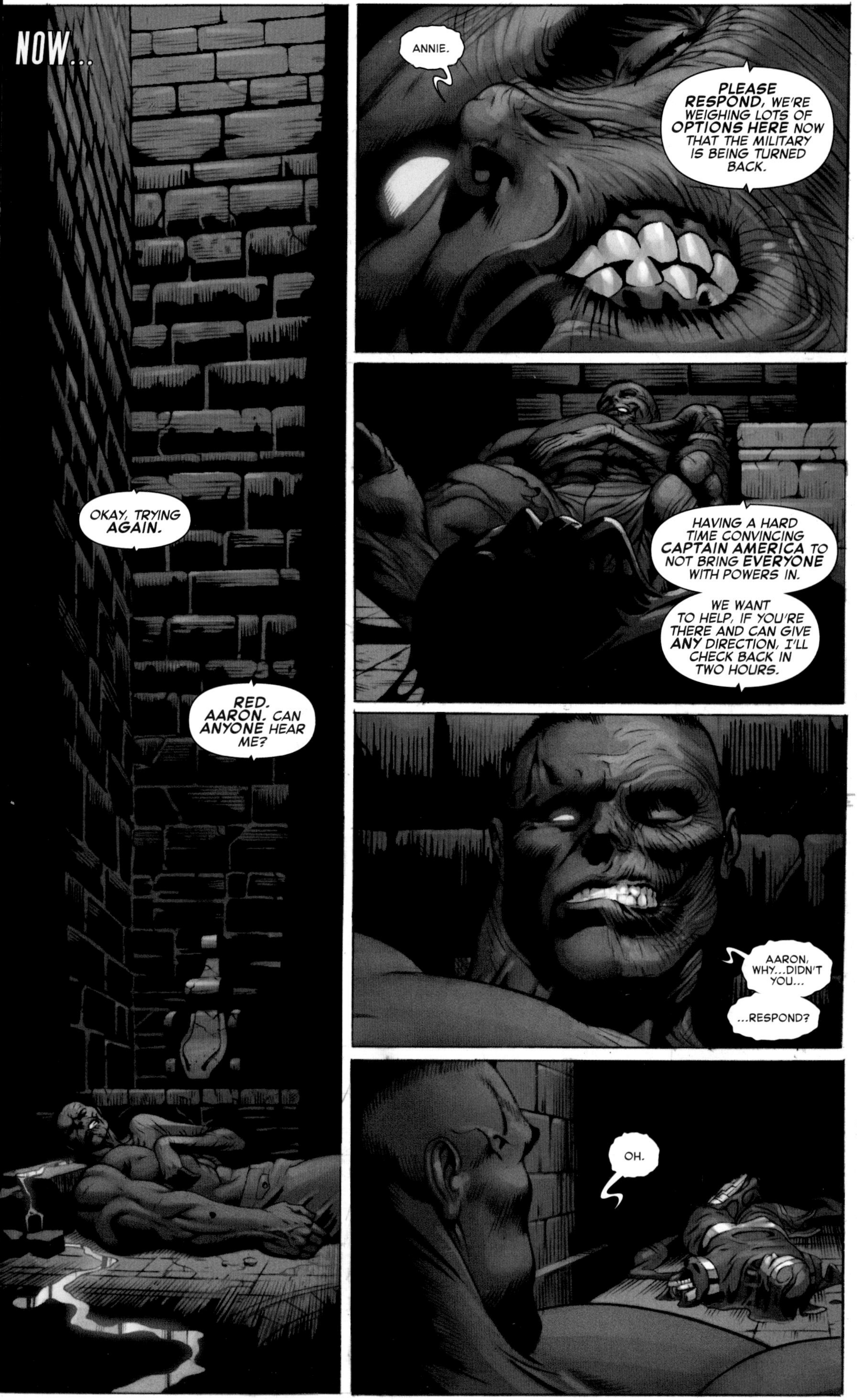
NOW...
OKAY, TRYING AGAIN.
RED. AARON. CAN ANYONE HEAR ME?
ANNIE.
PLEASE RESPOND, WE'RE WEIGHING LOTS OF OPTIONS HERE NOW THAT THE MILITARY IS BEING TURNED BACK.
HAVING A HARD TIME CONVINCING CAPTAIN AMERICA TO NOT BRING EVERYONE WITH POWERS IN.
WE WANT TO HELP, IF YOU'RE THERE AND CAN GIVE ANY DIRECTION, I'LL CHECK BACK IN TWO HOURS.
AARON, WHY...DIDN'T YOU...
...RESPOND?
OH.

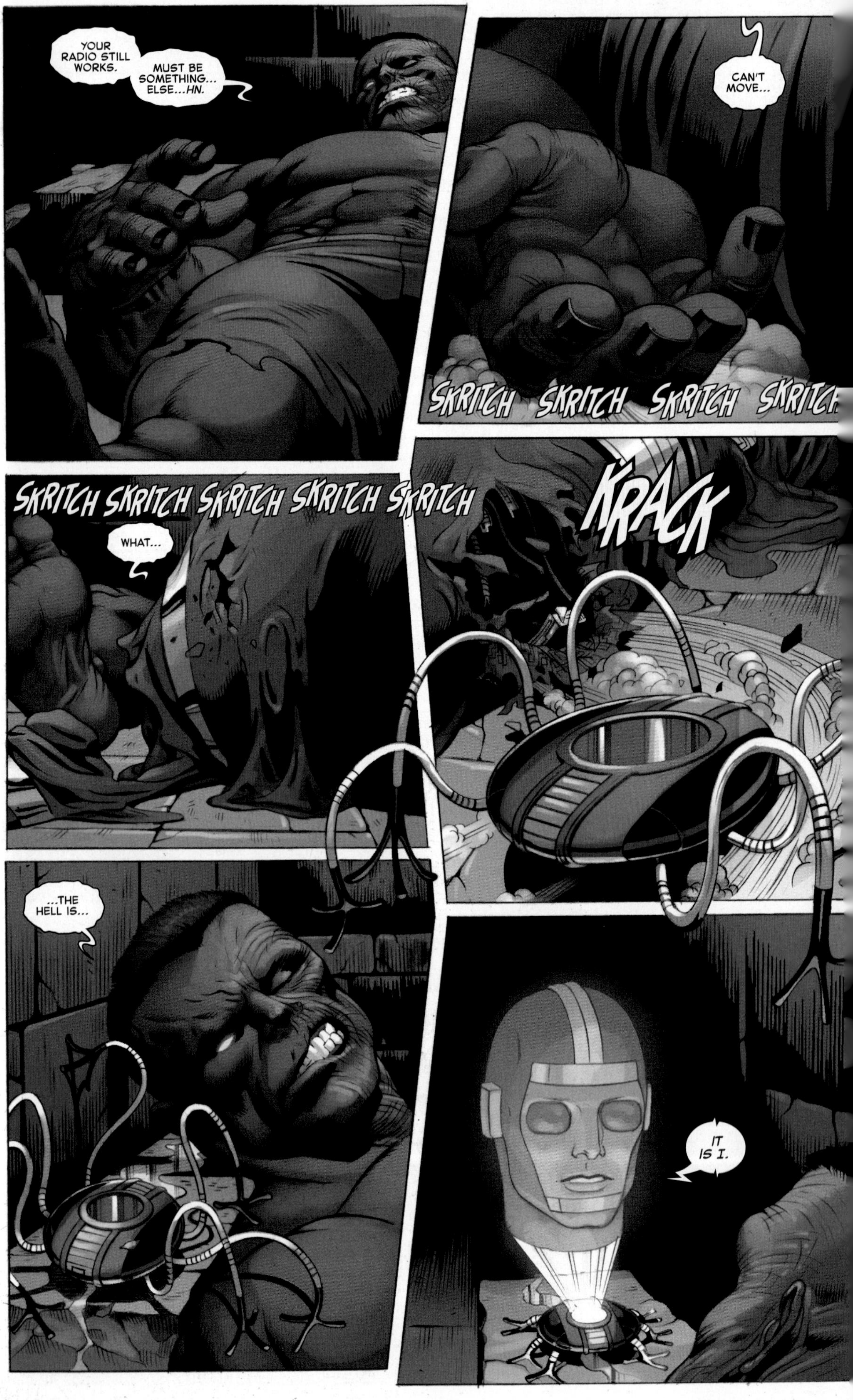
YOUR RADIO STILL WORKS.
MUST BE SOMETHING... ELSE...HN.
CAN'T MOVE...
SKRITCH SKRITCH SKRITCH SKRITCH
SKRITCH SKRITCH SKRITCH SKRITCH SKRITCH
WHAT...
KRACK
...THE HELL IS...
IT IS I.

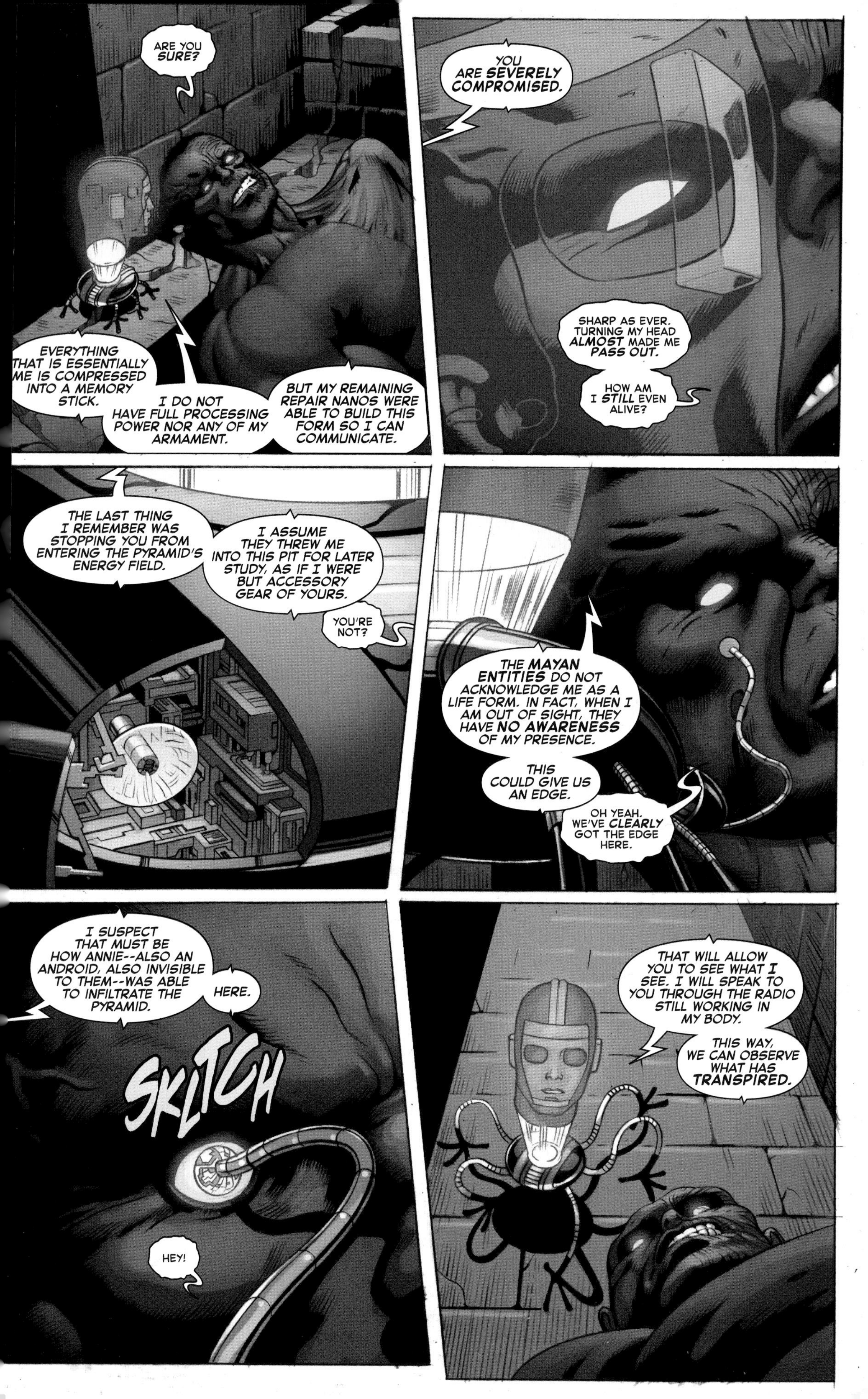

ARE YOU SURE?
EVERYTHING THAT IS ESSENTIALLY ME IS COMPRESSED INTO A MEMORY STICK.
I DO NOT HAVE FULL PROCESSING POWER NOR ANY OF MY ARMAMENT.
BUT MY REMAINING REPAIR NANOS WERE ABLE TO BUILD THIS FORM SO I CAN COMMUNICATE.
YOU ARE SEVERELY COMPROMISED.
SHARP AS EVER. TURNING MY HEAD ALMOST MADE ME PASS OUT.
HOW AM I STILL EVEN ALIVE?
THE LAST THING I REMEMBER WAS STOPPING YOU FROM ENTERING THE PYRAMID'S ENERGY FIELD.
I ASSUME THEY THREW ME INTO THIS PIT FOR LATER STUDY, AS IF I WERE BUT ACCESSORY GEAR OF YOURS.
YOU'RE NOT?
THE MAYAN ENTITIES DO NOT ACKNOWLEDGE ME AS A LIFE FORM. IN FACT, WHEN I AM OUT OF SIGHT, THEY HAVE NO AWARENESS OF MY PRESENCE.
THIS COULD GIVE US AN EDGE.
OH YEAH. WE'VE CLEARLY GOT THE EDGE HERE.
I SUSPECT THAT MUST BE HOW ANNIE--ALSO AN ANDROID, ALSO INVISIBLE TO THEM--WAS ABLE TO INFILTRATE THE PYRAMID.
HERE.
SKLTCH
HEY!
THAT WILL ALLOW YOU TO SEE WHAT I SEE. I WILL SPEAK TO YOU THROUGH THE RADIO STILL WORKING IN MY BODY.
THIS WAY, WE CAN OBSERVE WHAT HAS TRANSPIRED.

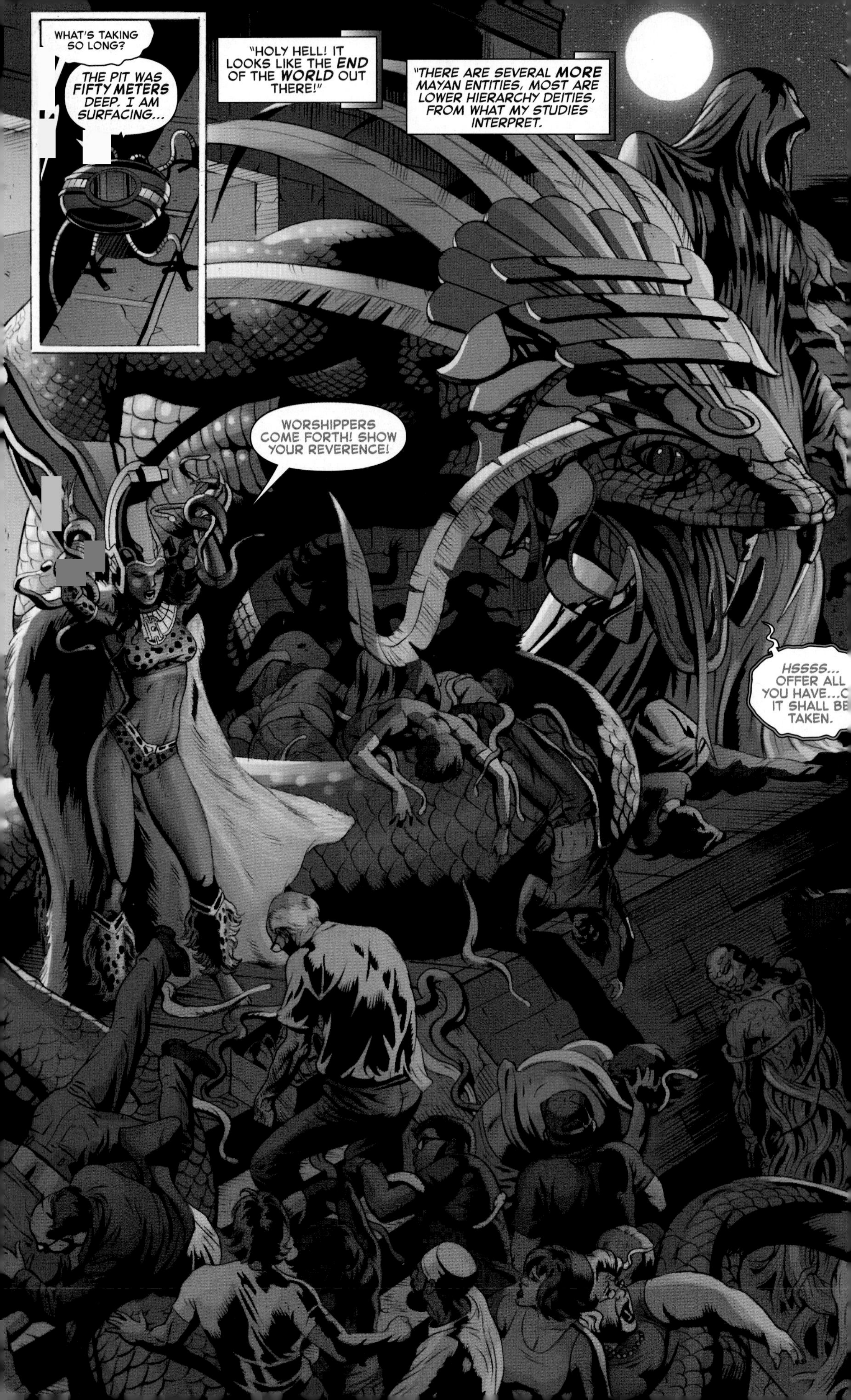
WHAT'S TAKING SO LONG?
THE PIT WAS FIFTY METERS DEEP. I AM SURFACING...
"HOLY HELL! IT LOOKS LIKE THE END OF THE WORLD OUT THERE!"
"THERE ARE SEVERAL MORE MAYAN ENTITIES, MOST ARE LOWER HIERARCHY DEITIES, FROM WHAT MY STUDIES INTERPRET.
WORSHIPPERS COME FORTH! SHOW YOUR REVERENCE!
HSSSS... OFFER ALL YOU HAVE...O IT SHALL BE TAKEN.

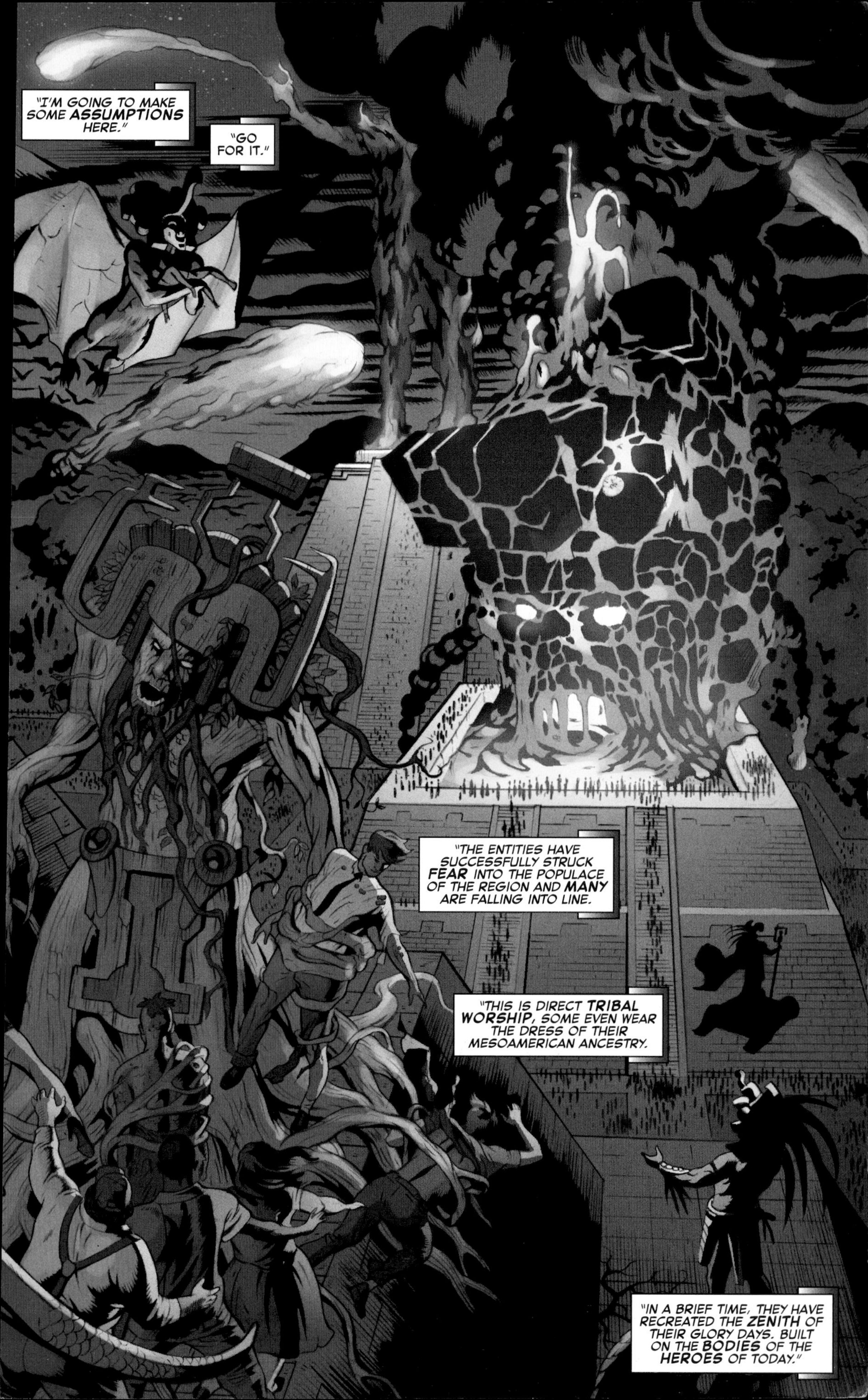
"I'M GOING TO MAKE SOME ASSUMPTIONS HERE."
"GO FOR IT."
"THE ENTITIES HAVE SUCCESSFULLY STRUCK FEAR INTO THE POPULACE OF THE REGION AND MANY ARE FALLING INTO LINE.
"THIS IS DIRECT TRIBAL WORSHIP, SOME EVEN WEAR THE DRESS OF THEIR MESOAMERICAN ANCESTRY.
"IN A BRIEF TIME, THEY HAVE RECREATED THE ZENITH OF THEIR GLORY DAYS. BUILT ON THE BODIES OF THE HEROES OF TODAY."

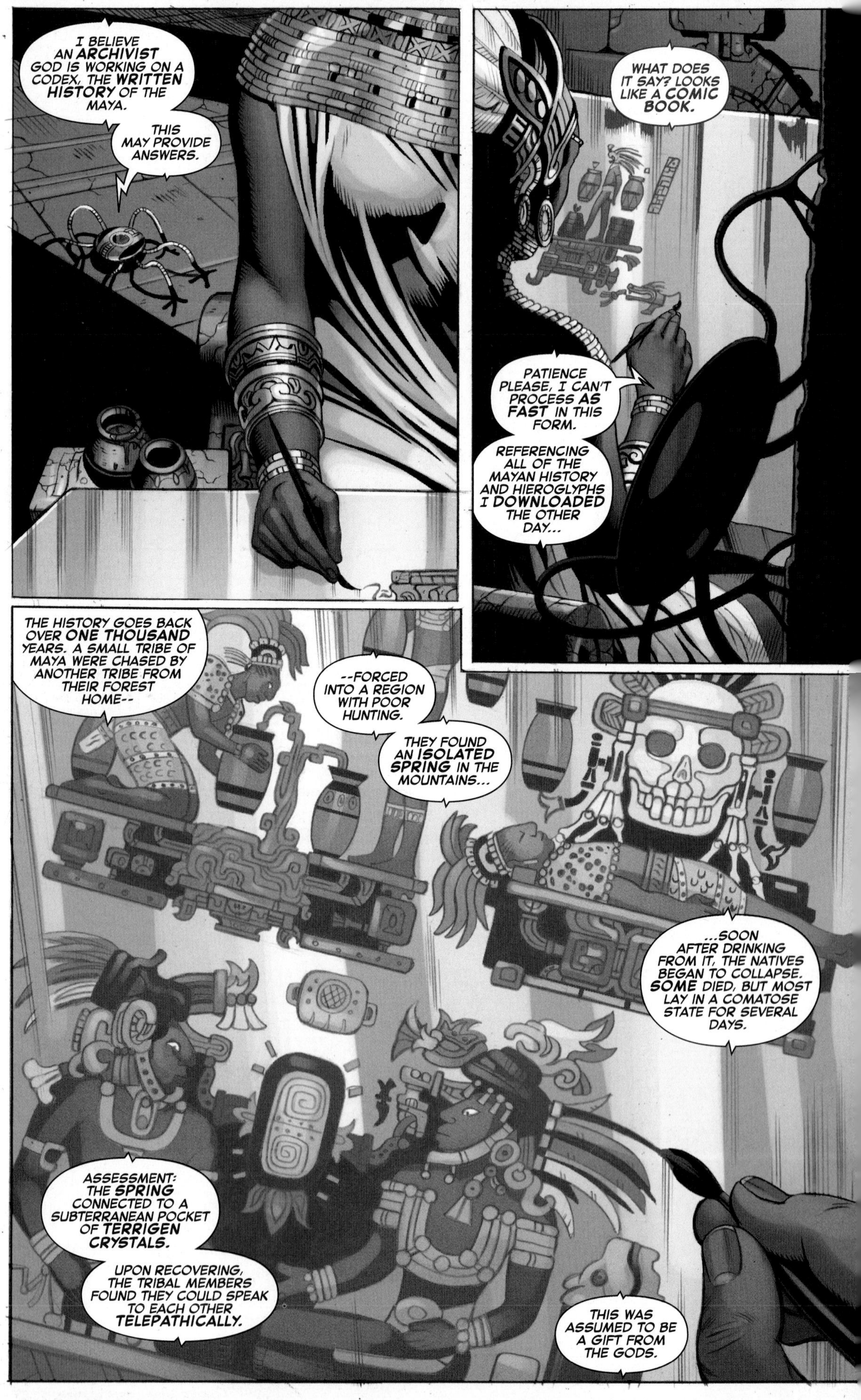
I BELIEVE AN ARCHIVIST GOD IS WORKING ON A CODEX, THE WRITTEN HISTORY OF THE MAYA.
THIS MAY PROVIDE ANSWERS.
WHAT DOES IT SAY? LOOKS LIKE A COMIC BOOK.
PATIENCE PLEASE, I CAN'T PROCESS AS FAST IN THIS FORM.
REFERENCING ALL OF THE MAYAN HISTORY AND HIEROGLYPHS I DOWNLOADED THE OTHER DAY...
THE HISTORY GOES BACK OVER ONE THOUSAND YEARS. A SMALL TRIBE OF MAYA WERE CHASED BY ANOTHER TRIBE FROM THEIR FOREST HOME--
--FORCED INTO A REGION WITH POOR HUNTING.
THEY FOUND AN ISOLATED SPRING IN THE MOUNTAINS...
...SOON AFTER DRINKING FROM IT, THE NATIVES BEGAN TO COLLAPSE. SOME DIED, BUT MOST LAY IN A COMATOSE STATE FOR SEVERAL DAYS.
ASSESSMENT: THE SPRING CONNECTED TO A SUBTERRANEAN POCKET OF TERRIGEN CRYSTALS.
UPON RECOVERING, THE TRIBAL MEMBERS FOUND THEY COULD SPEAK TO EACH OTHER TELEPATHICALLY.
THIS WAS ASSUMED TO BE A GIFT FROM THE GODS.

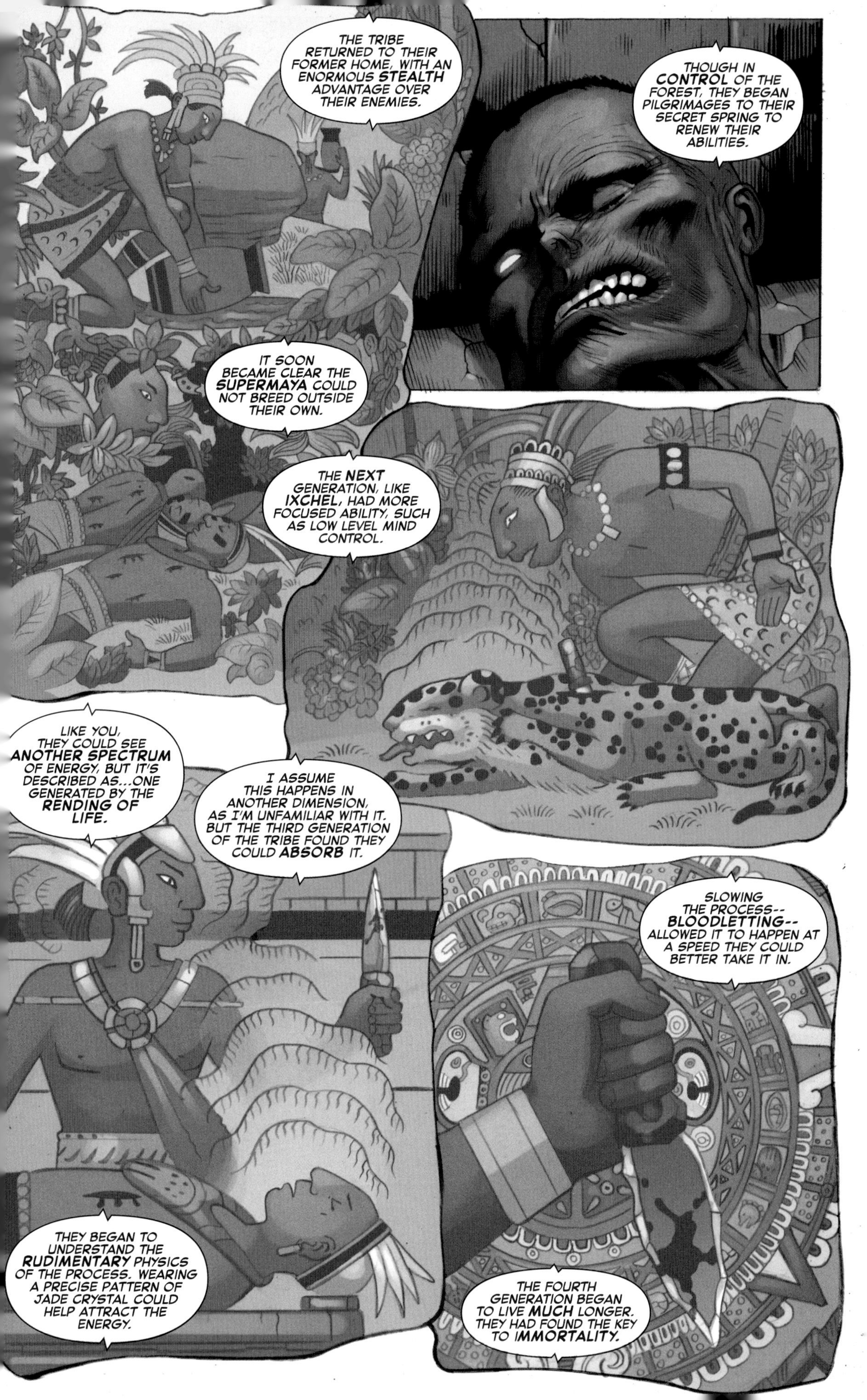
THE TRIBE RETURNED TO THEIR FORMER HOME, WITH AN ENORMOUS STEALTH ADVANTAGE OVER THEIR ENEMIES.
THOUGH IN CONTROL OF THE FOREST, THEY BEGAN PILGRIMAGES TO THEIR SECRET SPRING TO RENEW THEIR ABILITIES.
IT SOON BECAME CLEAR THE SUPERMAYA COULD NOT BREED OUTSIDE THEIR OWN.
THE NEXT GENERATION, LIKE IXCHEL, HAD MORE FOCUSED ABILITY, SUCH AS LOW LEVEL MIND CONTROL.
LIKE YOU, THEY COULD SEE ANOTHER SPECTRUM OF ENERGY, BUT IT'S DESCRIBED AS...ONE GENERATED BY THE RENDING OF LIFE.
I ASSUME THIS HAPPENS IN ANOTHER DIMENSION, AS I'M UNFAMILIAR WITH IT. BUT THE THIRD GENERATION OF THE TRIBE FOUND THEY COULD ABSORB IT.
SLOWING THE PROCESS--BLOODLETTING--ALLOWED IT TO HAPPEN AT A SPEED THEY COULD BETTER TAKE IT IN.
THEY BEGAN TO UNDERSTAND THE RUDIMENTARY PHYSICS OF THE PROCESS. WEARING A PRECISE PATTERN OF JADE CRYSTAL COULD HELP ATTRACT THE ENERGY.
THE FOURTH GENERATION BEGAN TO LIVE MUCH LONGER. THEY HAD FOUND THE KEY TO IMMORTALITY.

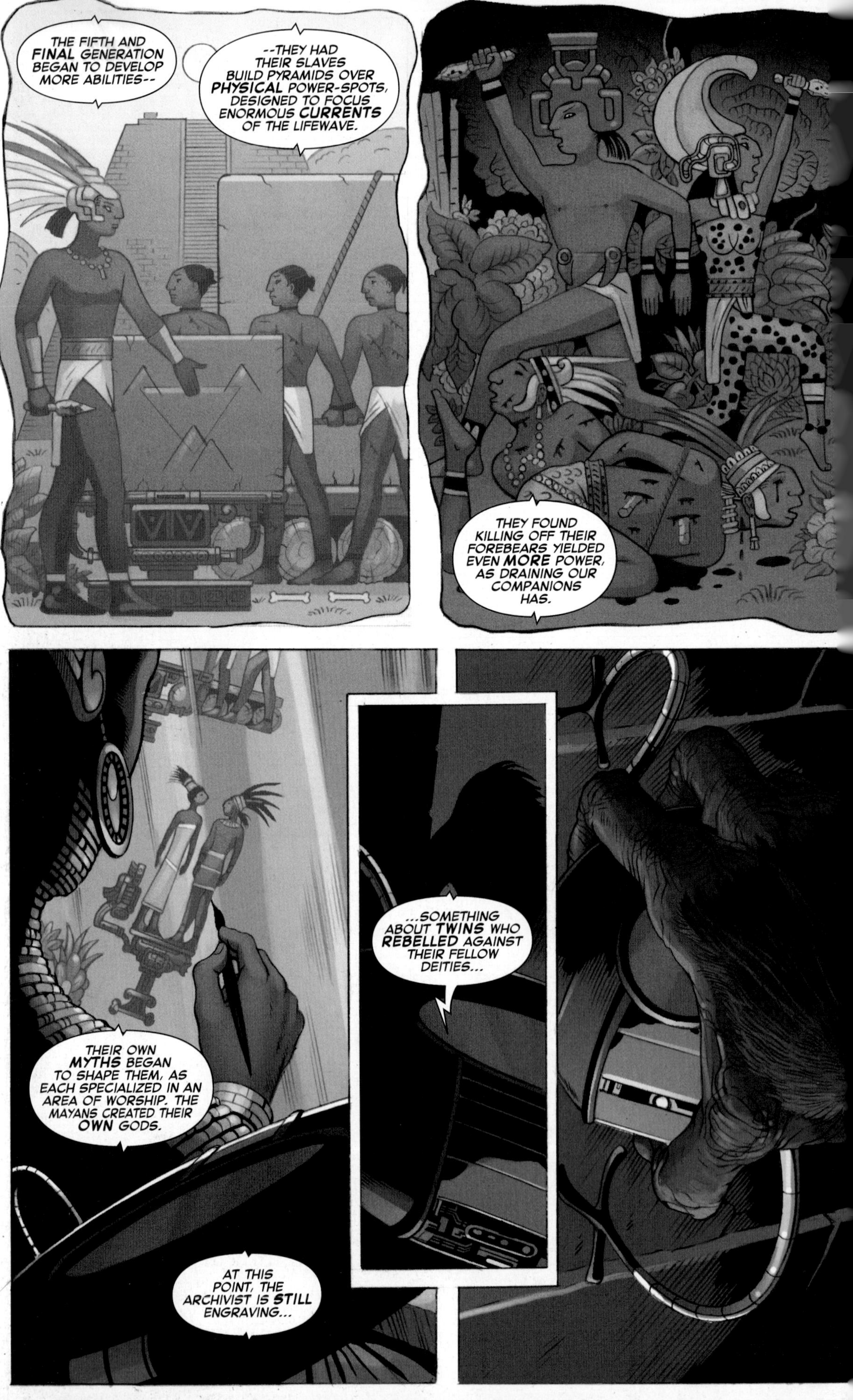
THE FIFTH AND FINAL GENERATION BEGAN TO DEVELOP MORE ABILITIES--
--THEY HAD THEIR SLAVES BUILD PYRAMIDS OVER PHYSICAL POWER-SPOTS, DESIGNED TO FOCUS ENORMOUS CURRENTS OF THE LIFEWAVE.
THEY FOUND KILLING OFF THEIR FOREBEARS YIELDED EVEN MORE POWER, AS DRAINING OUR COMPANIONS HAS.
THEIR OWN MYTHS BEGAN TO SHAPE THEM, AS EACH SPECIALIZED IN AN AREA OF WORSHIP. THE MAYANS CREATED THEIR OWN GODS.
AT THIS POINT, THE ARCHIVIST IS STILL ENGRAVING...
...SOMETHING ABOUT TWINS WHO REBELLED AGAINST THEIR FELLOW DEITIES...

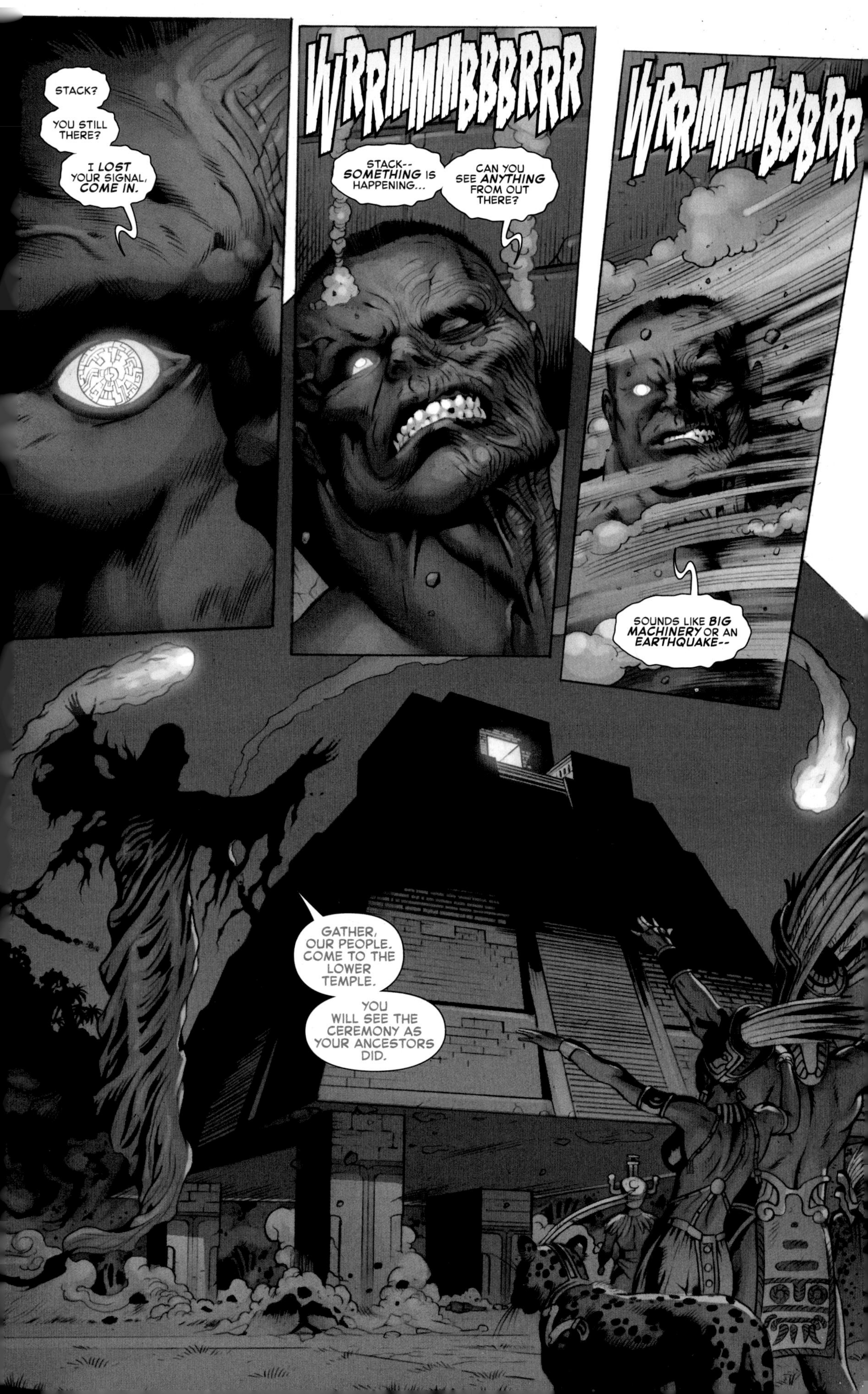
STACK?
YOU STILL THERE?
I LOST YOUR SIGNAL, COME IN.
WRRMMMMBBRRR
STACK-- SOMETHING IS HAPPENING...
CAN YOU SEE ANYTHING FROM OUT THERE?
WRRMMMMBBRR
SOUNDS LIKE BIG MACHINERY OR AN EARTHQUAKE--
GATHER, OUR PEOPLE. COME TO THE LOWER TEMPLE.
YOU WILL SEE THE CEREMONY AS YOUR ANCESTORS DID.

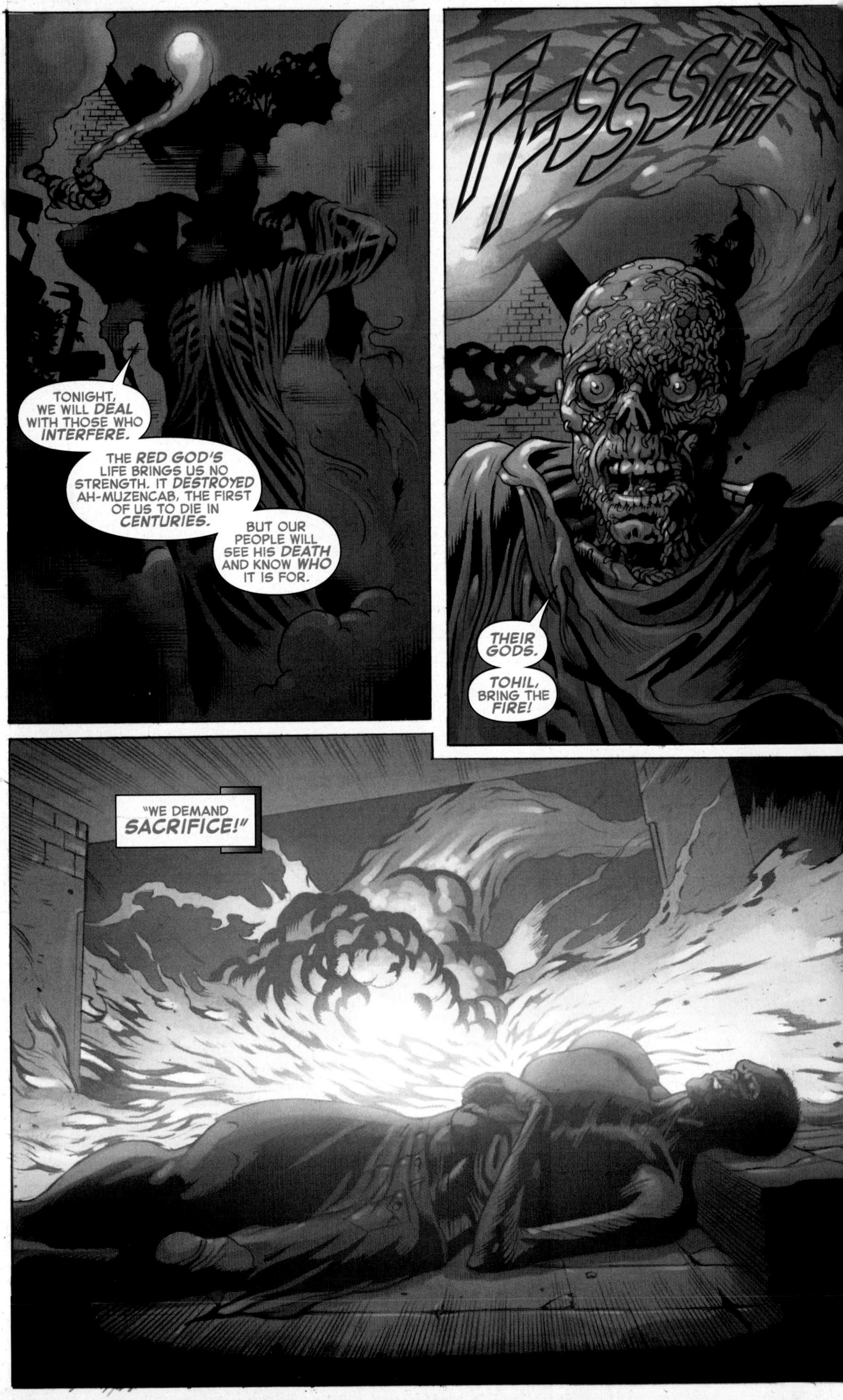
TONIGHT, WE WILL DEAL WITH THOSE WHO INTERFERE.
THE RED GOD'S LIFE BRINGS US NO STRENGTH. IT DESTROYED AH-MUZENCAB, THE FIRST OF US TO DIE IN CENTURIES.
BUT OUR PEOPLE WILL SEE HIS DEATH AND KNOW WHO IT IS FOR.
FSSSSHH
THEIR GODS.
TOHIL, BRING THE FIRE!
"WE DEMAND SACRIFICE!"

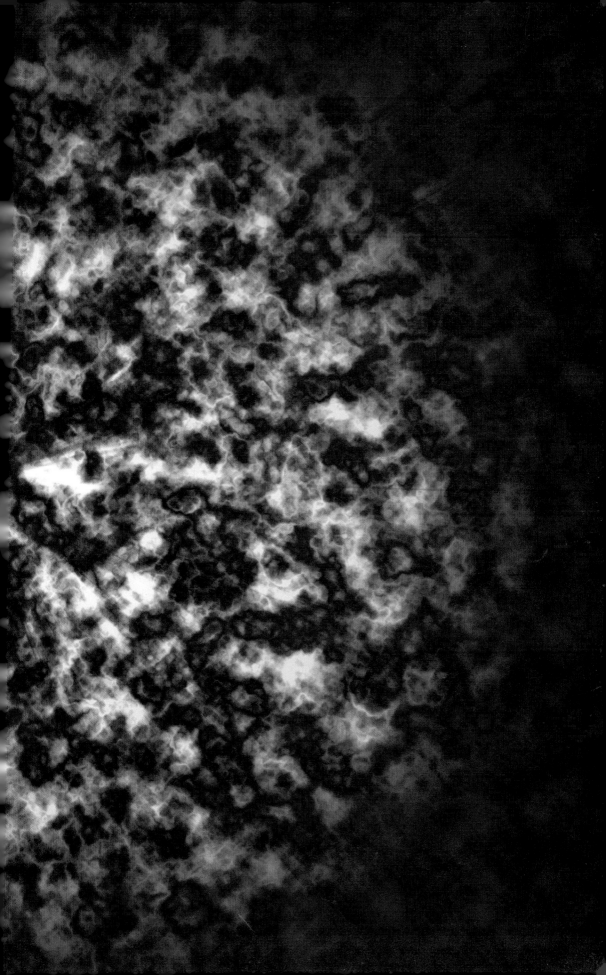

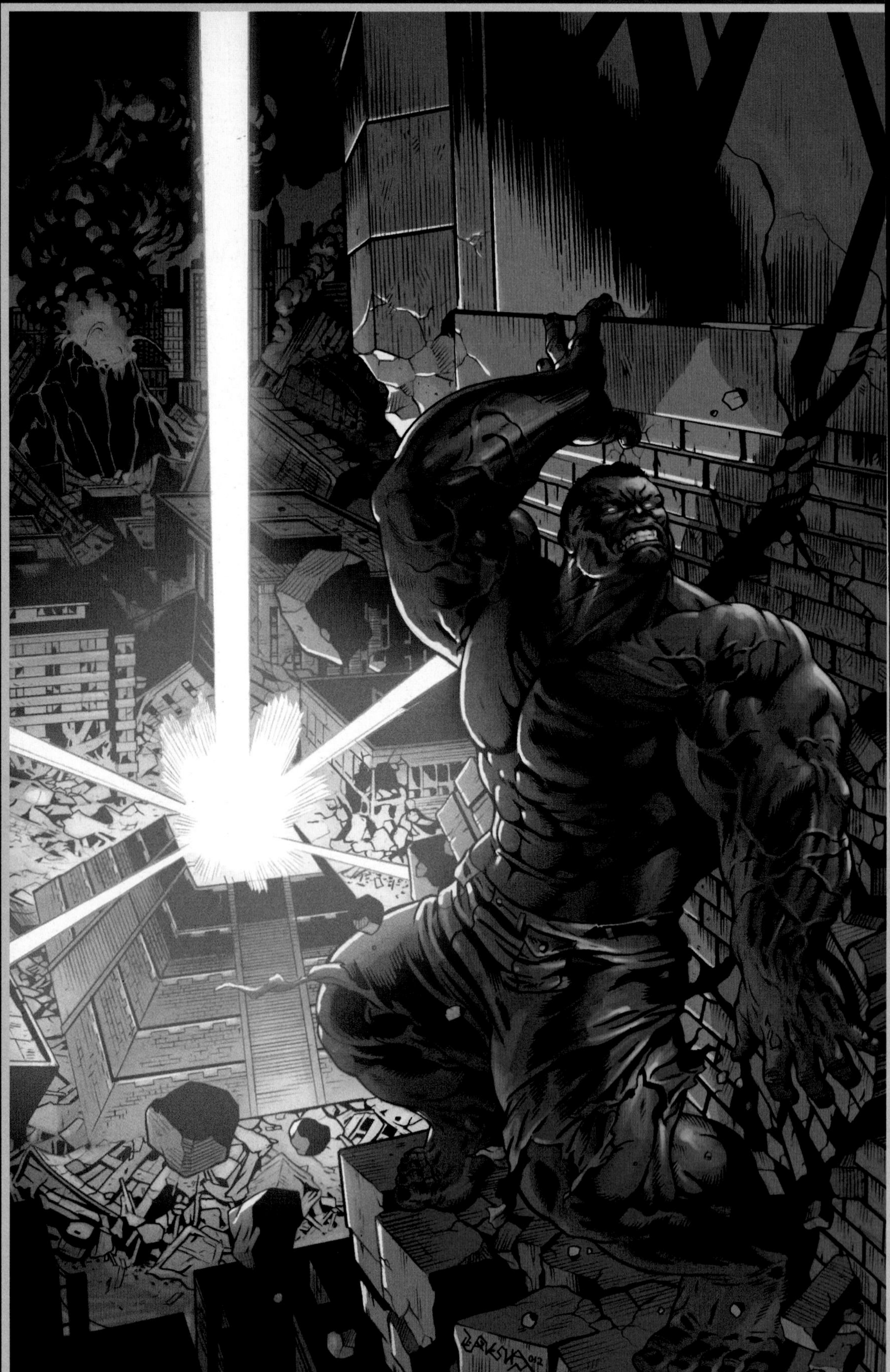

HULK #57

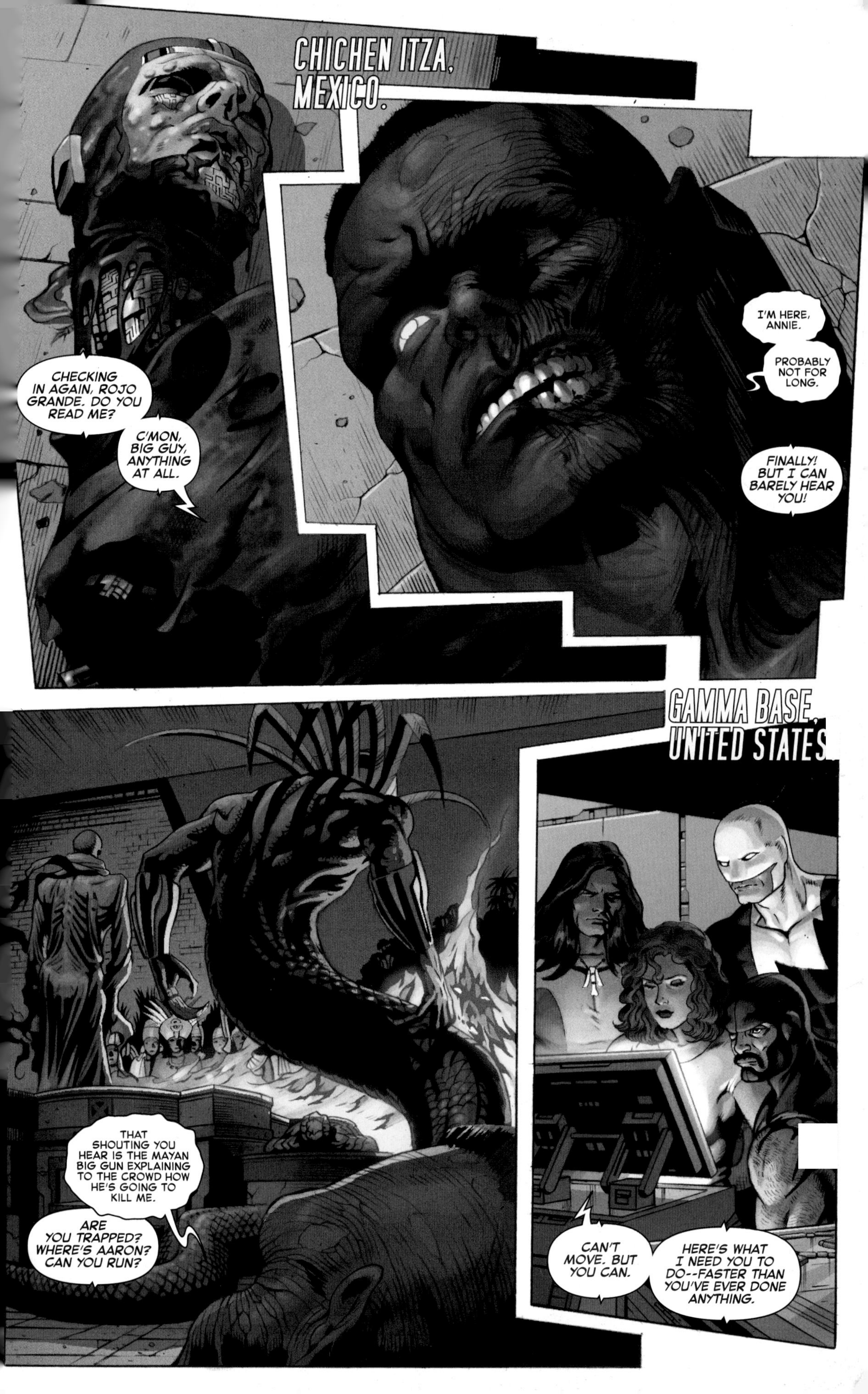
CHICHEN ITZA, MEXICO.
CHECKING IN AGAIN, ROJO GRANDE. DO YOU READ ME?
C'MON, BIG GUY, ANYTHING AT ALL.
I'M HERE, ANNIE.
PROBABLY NOT FOR LONG.
FINALLY! BUT I CAN BARELY HEAR YOU!
GAMMA BASE, UNITED STATES.
THAT SHOUTING YOU HEAR IS THE MAYAN BIG GUN EXPLAINING TO THE CROWD HOW HE'S GOING TO KILL ME.
ARE YOU TRAPPED? WHERE'S AARON? CAN YOU RUN?
CAN'T MOVE. BUT YOU CAN.
HERE'S WHAT I NEED YOU TO DO--FASTER THAN YOU'VE EVER DONE ANYTHING.

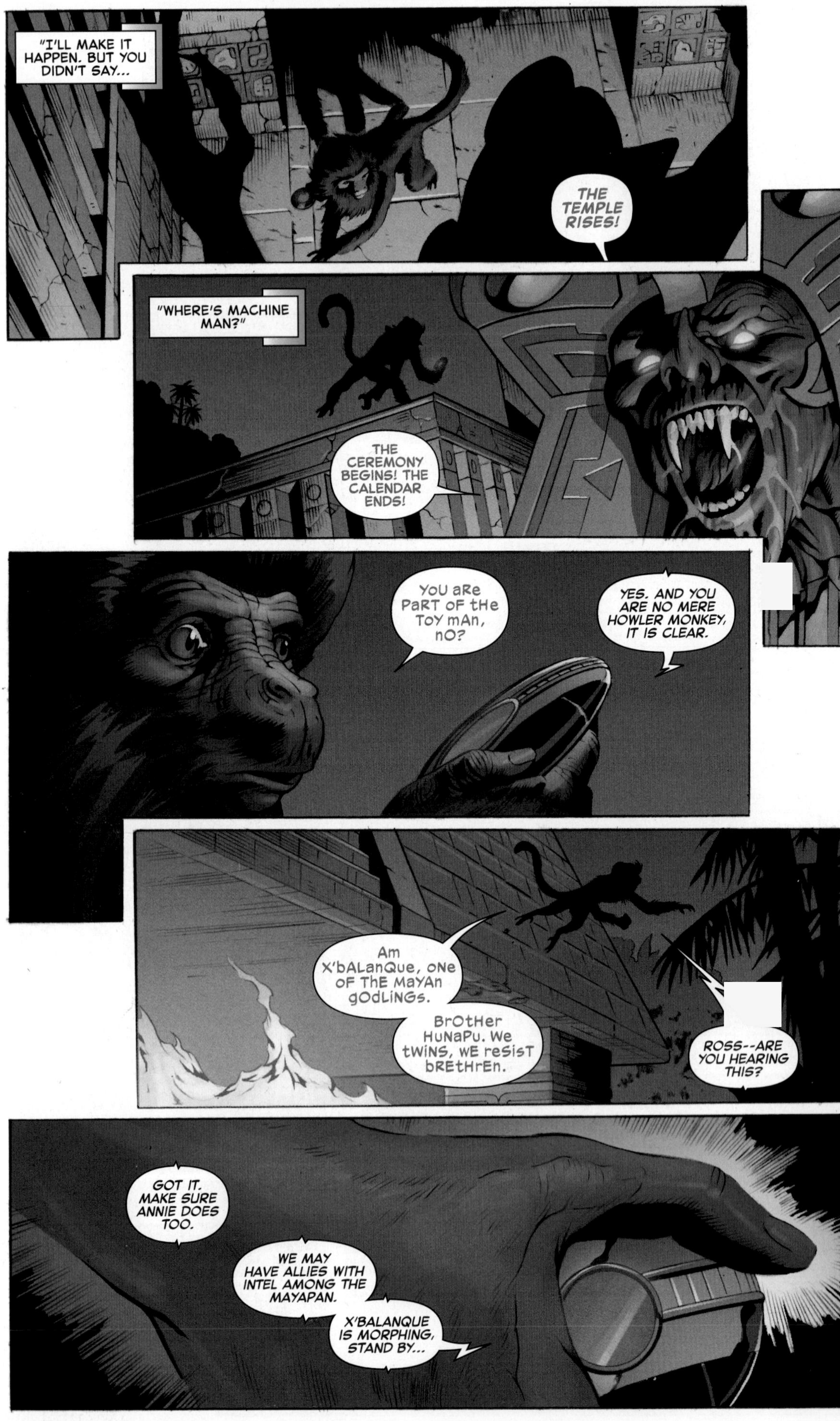
"I'LL MAKE IT HAPPEN. BUT YOU DIDN'T SAY...
THE TEMPLE RISES!
"WHERE'S MACHINE MAN?"
THE CEREMONY BEGINS! THE CALENDAR ENDS!
YOU ARE PART OF THE TOY MAN, NO?
YES. AND YOU ARE NO MERE HOWLER MONKEY, IT IS CLEAR.
AM X'BALANQUE, ONE OF THE MAYAN GODLINGS.
BROTHER HUNAPU. WE TWINS, WE RESIST BRETHREN.
ROSS--ARE YOU HEARING THIS?
GOT IT. MAKE SURE ANNIE DOES TOO.
WE MAY HAVE ALLIES WITH INTEL AMONG THE MAYAPAN.
X'BALANQUE IS MORPHING, STAND BY...

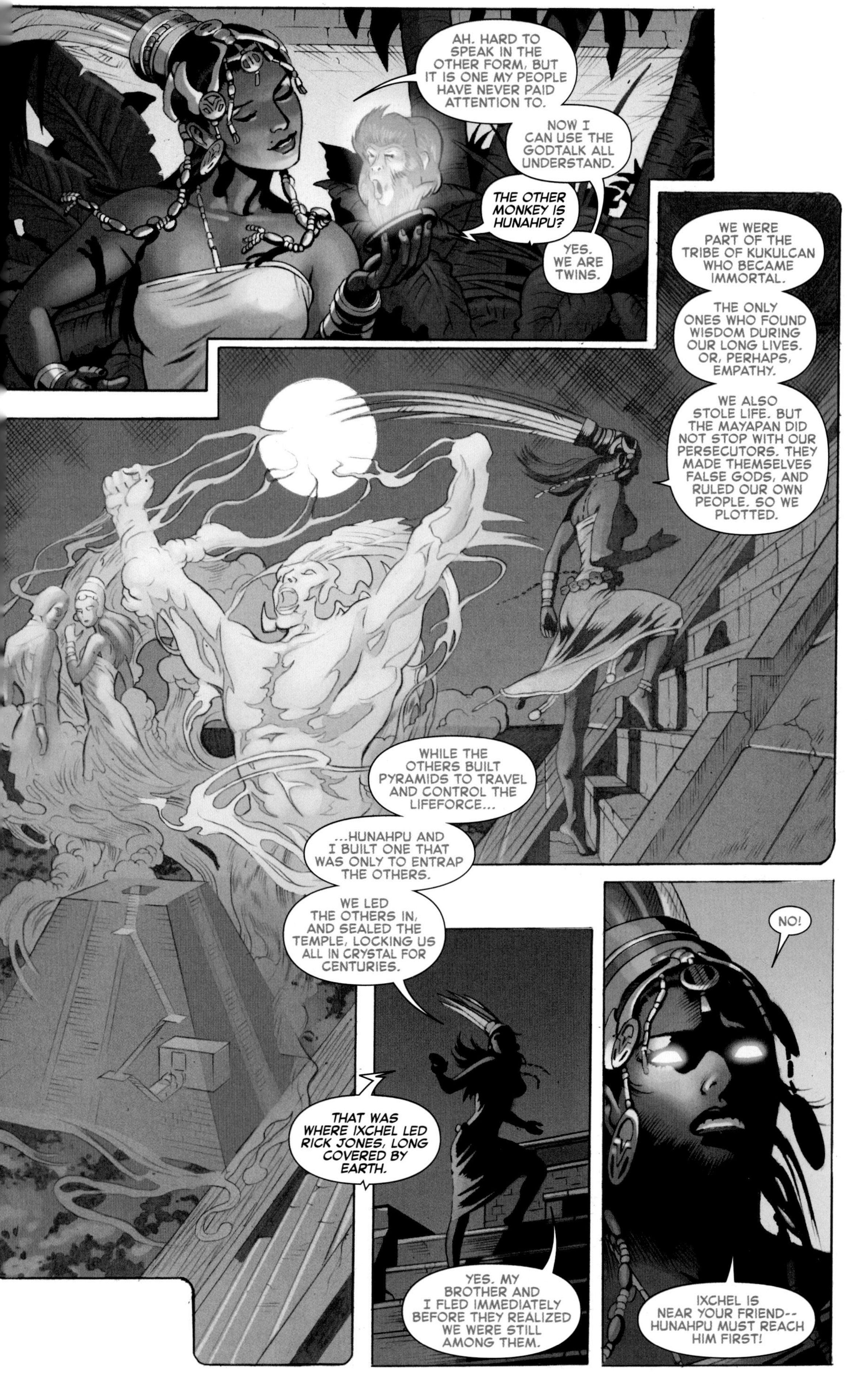
AH. HARD TO SPEAK IN THE OTHER FORM, BUT IT IS ONE MY PEOPLE HAVE NEVER PAID ATTENTION TO.
NOW I CAN USE THE GODTALK ALL UNDERSTAND.
THE OTHER MONKEY IS HUNAHPU?
YES. WE ARE TWINS.
WE WERE PART OF THE TRIBE OF KUKULCAN WHO BECAME IMMORTAL.
THE ONLY ONES WHO FOUND WISDOM DURING OUR LONG LIVES. OR, PERHAPS, EMPATHY.
WE ALSO STOLE LIFE. BUT THE MAYAPAN DID NOT STOP WITH OUR PERSECUTORS. THEY MADE THEMSELVES FALSE GODS, AND RULED OUR OWN PEOPLE. SO WE PLOTTED.
WHILE THE OTHERS BUILT PYRAMIDS TO TRAVEL AND CONTROL THE LIFEFORCE...
...HUNAHPU AND I BUILT ONE THAT WAS ONLY TO ENTRAP THE OTHERS.
WE LED THE OTHERS IN, AND SEALED THE TEMPLE, LOCKING US ALL IN CRYSTAL FOR CENTURIES.
THAT WAS WHERE IXCHEL LED RICK JONES, LONG COVERED BY EARTH.
YES. MY BROTHER AND I FLED IMMEDIATELY BEFORE THEY REALIZED WE WERE STILL AMONG THEM.
NO!
IXCHEL IS NEAR YOUR FRIEND-- HUNAHPU MUST REACH HIM FIRST!

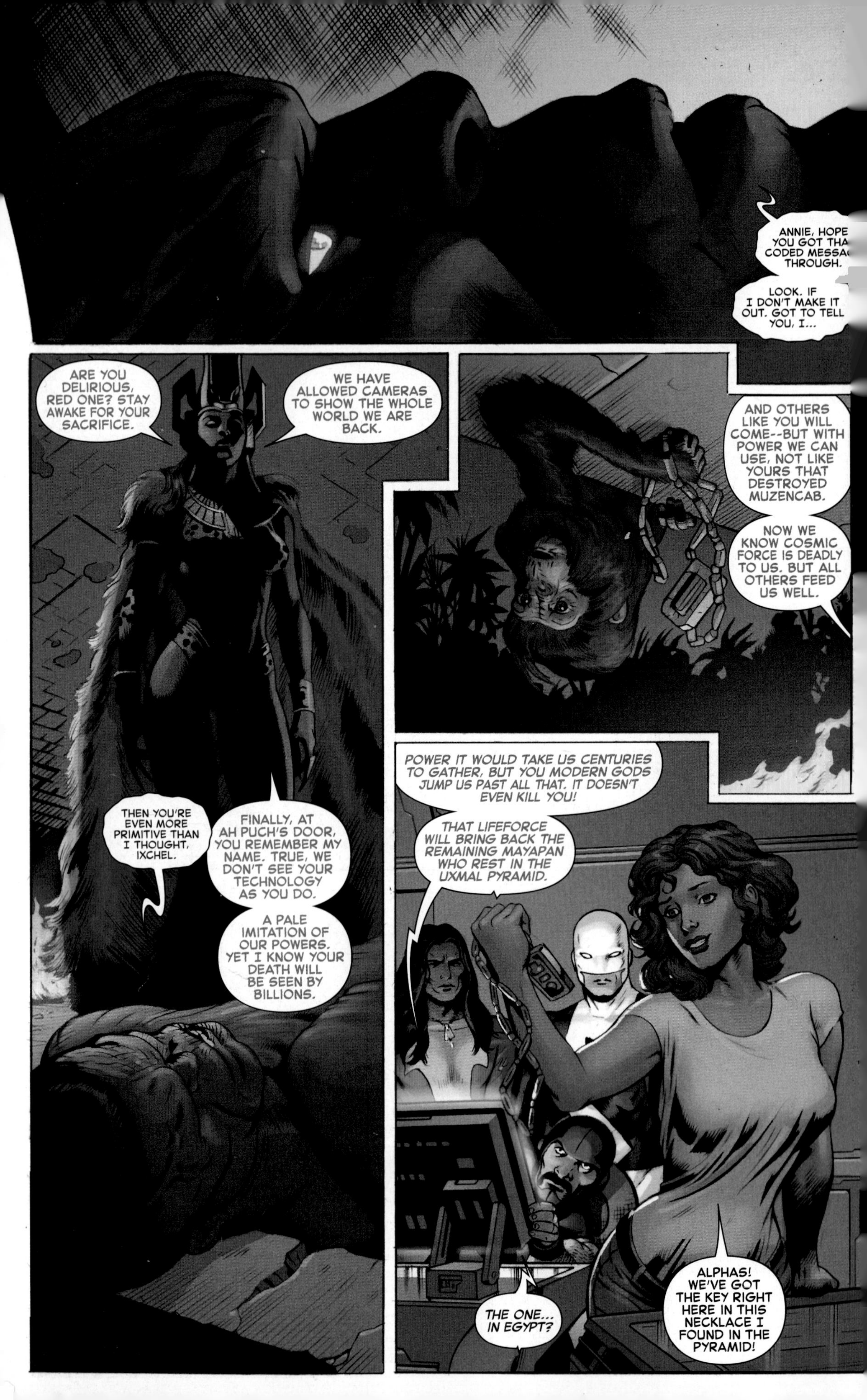
ANNIE, HOPE YOU GOT THA CODED MESSA THROUGH.
LOOK. IF I DON'T MAKE IT OUT. GOT TO TELL YOU, I...
ARE YOU DELIRIOUS, RED ONE? STAY AWAKE FOR YOUR SACRIFICE.
WE HAVE ALLOWED CAMERAS TO SHOW THE WHOLE WORLD WE ARE BACK.
THEN YOU'RE EVEN MORE PRIMITIVE THAN I THOUGHT, IXCHEL.
FINALLY, AT AH PUCH'S DOOR, YOU REMEMBER MY NAME. TRUE, WE DON'T SEE YOUR TECHNOLOGY AS YOU DO.
A PALE IMITATION OF OUR POWERS. YET I KNOW YOUR DEATH WILL BE SEEN BY BILLIONS.
AND OTHERS LIKE YOU WILL COME--BUT WITH POWER WE CAN USE, NOT LIKE YOURS THAT DESTROYED MUZENCAB.
NOW WE KNOW COSMIC FORCE IS DEADLY TO US. BUT ALL OTHERS FEED US WELL.
POWER IT WOULD TAKE US CENTURIES TO GATHER, BUT YOU MODERN GODS JUMP US PAST ALL THAT. IT DOESN'T EVEN KILL YOU!
THAT LIFEFORCE WILL BRING BACK THE REMAINING MAYAPAN WHO REST IN THE UXMAL PYRAMID.
THE ONE... IN EGYPT?
ALPHAS! WE'VE GOT THE KEY RIGHT HERE IN THIS NECKLACE I FOUND IN THE PYRAMID!

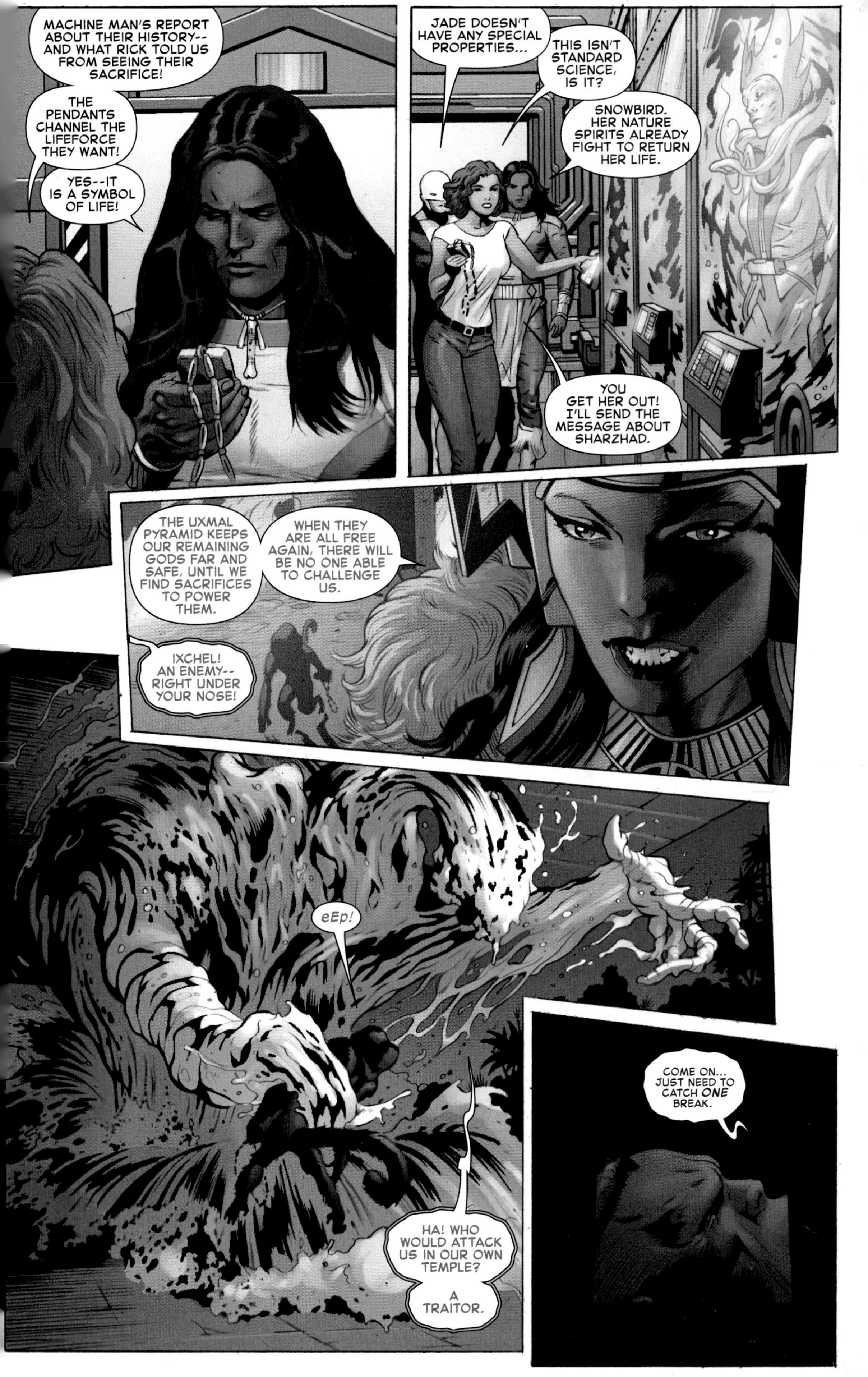
MACHINE MAN'S REPORT ABOUT THEIR HISTORY--AND WHAT RICK TOLD US FROM SEEING THEIR SACRIFICE!
THE PENDANTS CHANNEL THE LIFEFORCE THEY WANT!
YES--IT IS A SYMBOL OF LIFE!
JADE DOESN'T HAVE ANY SPECIAL PROPERTIES...
THIS ISN'T STANDARD SCIENCE, IS IT?
SNOWBIRD. HER NATURE SPIRITS ALREADY FIGHT TO RETURN HER LIFE.
YOU GET HER OUT! I'LL SEND THE MESSAGE ABOUT SHARZHAD.
THE UXMAL PYRAMID KEEPS OUR REMAINING GODS FAR AND SAFE, UNTIL WE FIND SACRIFICES TO POWER THEM.
WHEN THEY ARE ALL FREE AGAIN, THERE WILL BE NO ONE ABLE TO CHALLENGE US.
IXCHEL! AN ENEMY--RIGHT UNDER YOUR NOSE!
eEp!
HA! WHO WOULD ATTACK US IN OUR OWN TEMPLE?
A TRAITOR.
COME ON... JUST NEED TO CATCH ONE BREAK.

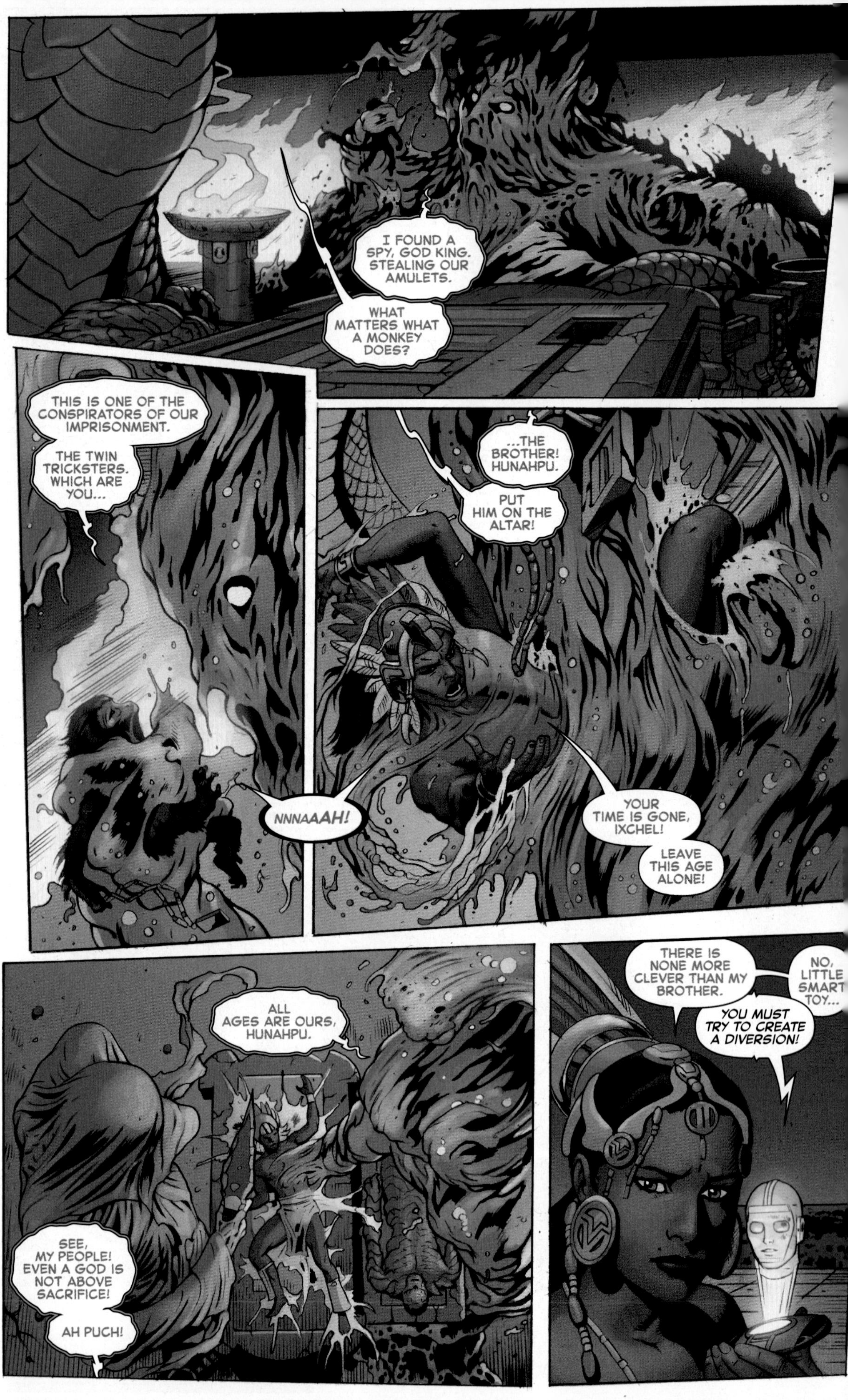
I FOUND A SPY, GOD KING. STEALING OUR AMULETS.
WHAT MATTERS WHAT A MONKEY DOES?
THIS IS ONE OF THE CONSPIRATORS OF OUR IMPRISONMENT.
THE TWIN TRICKSTERS. WHICH ARE YOU...
...THE BROTHER! HUNAHPU.
PUT HIM ON THE ALTAR!
NNNAAAH!
YOUR TIME IS GONE, IXCHEL!
LEAVE THIS AGE ALONE!
ALL AGES ARE OURS, HUNAHPU.
SEE, MY PEOPLE! EVEN A GOD IS NOT ABOVE SACRIFICE!
AH PUCH!
THERE IS NONE MORE CLEVER THAN MY BROTHER.
NO, LITTLE SMART TOY...
YOU MUST TRY TO CREATE A DIVERSION!

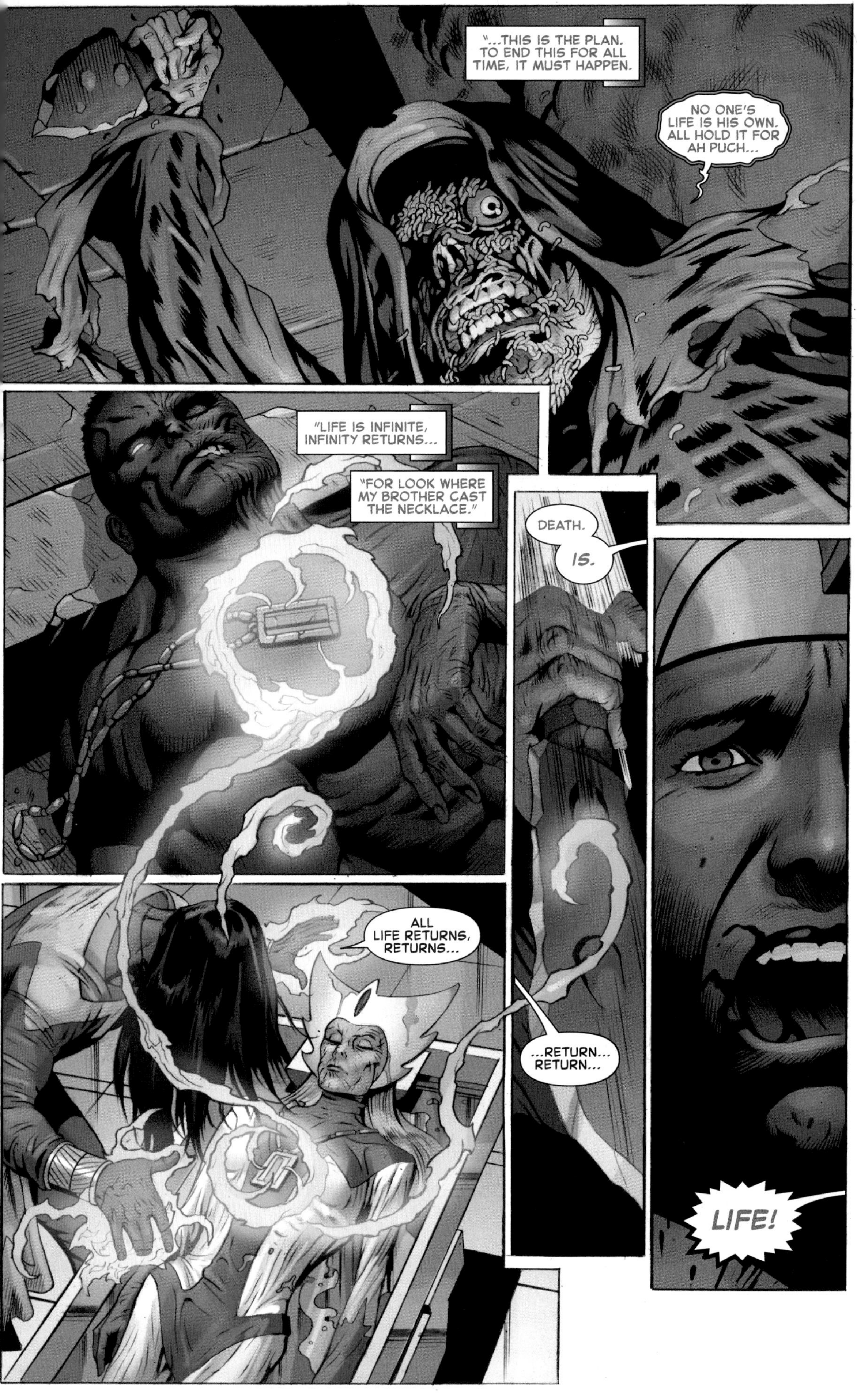
"...THIS IS THE PLAN. TO END THIS FOR ALL TIME, IT MUST HAPPEN.
NO ONE'S LIFE IS HIS OWN. ALL HOLD IT FOR AH PUCH...
"LIFE IS INFINITE, INFINITY RETURNS...
"FOR LOOK WHERE MY BROTHER CAST THE NECKLACE."
DEATH.
IS.
ALL LIFE RETURNS, RETURNS...
...RETURN... RETURN...
LIFE!

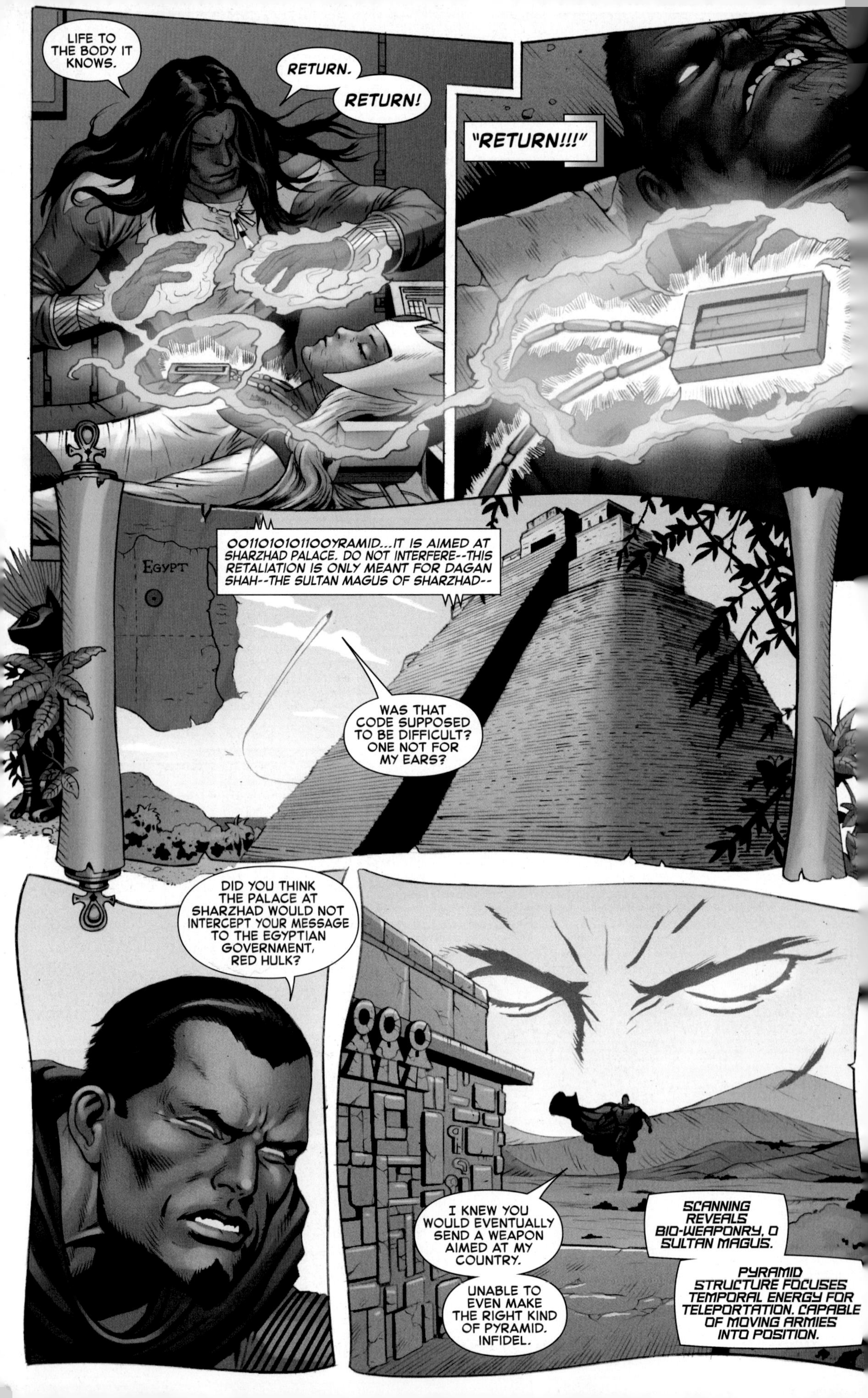
LIFE TO THE BODY IT KNOWS.
RETURN.
RETURN!
"RETURN!!!"
0011010101100YRAMID...IT IS AIMED AT SHARZHAD PALACE. DO NOT INTERFERE--THIS RETALIATION IS ONLY MEANT FOR DAGAN SHAH--THE SULTAN MAGUS OF SHARZHAD--
EGYPT
WAS THAT CODE SUPPOSED TO BE DIFFICULT? ONE NOT FOR MY EARS?
DID YOU THINK THE PALACE AT SHARZHAD WOULD NOT INTERCEPT YOUR MESSAGE TO THE EGYPTIAN GOVERNMENT, RED HULK?
I KNEW YOU WOULD EVENTUALLY SEND A WEAPON AIMED AT MY COUNTRY.
UNABLE TO EVEN MAKE THE RIGHT KIND OF PYRAMID. INFIDEL.
SCANNING REVEALS BIO-WEAPONRY, O SULTAN MAGUS.
PYRAMID STRUCTURE FOCUSES TEMPORAL ENERGY FOR TELEPORTATION. CAPABLE OF MOVING ARMIES INTO POSITION.

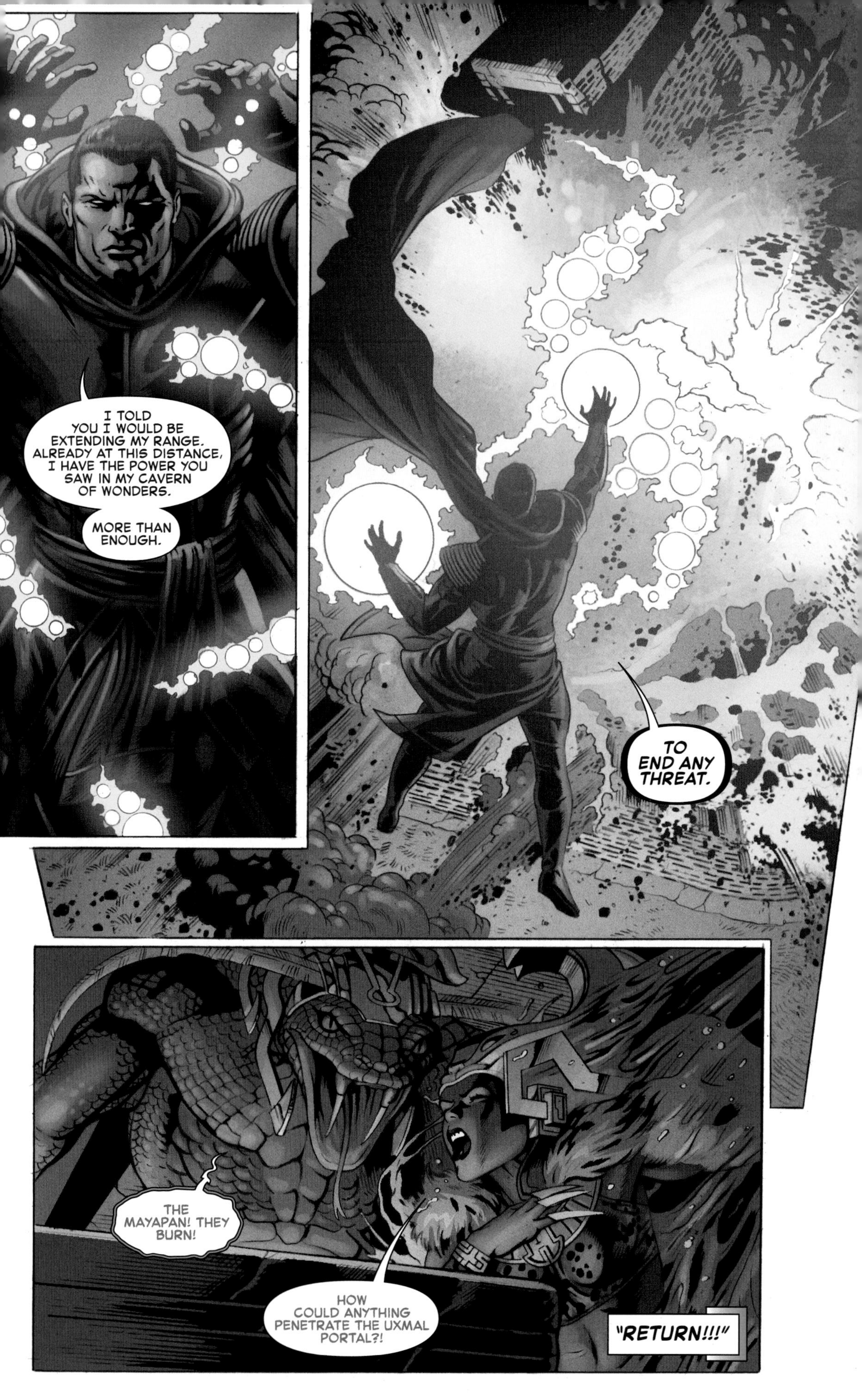
I TOLD YOU I WOULD BE EXTENDING MY RANGE. ALREADY AT THIS DISTANCE, I HAVE THE POWER YOU SAW IN MY CAVERN OF WONDERS.
MORE THAN ENOUGH.
TO END ANY THREAT.
THE MAYAPAN! THEY BURN!
HOW COULD ANYTHING PENETRATE THE UXMAL PORTAL?!
"RETURN!!!"

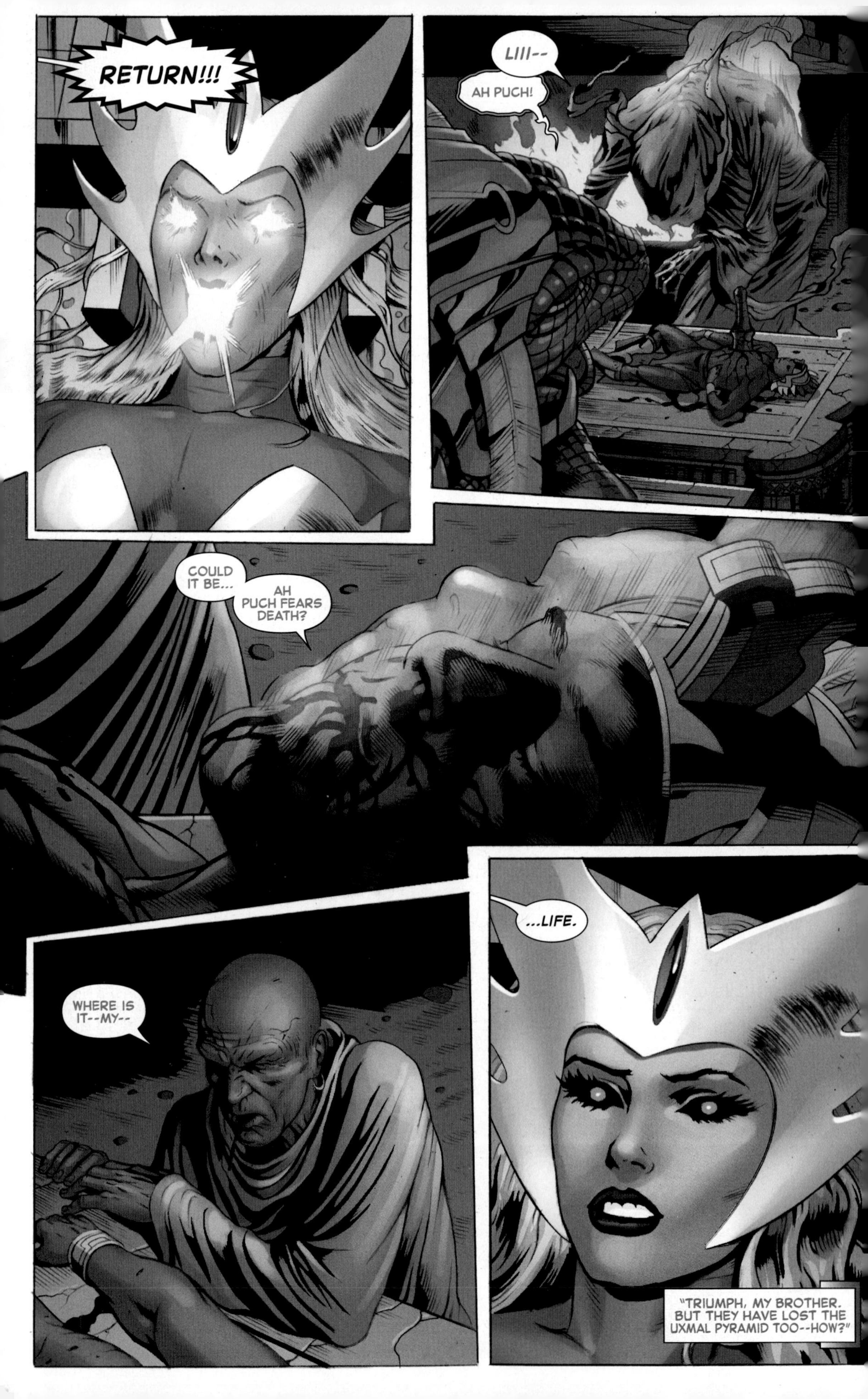
RETURN!!!
LIII--
AH PUCH!
COULD IT BE...
AH PUCH FEARS DEATH?
WHERE IS IT--MY--
...LIFE.
"TRIUMPH, MY BROTHER. BUT THEY HAVE LOST THE UXMAL PYRAMID TOO--HOW?"

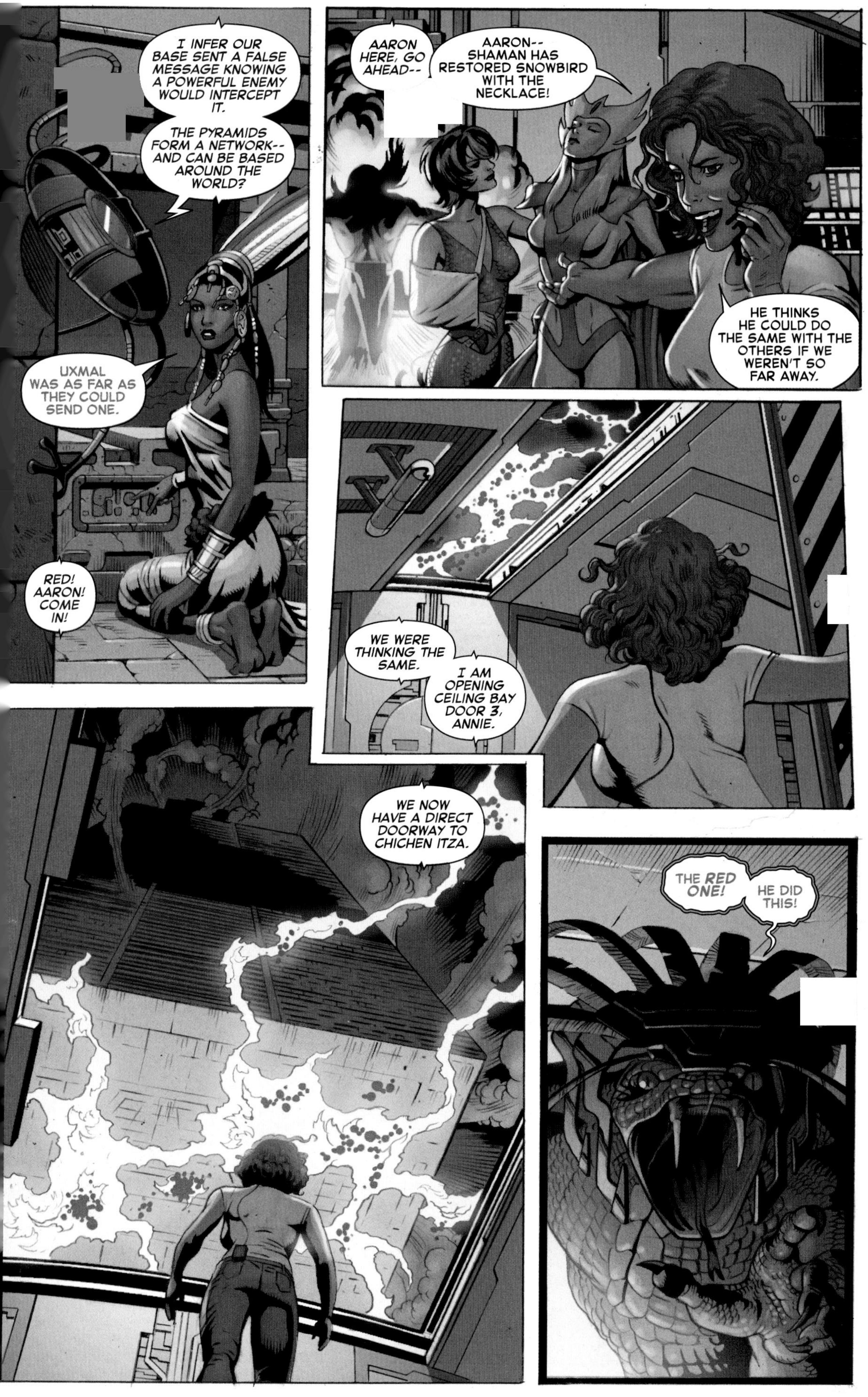
I INFER OUR BASE SENT A FALSE MESSAGE KNOWING A POWERFUL ENEMY WOULD INTERCEPT IT.
THE PYRAMIDS FORM A NETWORK--AND CAN BE BASED AROUND THE WORLD?
UXMAL WAS AS FAR AS THEY COULD SEND ONE.
RED! AARON! COME IN!
AARON HERE, GO AHEAD--
AARON--SHAMAN HAS RESTORED SNOWBIRD WITH THE NECKLACE!
HE THINKS HE COULD DO THE SAME WITH THE OTHERS IF WE WEREN'T SO FAR AWAY.
WE WERE THINKING THE SAME.
I AM OPENING CEILING BAY DOOR 3, ANNIE.
WE NOW HAVE A DIRECT DOORWAY TO CHICHEN ITZA.
THE *RED ONE!*
HE DID THIS!

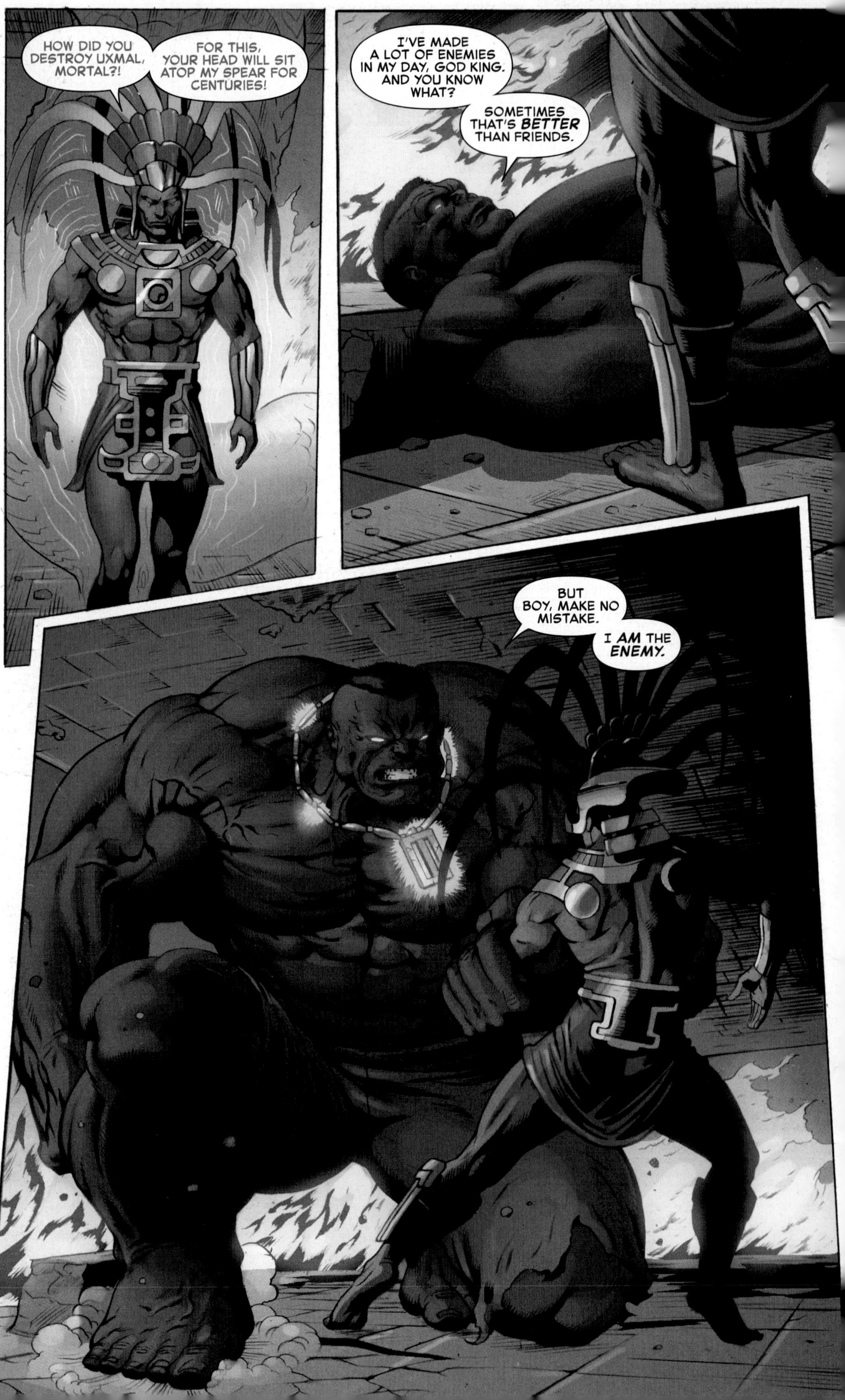
HOW DID YOU DESTROY UXMAL, MORTAL?!
FOR THIS, YOUR HEAD WILL SIT ATOP MY SPEAR FOR CENTURIES!
I'VE MADE A LOT OF ENEMIES IN MY DAY, GOD KING. AND YOU KNOW WHAT?
SOMETIMES THAT'S BETTER THAN FRIENDS.
BUT BOY, MAKE NO MISTAKE.
I AM THE ENEMY.

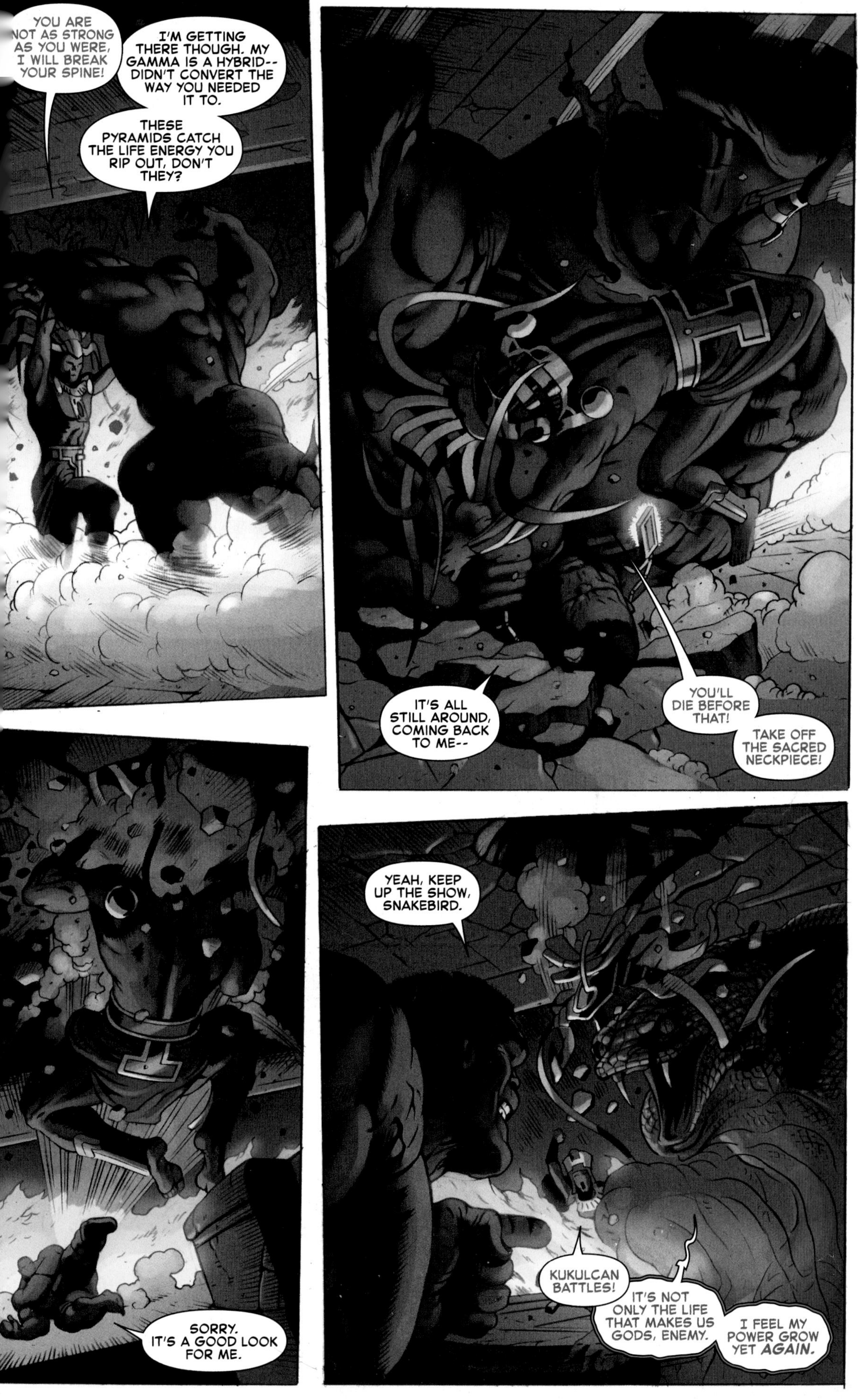
YOU ARE NOT AS STRONG AS YOU WERE, I WILL BREAK YOUR SPINE!
I'M GETTING THERE THOUGH. MY GAMMA IS A HYBRID-- DIDN'T CONVERT THE WAY YOU NEEDED IT TO.
THESE PYRAMIDS CATCH THE LIFE ENERGY YOU RIP OUT, DON'T THEY?
IT'S ALL STILL AROUND, COMING BACK TO ME--
YOU'LL DIE BEFORE THAT!
TAKE OFF THE SACRED NECKPIECE!
SORRY. IT'S A GOOD LOOK FOR ME.
YEAH, KEEP UP THE SHOW, SNAKEBIRD.
KUKULCAN BATTLES!
IT'S NOT ONLY THE LIFE THAT MAKES US GODS, ENEMY.
I FEEL MY POWER GROW YET AGAIN.

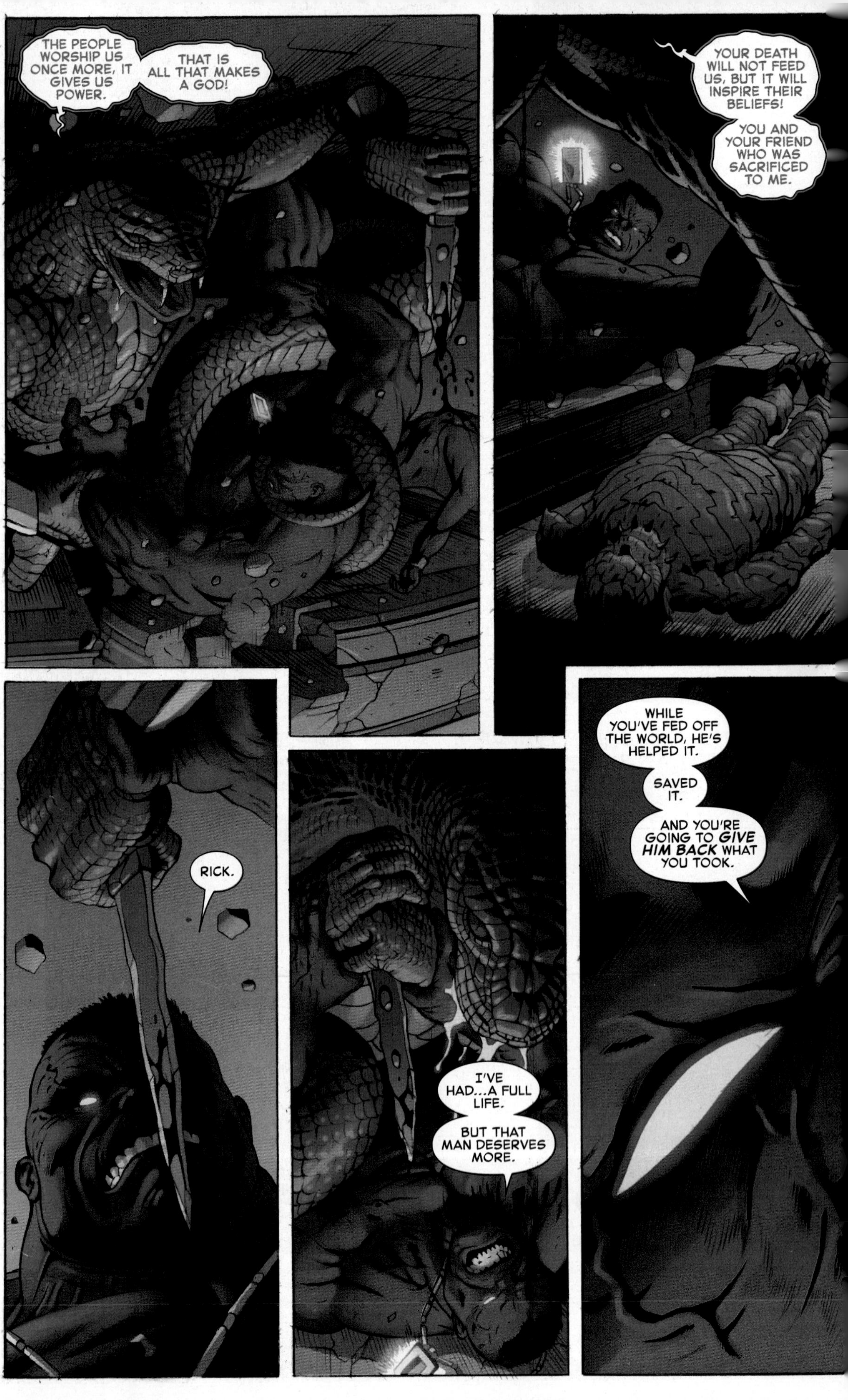
THE PEOPLE WORSHIP US ONCE MORE, IT GIVES US POWER.
THAT IS ALL THAT MAKES A GOD!
YOUR DEATH WILL NOT FEED US, BUT IT WILL INSPIRE THEIR BELIEFS!
YOU AND YOUR FRIEND WHO WAS SACRIFICED TO ME.
RICK.
I'VE HAD...A FULL LIFE.
BUT THAT MAN DESERVES MORE.
WHILE YOU'VE FED OFF THE WORLD, HE'S HELPED IT.
SAVED IT.
AND YOU'RE GOING TO GIVE HIM BACK WHAT YOU TOOK.

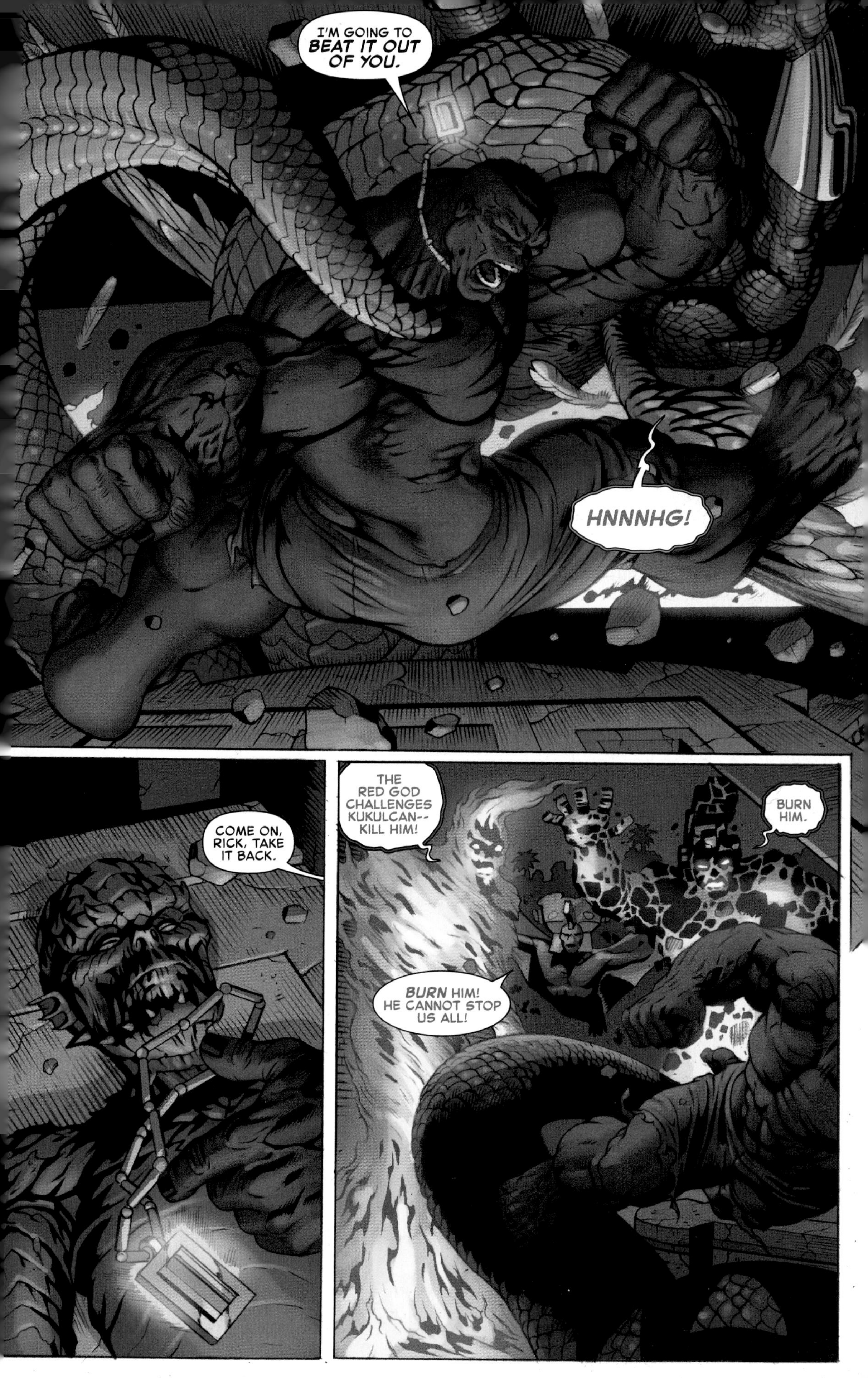
I'M GOING TO BEAT IT OUT OF YOU.
HNNNHG!
COME ON, RICK, TAKE IT BACK.
THE RED GOD CHALLENGES KUKULCAN-- KILL HIM!
BURN HIM.
BURN HIM! HE CANNOT STOP US ALL!

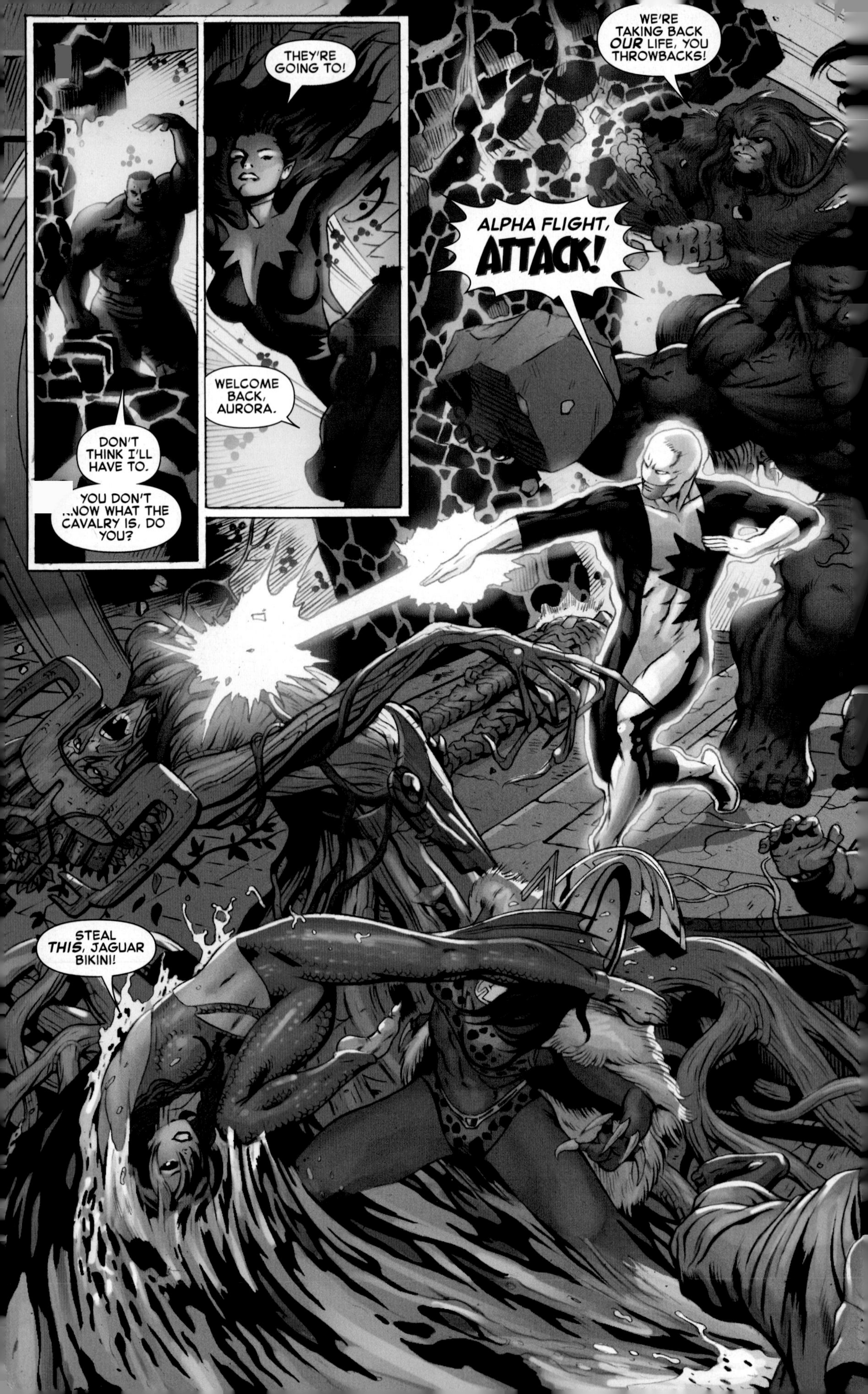
DON'T THINK I'LL HAVE TO.
YOU DON'T NOW WHAT THE CAVALRY IS, DO YOU?
THEY'RE GOING TO!
WELCOME BACK, AURORA.
WE'RE TAKING BACK OUR LIFE, YOU THROWBACKS!
ALPHA FLIGHT, ATTACK!
STEAL THIS, JAGUAR BIKINI!

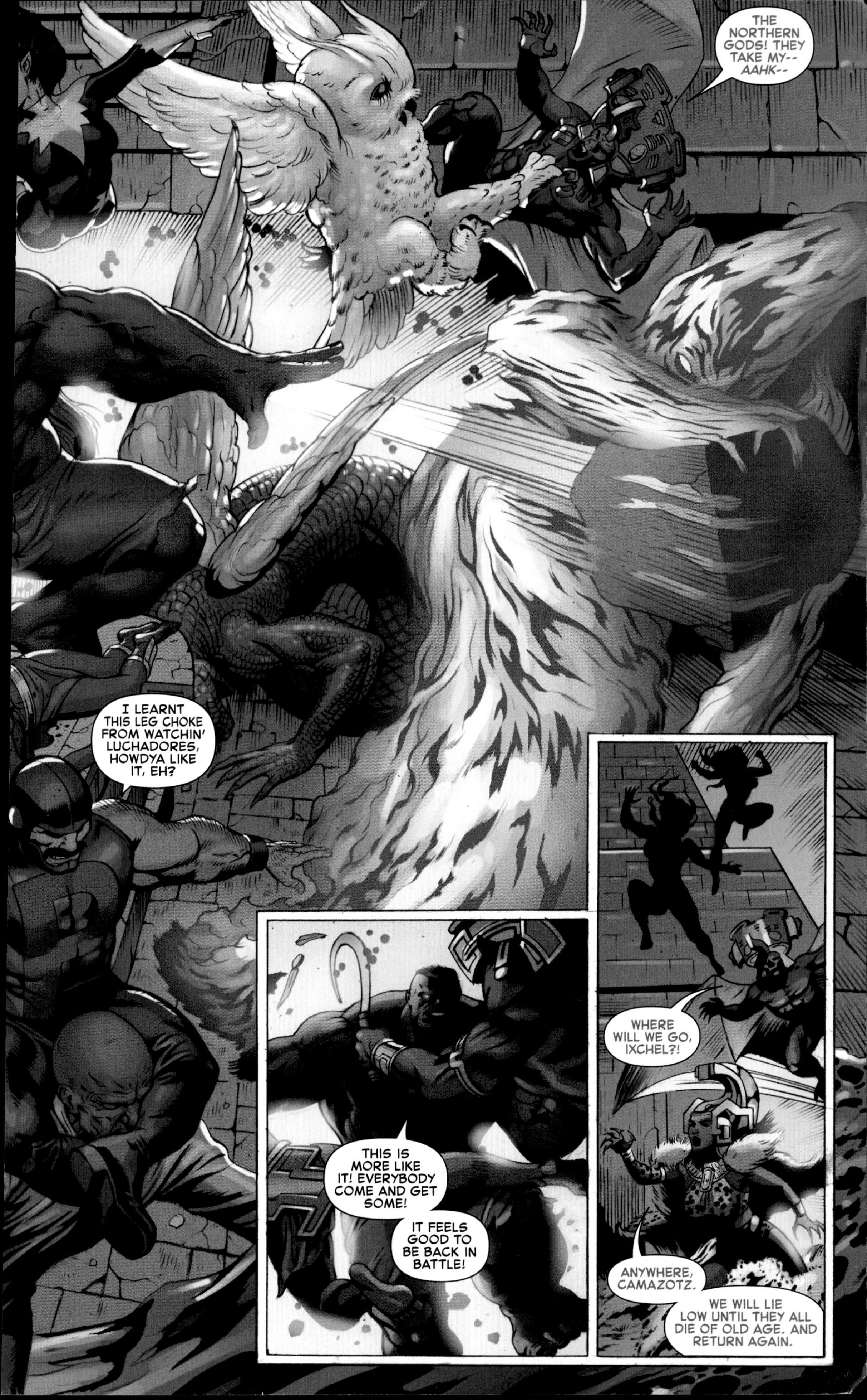
THE NORTHERN GODS! THEY TAKE MY-- AAHK--
I LEARNT THIS LEG CHOKE FROM WATCHIN' LUCHADORES, HOWDYA LIKE IT, EH?
THIS IS MORE LIKE IT! EVERYBODY COME AND GET SOME!
IT FEELS GOOD TO BE BACK IN BATTLE!
WHERE WILL WE GO, IXCHEL?!
ANYWHERE, CAMAZOTZ.
WE WILL LIE LOW UNTIL THEY ALL DIE OF OLD AGE. AND RETURN AGAIN.

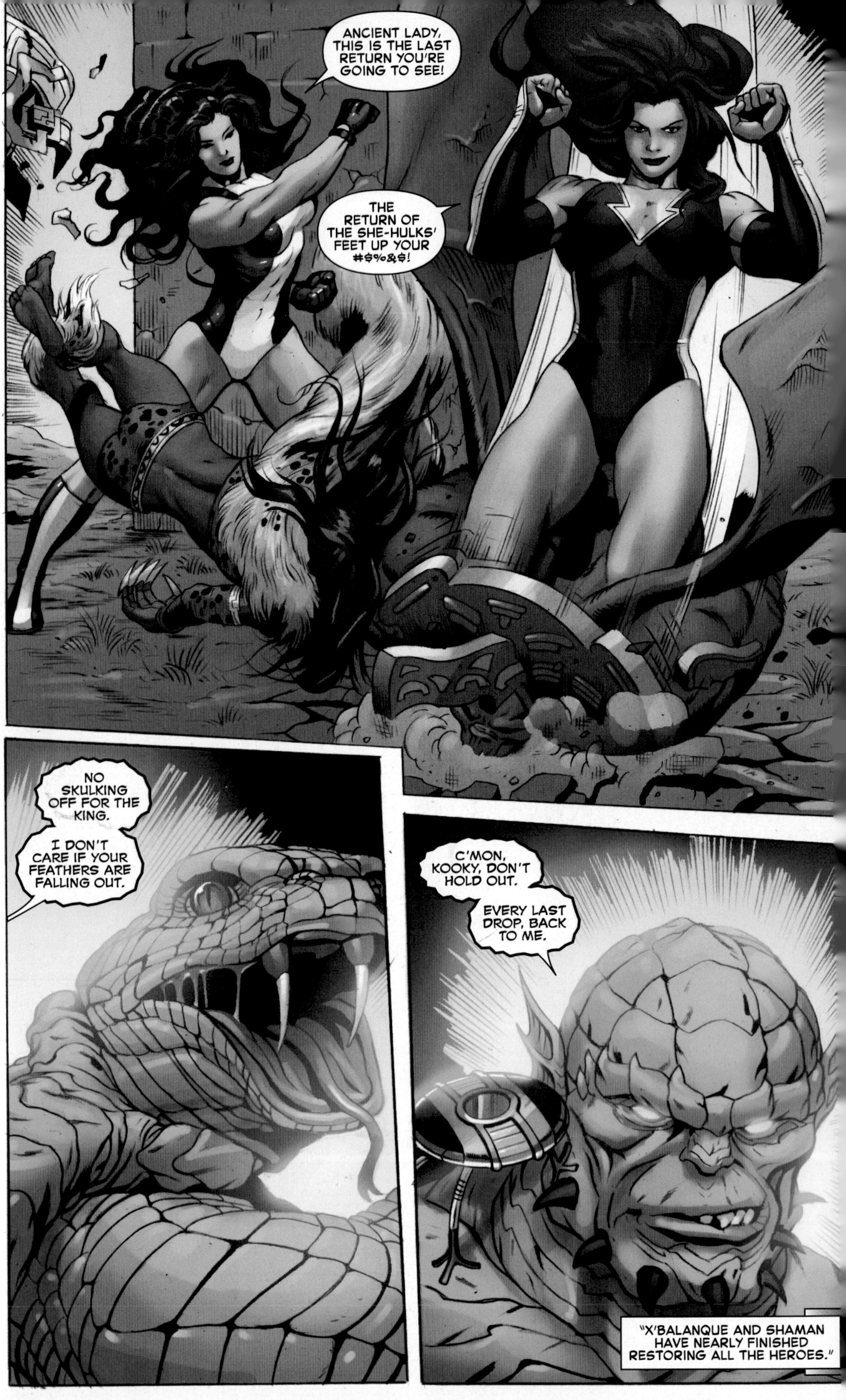

ANCIENT LADY, THIS IS THE LAST RETURN YOU'RE GOING TO SEE!
THE RETURN OF THE SHE-HULKS' FEET UP YOUR #$%&$!
NO SKULKING OFF FOR THE KING.
I DON'T CARE IF YOUR FEATHERS ARE FALLING OUT.
C'MON, KOOKY, DON'T HOLD OUT.
EVERY LAST DROP, BACK TO ME.
"X'BALANQUE AND SHAMAN HAVE NEARLY FINISHED RESTORING ALL THE HEROES."

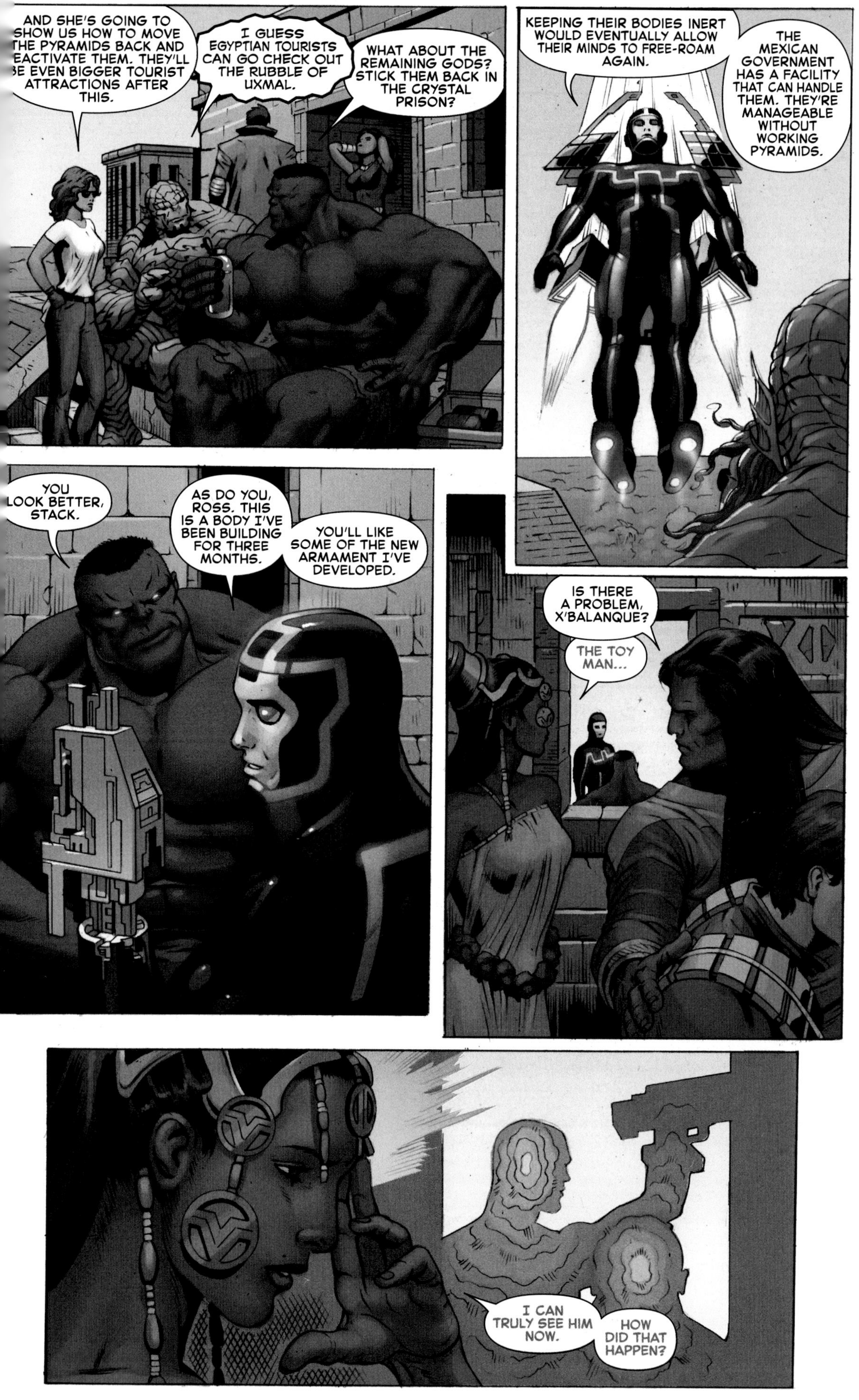
AND SHE'S GOING TO SHOW US HOW TO MOVE THE PYRAMIDS BACK AND REACTIVATE THEM. THEY'LL BE EVEN BIGGER TOURIST ATTRACTIONS AFTER THIS.
I GUESS EGYPTIAN TOURISTS CAN GO CHECK OUT THE RUBBLE OF UXMAL.
WHAT ABOUT THE REMAINING GODS? STICK THEM BACK IN THE CRYSTAL PRISON?
KEEPING THEIR BODIES INERT WOULD EVENTUALLY ALLOW THEIR MINDS TO FREE-ROAM AGAIN.
THE MEXICAN GOVERNMENT HAS A FACILITY THAT CAN HANDLE THEM. THEY'RE MANAGEABLE WITHOUT WORKING PYRAMIDS.
YOU LOOK BETTER, STACK.
AS DO YOU, ROSS. THIS IS A BODY I'VE BEEN BUILDING FOR THREE MONTHS.
YOU'LL LIKE SOME OF THE NEW ARMAMENT I'VE DEVELOPED.
IS THERE A PROBLEM, X'BALANQUE?
THE TOY MAN...
I CAN TRULY SEE HIM NOW.
HOW DID THAT HAPPEN?

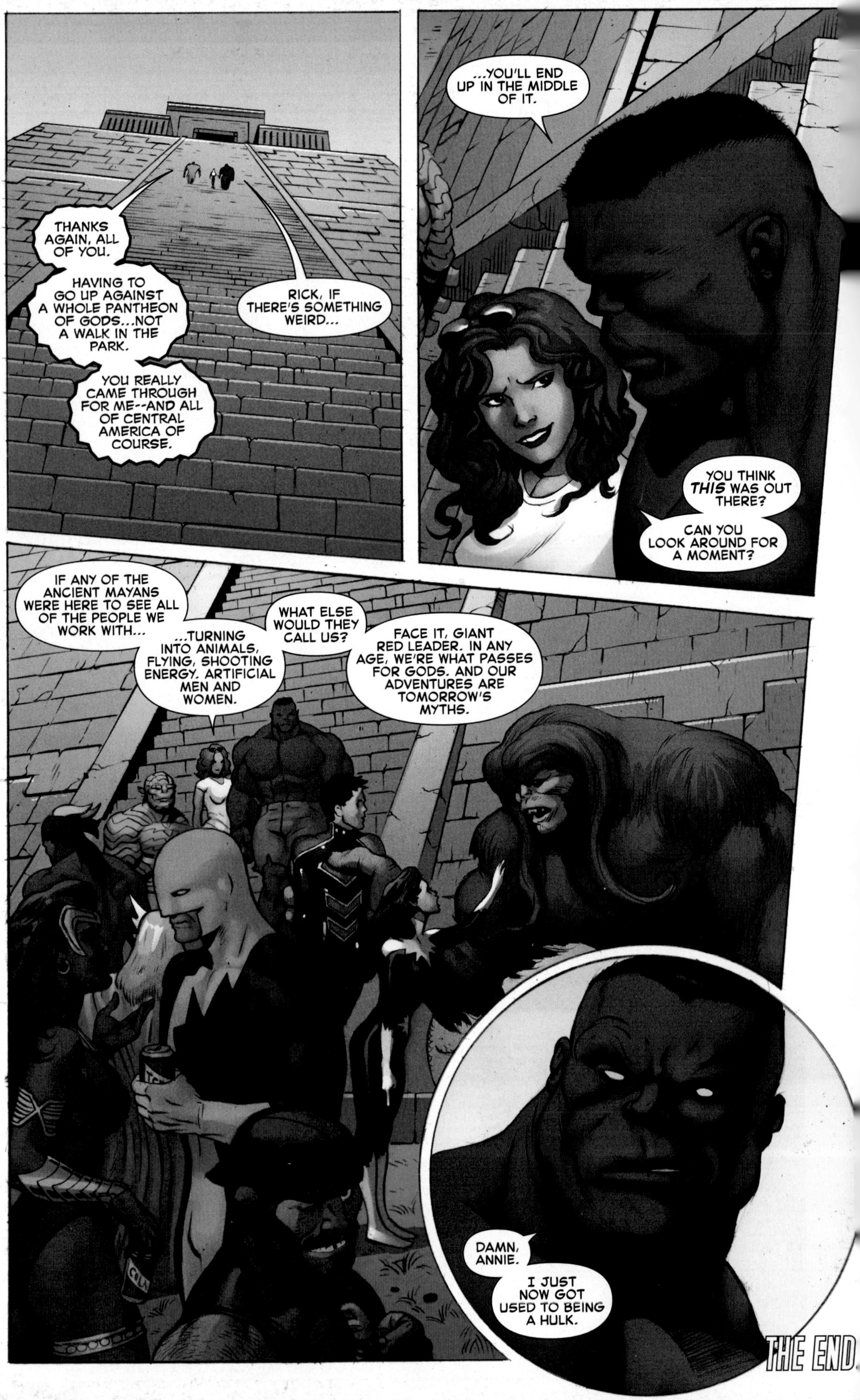
THANKS AGAIN, ALL OF YOU.
HAVING TO GO UP AGAINST A WHOLE PANTHEON OF GODS...NOT A WALK IN THE PARK.
YOU REALLY CAME THROUGH FOR ME--AND ALL OF CENTRAL AMERICA OF COURSE.
RICK, IF THERE'S SOMETHING WEIRD...
...YOU'LL END UP IN THE MIDDLE OF IT.
YOU THINK *THIS* WAS OUT THERE?
CAN YOU LOOK AROUND FOR A MOMENT?
IF ANY OF THE ANCIENT MAYANS WERE HERE TO SEE ALL OF THE PEOPLE WE WORK WITH...
...TURNING INTO ANIMALS, FLYING, SHOOTING ENERGY. ARTIFICIAL MEN AND WOMEN.
WHAT ELSE WOULD THEY CALL US?
FACE IT, GIANT RED LEADER. IN ANY AGE, WE'RE WHAT PASSES FOR GODS. AND OUR ADVENTURES ARE TOMORROW'S MYTHS.
DAMN, ANNIE.
I JUST NOW GOT USED TO BEING A HULK.
THE END

GENERAL'S END

Well THAT was a ride, wasn't it?

Red Hulk smashed his way into the world of our big green hero/monster five years ago and didn't make a lot of friends at first. Unless you consider The Leader and M.O.D.O.K. good friends, which I wouldn't.

Red challenged The Hulk and fell, and that's the point that defined his character. Most foes skulk off, lick their wounds and plot revenge, to keep showing up later with new schemes and attacks. But Red accepted that he was beaten. It wasn't just new powerhouse Red Hulk admitting that, it was lifelong antagonist General Thaddeus Ross finally acknowledging his war with The Hulk was over, ending a destructive cycle at long last.

And then he moved on with his life. Captain America came in to offer direction (as he does) and it paid off. Red Hulk started using that ridiculous amount of power and his tactician's mind to stomp other world threats. He regained purpose. And now he can wake up without thinking of how much he hates Banner every day.

The Red Hulk is also literally moving on from this book. If you haven't heard the news yet, he will now be heading up a title I'm familiar with (that's a hint). It's a perfect next step forward for the four-star fighter that you can follow into new territory.

But wait—we've still got a Hulk book here, and there's someone still relatively new to the Gamma Family with a story to explore—though she's been in the Hulk mythos from day one. Beginning next issue, our focus turns to BETTY ROSS, daughter of the General, former lover of the man-monster, and integral part of the world of Hulk for 50 years!

Her arc is going in a very different direction as we learn some dark truths about the Marvel Universe, and I'll say more about it then.

I'll be joined by phenomenal artists Carlo Pagulayan and Wellinton Alves, and I can't wait for you to see it—it's stunning.

As we feel the gamma hit us and we start to change again into something new and explosive, I'd like to thank editor Mark Paniccia for guiding this rocket ever higher along the way. He and Jeph Loeb and Ed McGuinness set up a lot of dynamic elements to work with, and I can't ask for more. I'm also indebted to the artists who pulled off wildly improbable adventures month after month, beginning with Gabriel Hardman, who truly set the tone for this era of Hulk. Mark also prefers top-level artists on his books, so I was lucky enough to then work with Patrick Zircher, Elena Casagrande, Dan Breretan, Ed, Carlo, and finishing off strong with Dale Eaglesham.

Thanks most of all to you for reading along and spreading the word about what we're doing here. I'll see you in October.

Jeff Parker

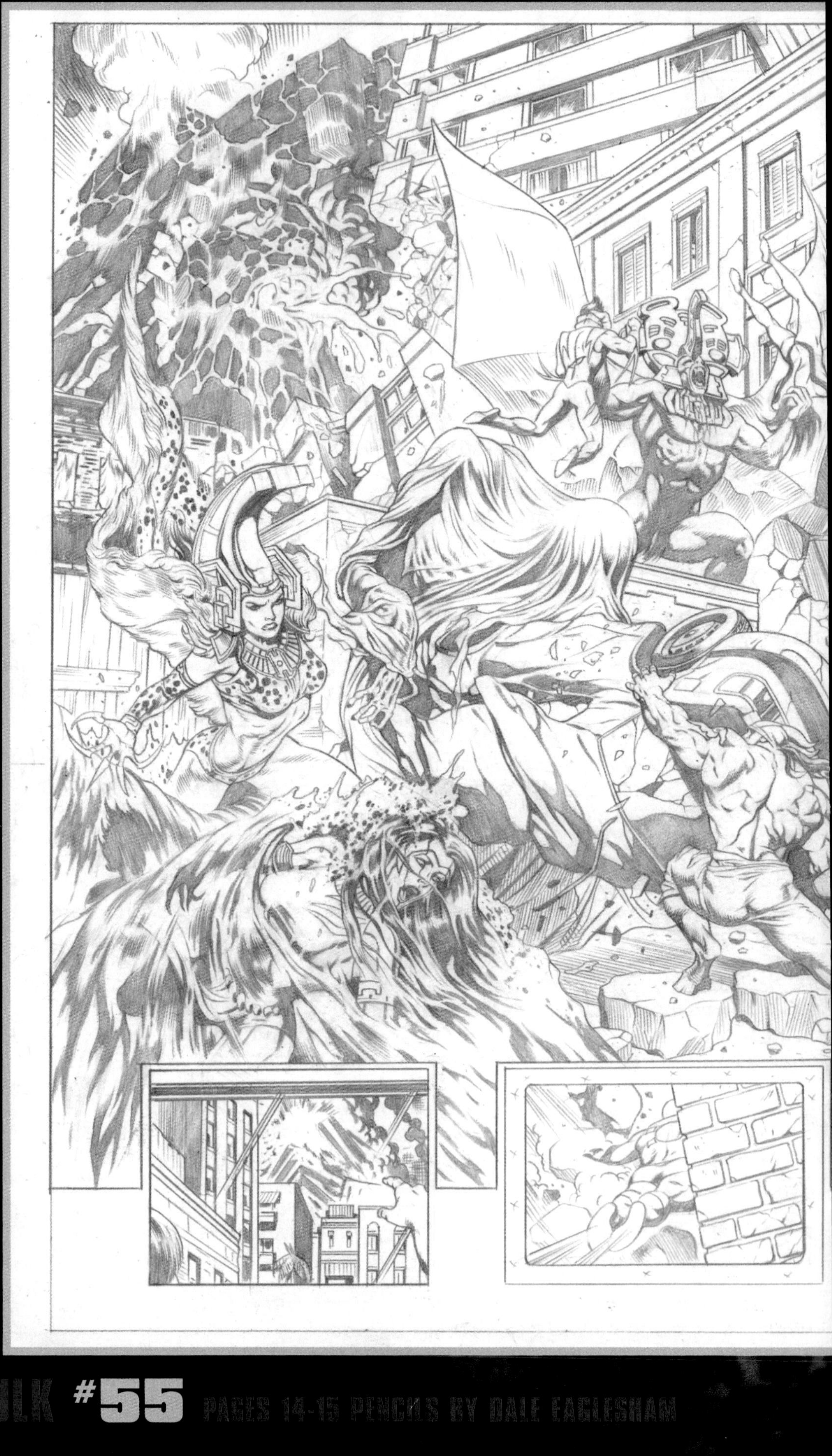

HULK #55 PAGES 14-15 PENCILS BY DALE EAGLESHAM

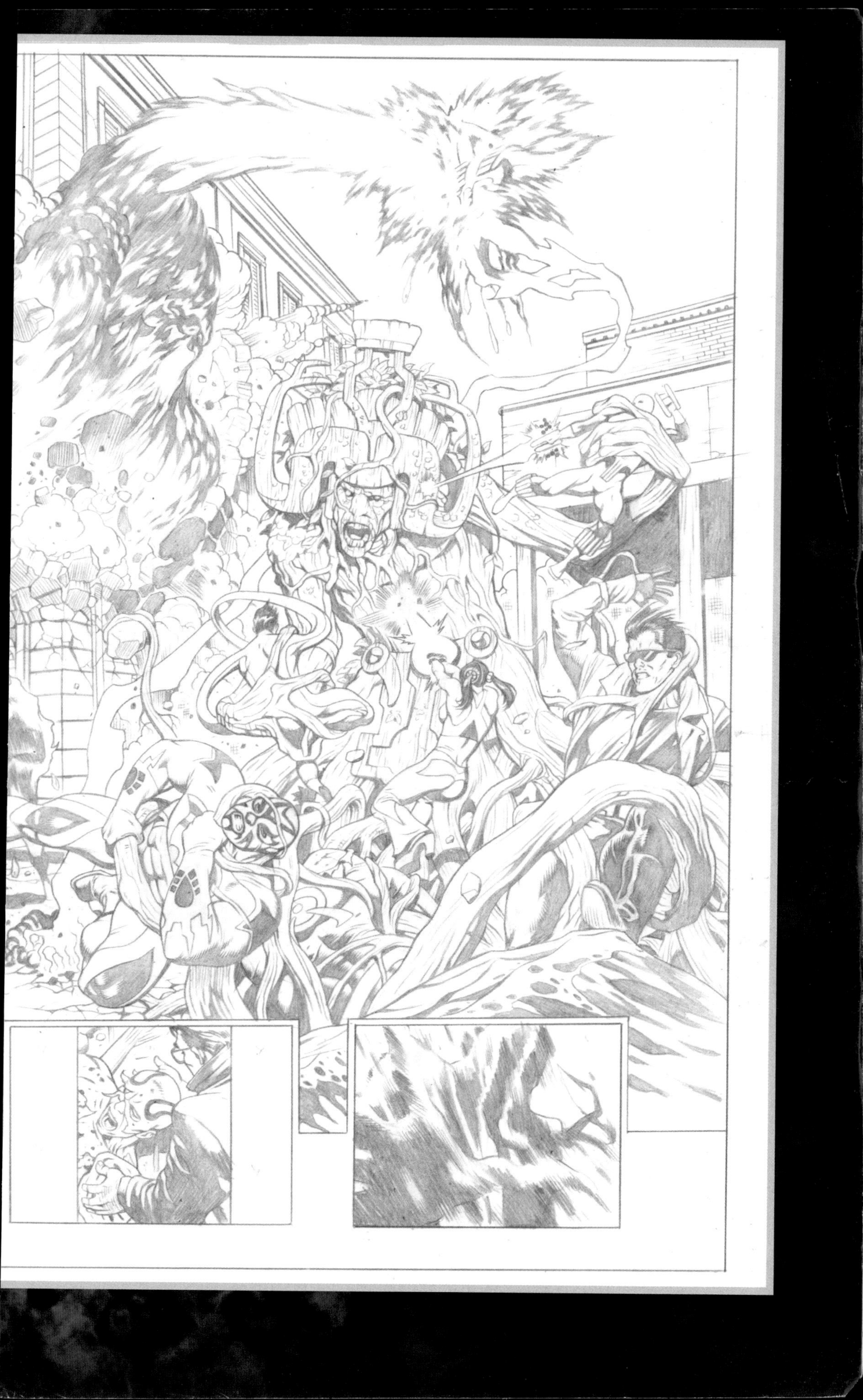

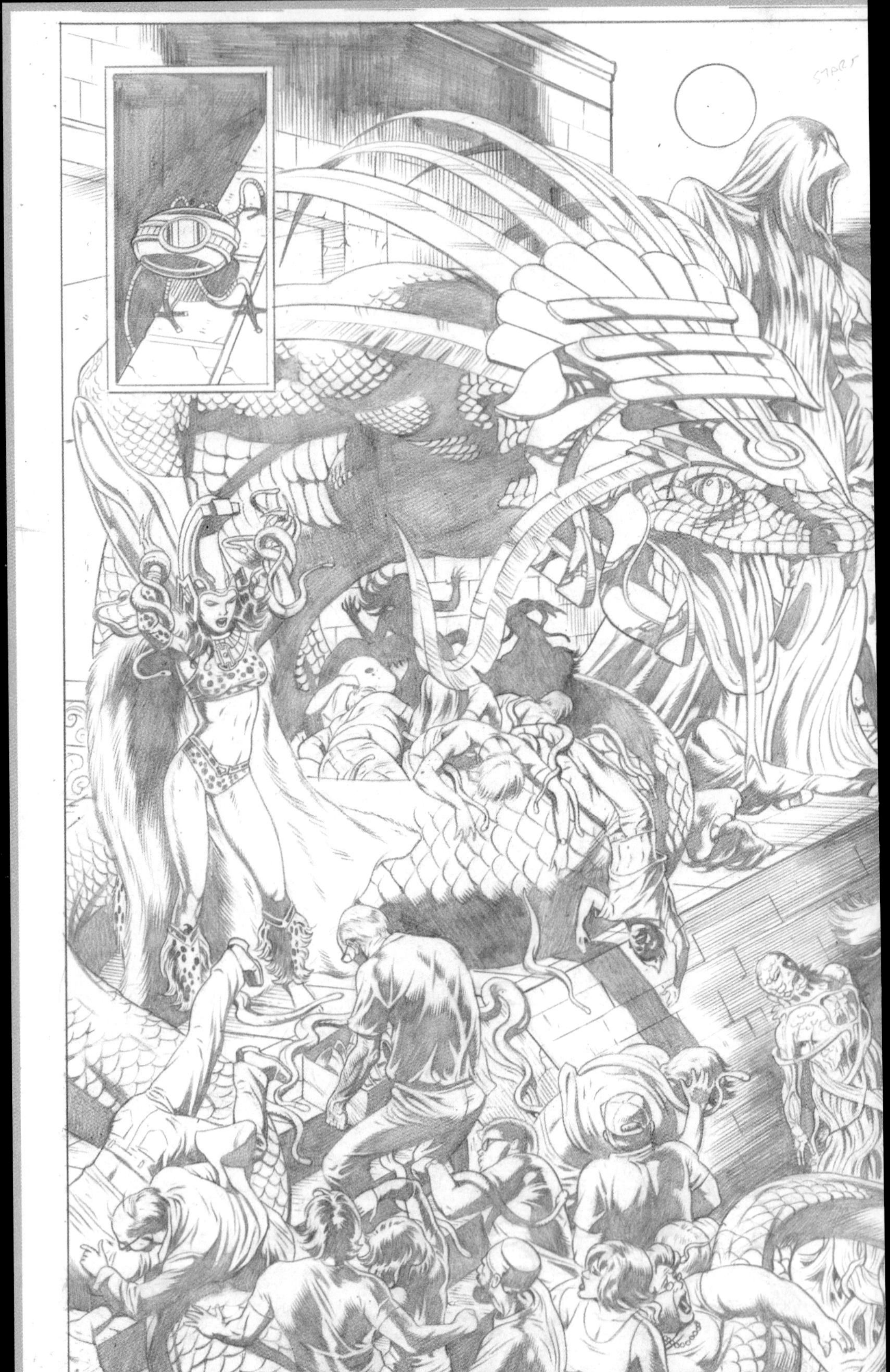
START

HULK #56 PAGES 14-15 PENCILS BY DALE EAGLESHAM

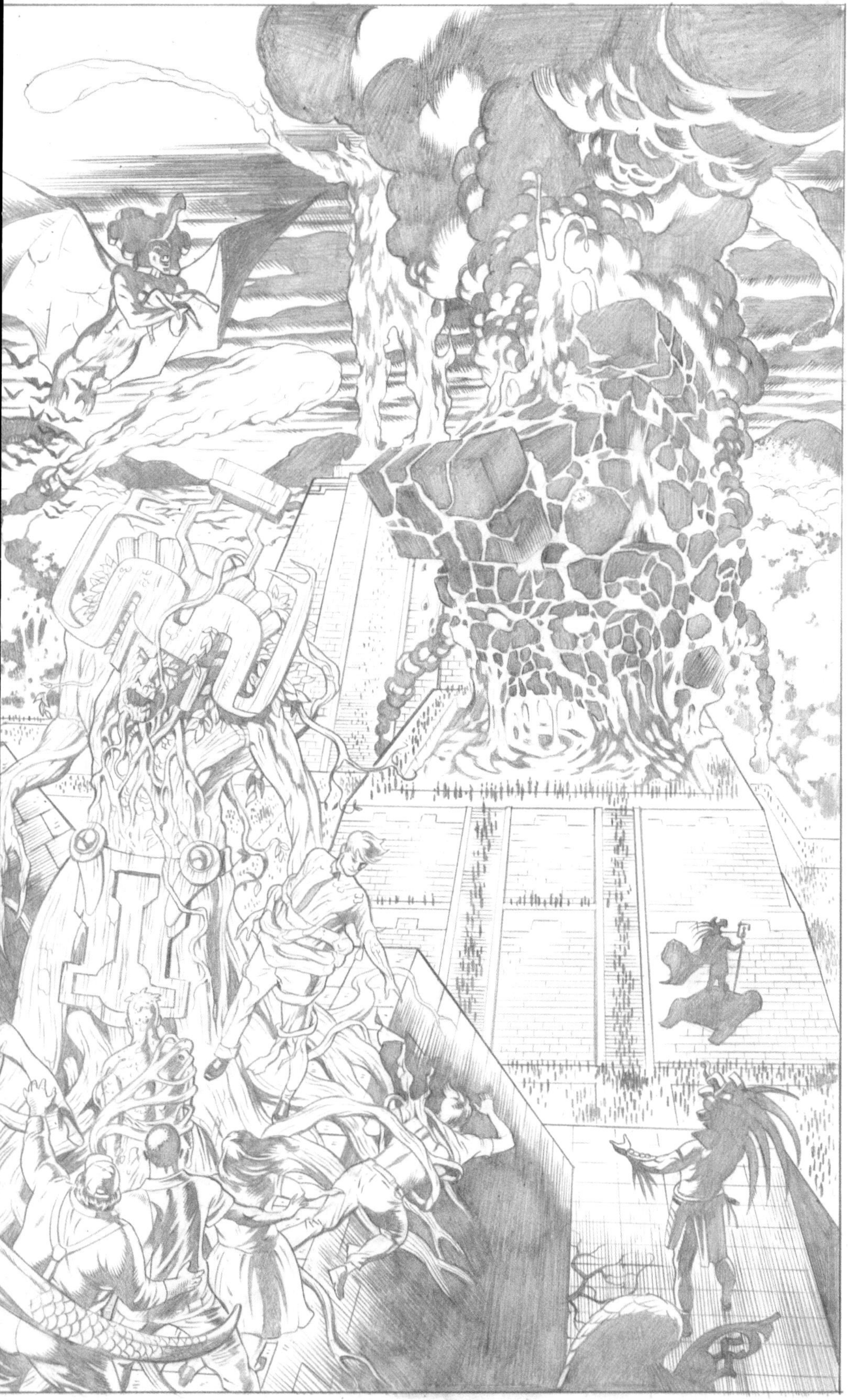

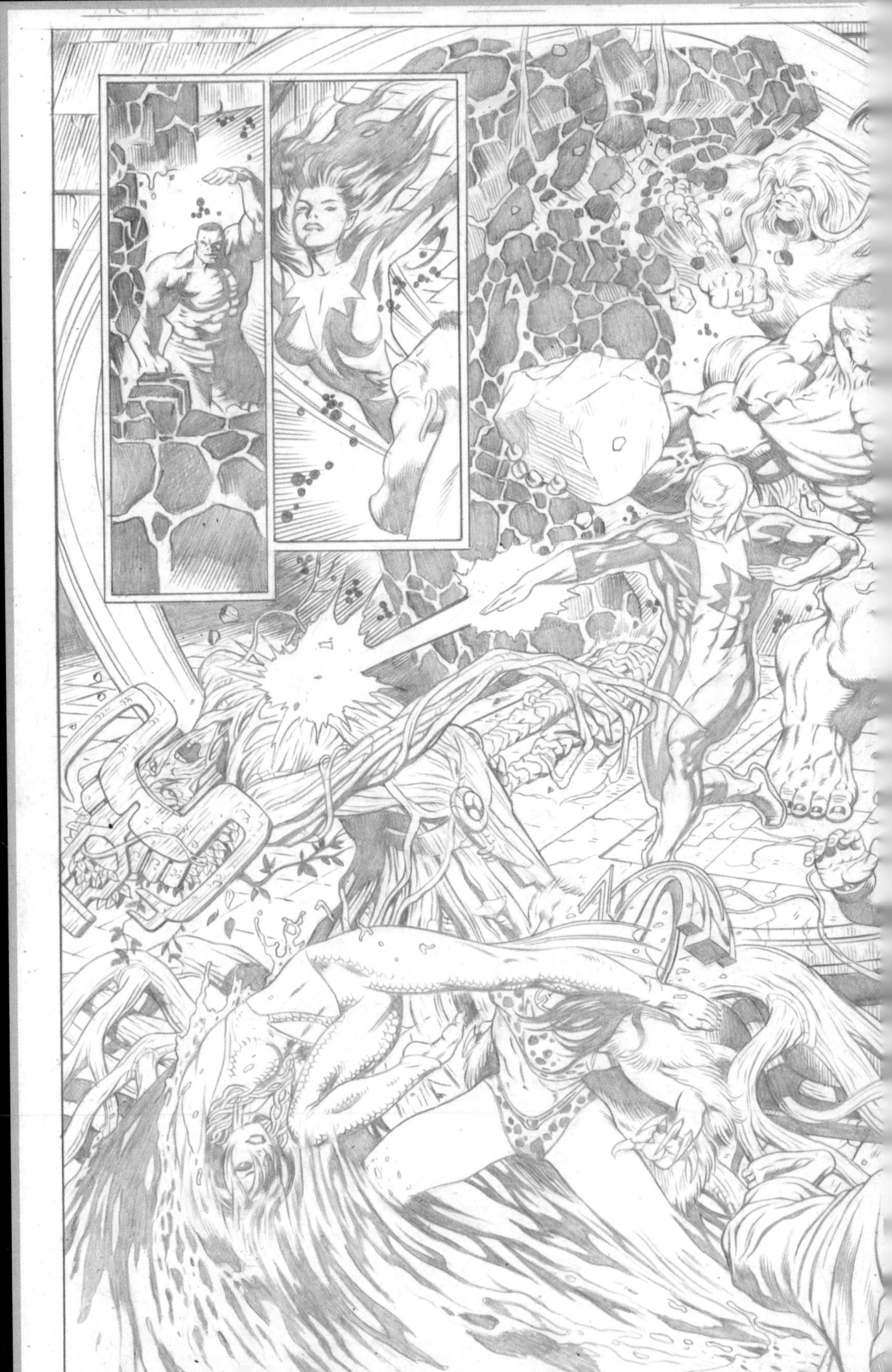

HULK #57 PAGES 16-17 PENCILS BY DALE EAGLESHAM

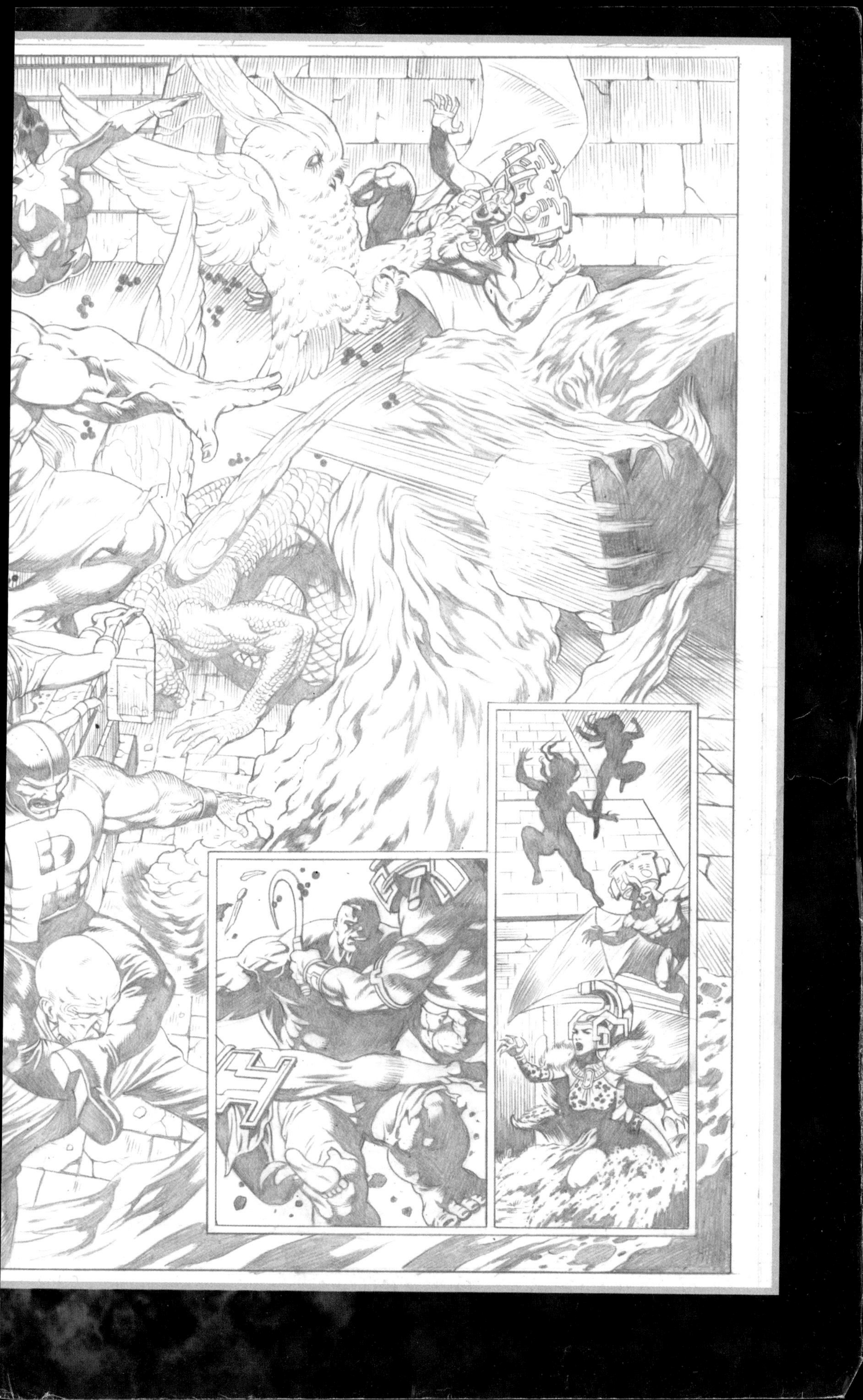

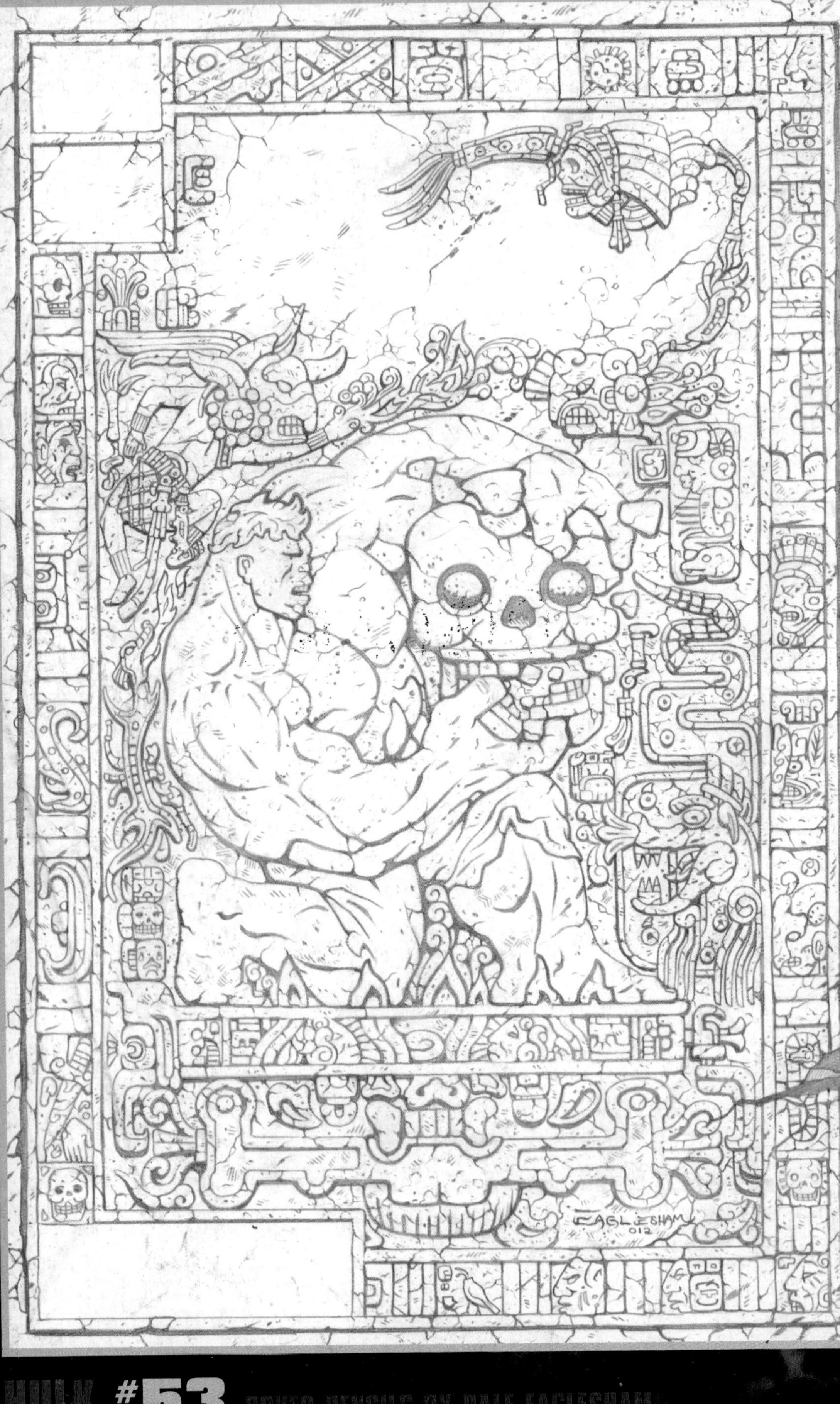
EAGLESHAM
012

HULK #53 COVER PENCILS BY DALE EAGLESHAM